The Oxfordian Shakespeare Series

William Shakespeare

OTHELLO
THE MOOR OF
VENICE

With an introduction and fully annotated from an Oxfordian perspective by
Ren Draya, professor of British and American literature at Blackburn College,
and Richard F. Whalen, co-general editor of the series

Horatio Editions - Llumina Press

The Oxfordian Shakespeare Series

General Editors

Richard F. Whalen, author of *Shakespeare Who Was He?
The Oxford Challenge to the Bard of Avon.*

= The ` River"

Daniel L. Wright, director of the Shakespeare Authorship
Research Center and professor of English, Concordia
University, Portland, Oregon.

ISBN: 978-1-60594-439-5

Printed in the United States of America by Llumina Press

Library of Congress Control Number: 2010922598

Horatio Editions
PO Box 1084 Truro MA 02666
RFWhalen@Comcast. net

Design, production and distribution by Llumina Press www. Llumina.com

Llumina
Press

Contents

Verité

For truth is truth, though ever so old, and time cannot make that false which once was true.

    Edward de Vere, seventeenth Earl of Oxford

Verité

For truth is truth
To the end of reckoning.

    William Shakespeare, *Measure for Measure*

[handwritten annotations:]

Two Speаus

2 shaking are OX's
speurs crest

Poems

Sonnets

= ↑ ✕ → ↑↓

Two crossing
spears

Imagine shaking spears two movement

Anthony & Cleopatra

Ox's crest

Preface

Edward De Vair / Fair /

This Oxfordian Shakespeare Series offers a frankly different view of the Shakespeare plays and their author. It takes the view that the great poet and dramatist was Edward de Vere, the seventeenth Earl of Oxford, writing under the pen name "William Shakespeare," and was not the man from Stratford-on-Avon, known there as Shakspere. *NB ⊘ 'Shakspur'*

Supporting this view are the many correspondences in the plays to Oxford's life and times. The case that Oxford wrote Shakespeare becomes more compelling as these correspondences, clear allusions and direct references multiply in many of the plays, especially in *Hamlet*, *Othello*, *Antony and Cleopatra*, *The Merchant of Venice*, and *All's Well That Ends Well*.

For almost a century, Oxfordian scholars have been researching Oxford's life and the Shakespeare works. Their efforts have turned up a wealth of evidence for his authorship and many insights that inform the plays. The editors of the plays in this series have drawn on their scholarship and also on the scholarship of "Stratfordian" professors, whose discoveries and observations not infrequently can be seen to support the case for Oxford. For readers and theatergoers, the result is a better understanding of the author's intention and design and a greatly enhanced understanding and appreciation of the plays as literary masterpieces.

In recent decades, support for Oxford as Shakespeare has been growing rapidly. Many notable writers, actors, directors, lawyers and judges are among those who have become persuaded that Oxford was the true author. In a breakthrough that augurs well for "Oxfordians," a fair number of university professors have also seen merit in the case for Oxford. Several have become convinced that Oxford was Shakespeare and eight of them have agreed to edit plays in this series.

Knowing how Oxford drew on his life experience, wide reading, travels and his deepest concerns can greatly enrich the reader's appreciation of his literary accomplishment and open new avenues for study and research for students and professors. Theater directors and actors will find new and intriguing ways to interpret the plays, which take on new meanings. The plot line has more nuances. The characters have more depth and complexity, and the interactions among them are more dramatic. Audiences who accept Oxford as the dramatist

1

will find richer meanings in the plays and enjoy a greater appreciation of the interactions among the characters.

The introduction to each play and the line notes call attention to the allusions and direct references to Oxford's life experience as a ranking courtier in Queen Elizabeth's court and a traveler in Italy, France and Scotland. The line notes also clarify words, phrases and constructions that may be unfamiliar but that are important to an understanding of a passage. They explain words and phrases that had quite different meanings four centuries ago. Some of the word play, puns and unusual metaphors require translation for today's reader and theatergoer. As in all modern-day editions of the Shakespeare plays, the play texts have been modernized for easier reading and understanding.

Ox travelled
to Scotland
to France
to Italy

coat of Arms:
spear "shaking"

literary
Name b/c Ox's crest
Family

genius

was two shaking Spears:

ie
ridicule

meant to inspire
English loyalty

in face of Spanish
intention to invade "Armada"
England — but Act of God
sank fleet of Sp. (Armada)
by a mega storm.

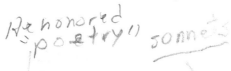
He honored "poetry" sonnets

Overview

He was one of the "best for comedy" in the Elizabethan Age. Among Queen Elizabeth's courtiers, he was "most excellent...in the rare devices of poetry." He excelled "in letters...many Latin verses...yea, even more English verses." He was among those "who honored poesie with their pens and practice." And tellingly, he was considered first among courtier writers "who have written excellently well, as it would appear, if their doings could be found out and made public."

Fair These comments by Elizabethan literary critics all referred to Edward de Vere, the seventeenth Earl of Oxford (1550-1604), who, in the view of many who have studied his life story as well as the Shakespeare plays and poems, was Elizabeth's chief poet-playwright, whose plays appeared under the pseudonym "William Shakespeare." Like all great writers of genius, he drew on his life experience and deepest concerns. His rich, turbulent, controversial life in London and Elizabeth's court and his travels in France, Italy and Scotland fit the profile of a man who would have written the works of Shakespeare. His authorship of the poems and plays, although not verified in historical documents, was likely an open secret. It was known in court and theater circles, but it was not a fact to be published and for two reasons: The plays commented on court persons and affairs, sometimes satirically; and writing plays performed in the "vulgar" public theaters and publishing them were considered far beneath the dignity of the nobility. And so Oxford used the pen name William Shakespeare, which has become the most famous name in world literature.

As the seventeenth Earl of Oxford and Lord Great Chamberlain of England, Edward de Vere was one of the top ranking noblemen in Queen Elizabeth's court. She and her courtiers were the primary audience for the Shakespeare plays. They were a literate and knowing audience that would appreciate the intricate plots, sophisticated language, allusions to the queen and the veiled satire of court figures such as the lampoon of Lord Burghley, Oxford's father-in-law, as Polonius in *Hamlet*.

The Shakespeare plays, as many scholars have long noted, were written perceptively and authoritatively from the point of view of a nobleman and courtier at the center of political power. They are almost exclusively about the ambitions, crimes, loves, foolishness, cowardice and bravery of monarchs, the nobility, aristocrats and political leaders, including the way they use and mis-use political power. The plays demonstrate the playwright's profound understanding of history from the perspective of one who was deeply educated in the humanistic arts, classical literature and the worlds of antiquity and

3

who had read widely in works that had not yet been translated into English, although they are recognized as important sources for several Shakespeare plays.

The point of view of the Shakespeare plays is that of an aristocrat, not a commoner such as Shakspere of Stratford. Characters from the ranks of commoners are buffoons, dolts and figures of fun; they are to be appreciated usually as comic relief and occasionally for their earthy folk wisdom.

His Life

Edward de Vere saw his first theatrical performances as a youngster at Hedingham Castle, where he was born in 1550, eight years before Elizabeth became queen. His father, the sixteenth Earl of Oxford, maintained a troupe of actors. When Edward was eleven, Queen Elizabeth and her entourage stayed at Hedingham almost a week, and plays were among the usual entertainments for the queen when noblemen such as Edward's father were called upon to host the royal entourage visiting their castles during the queen's "progresses" around England.

When his father died in 1562, young Edward inherited the earldom of Oxford and the vast properties that went with it. Even though his mother was living, under English feudal law Edward became a ward of the Crown until he reached the age of twenty-one. As a ward, he was sent to London to live with William Cecil, later Lord Burghley, master of the court of wards, minister of state and the queen's chief counselor throughout most of her reign. Polonius, a caricature of Burghley, is the king's chief counselor in *Hamlet*, the play that most impressively reflects Oxford's life and concerns. For example, Polonius lectures his son with maxims on how to behave in Paris. So did Burghley. Hamlet is captured at sea by pirates. So was Oxford, twice, and details of one of them match details in *Hamlet*. And there are many more parallels between the play and Oxford's life. Even Stratfordian scholars have described the play as seeming to be Shakespeare's most autobiographical.

Edward spent his teenage years at Cecil's mansion, which was well-known as a center for study and learning. Cecil supervised the education of many of the aristocratic wards and amassed one of the largest libraries in England. Many of the books are known to have been sources for the Shakespeare plays and poems. Edward's education in his pre-teens was at the home of Sir Thomas Smith, a renowned scholar and diplomat. His tutors found him an avid and precocious student. One of them owned the only extant manuscript of the Anglo-Saxon *Beowulf*, a work that makes a curious appearance in *Hamlet*. Another tutor, an historian and translator, would even observe that Edward was "too much addicted" to learning. The universities of Cambridge and Oxford awarded him degrees, and he enrolled at Gray's Inn, one of London's four Inns of Court, where young men studied law. Later in life, he would serve as one of the judges in two high-profile treason trials, the trial in 1587 of Mary Queen of Scots and the trials in 1601 of the earls of Essex and Southampton. Law scholars and judges find a profound knowledge of law throughout Shakespeare's works.

One of Cecil's retainers was Edward's uncle, Arthur Golding, a scholar-translator who helped manage Edward's estates and probably oversaw his education. When Edward was in his mid-teens, the first translation into English of Ovid's *Metamorphoses* was published, with Golding listed as the putative author. All scholars agree that the translation (even today considered the best) was, along with the Geneva edition of the Bible, the most important influence on the works of Shakespeare. The racy translation, however, is very different from and far superior to Golding's other writings, which were mostly translations of pious, religious books. It is likely that Golding's brilliant nephew may have done most, if not all, of the translating. Cecil's gardener, too, was a published scholar whom Edward would have known; he was the most noted English horticulturist of the time, and Shakespeare's works are full of detailed, accurate references to a wide range of plants and flowers, cultivated and wild, the kind of information that would transcend the knowledge of a casual observer but would proceed from one learned in botany.

Oxford was a published poet, but the only verse found under his name, initials, or a recognized pseudonym is a handful of songs and poems, most of them from his early teenage years. They are, nevertheless, considered to be some of the best poems and song lyrics by an early Elizabethan courtier-writer. Although he was hailed during his lifetime as an excellent playwright, no plays published under his name, or even mention of specific plays, have been found. They would appear under his Shakespeare pseudonym, as would the Sonnets.

When Oxford turned twenty-one, he and Cecil's daughter, Anne, were married. Queen Elizabeth attended the ceremony in Westminster Abbey. As a leading nobleman at court, Oxford could observe the power politics of courtiers and their many intrigues. Plotting, scheming and deceptions, sometimes playful and sometimes murderous in their purposes, are at the core of Shakespeare's plays, and all the principal characters are kings, queens, dukes, earls, countesses and other members of the nobility. The one exception is in *The Merry Wives of Windsor*, but the castle at Windsor is where young Oxford spent several weeks recuperating from an illness; and in the play the suitor who finally wins the hand of Anne Page is the only nobleman in the play. He is a man "too great of birth . . . who capers, dances, writes verse and speaks merrily." An apt description of the Earl of Oxford.

When Oxford was in his early twenties, he traveled on the Continent for about fifteen months, and the Shakespeare plays that are set principally in Italy and France exhibit first-hand knowledge of their geography and landmarks, especially in the cities of northern Italy–Venice, Milan, Padua, Florence, Sienna and Verona. He had served with the military in Scotland, and *Macbeth* shows first-hand knowledge of Scotland--its geography, clans, mores, laws and even its unusual weather.

When he was in his late twenties, court records list eleven plays that were performed for Queen Elizabeth but the records do not name the author of the plays, and none of them have been found. Many of the titles, however, suggest Shakespeare plays that appeared later. For example, "The Historie of Error" may well have been an early *Comedy of Errors*; "The Historie of the Solitarie Knight" could have been *Timon of Athens*; and "The Historie of the Rape of the Second Helene" may have been an early version of *All's Well That Ends Well*. In *All's Well,* the heroine, Helena, tricks her recalcitrant husband into bedding her in the dark thinking she is another woman. Published rumors had it that Oxford was a victim of this same bizarre bed trick when he was twenty-four years old and had been married for three years.

Oxford was immersed in the world of the theater, not just as a playwright but also as a patron of acting companies, employer of playwrights and at least once as a performer, in a court entertainment called a "masque." He was the patron of at least two acting companies that appeared regularly in Queen Elizabeth's court. John Lyly and Anthony Munday, both playwrights, served as his secretaries. Scholars see many resemblances between their plays and the Shakespeare plays.

While writing poems and plays, Oxford was living a full, even tumultuous, life. Besides traveling on the Continent and going on military expeditions, he produced pageants and extravaganzas for the queen and won jousting tournaments held in her honor. He exhibited an eccentric and mercurial temperament, spent extravagantly, got into rancorous disputes with other courtiers and fought with his enemies in the streets of London (shades of *Romeo and Juliet*). After a long estrangement from his first wife, he fathered five children with her and an illegitimate child with Anne Vavasor, one of the queen's Ladies in Waiting, much to Elizabeth's displeasure. She sent both Oxford and his mistress to the Tower of London for their transgressions. Although Elizabeth was quick to banish him from her court when he dared to disobey or displease her, it was never for long. Banishment and reconciliation are recurring themes in the Shakespeare plays.

When Oxford was in favor, he delighted the queen with his dancing, his wit and his theatricals. In 1586, she awarded him an extraordinary grant of a thousand pounds a year for life, the equivalent of hundreds of thousands of dollars in today's money. She gave no reason for it and required no accounting. One explanation is that she did this because she had managed to appropriate

Othello

for her treasury much of his wealth and estates in his younger years and then decided he needed the cash to maintain a lifestyle suitable for a leading nobleman. She also loved theatrical entertainments and, although notoriously tight-fisted, she may well have been backing Oxford as her court playwright and theatrical impresario. The queen's successor, King James, whose wife also loved plays and theatricals, would continue the grant until Oxford's death.

The Earl of Oxford was not the stereotypical aristocrat of dignity, decorum and rectitude. Far from it. By all accounts, he was a difficult, improvident, eccentric aristocrat of many contradictions. He could clown in processions in the London streets to make the people laugh. While some heaped scurrilous abuse on him, others gave him lavish praise. His contemporaries, including King James, referred to him as "Great Oxford" and "great-souled." He was called "peerless in England" by the scholar Gabriel Harvey in a speech made before the queen, but he was also seen as "a passing singular odd man." His mercurial temperament may be understood in the light of findings by modern-day psychologists who hold that many writers of genius experience the mood swings from despair to euphoria that seem to have characterized Oxford's personality—and the personalities of many of the conflicted leading characters in the Shakespeare plays.

Remarried after the death of his first wife, Oxford lived his last years in Hackney near the market town of Stratford-at-Bow on the outskirts of London. During the last eight years of his life (1597-1604), a surge of twelve Shakespeare plays poured from the presses—five in one year alone. The first edition of *Hamlet* appeared in 1603 and the second, a much-improved edition, in 1604 the year Oxford died. It was as if the author were making final revisions to his plays and releasing them for publication.

Oxford died at age fifty-four, a year after the death of Queen Elizabeth. Through his improvident spending and the queen's manipulations of his finances, he had lost almost all of his income-producing estates, upon which rested the reputation and power of a titled aristocrat. He was interred in St. Augustine's Church at Hackney. A nephew reported that his body was later removed to Westminster in London, but Westminster Abbey has no record of it. Church records at the Abbey were not maintained until 1616. The church at Hackney was torn down two centuries later, and the whereabouts of Oxford's remains is unknown. "Though I once gone to all the world must die." (Sonnet 81)

After his death in 1604, no new plays were published with any sign of being authorized releases until 1623, when thirty-six Shakespeare plays were published in the First Folio. Half had never before been in print. The First Folio was dedicated to the earls of Pembroke and Montgomery who were brothers, and Montgomery was Oxford's son-in-law. Pembroke, who had at one time been betrothed to another of Oxford's daughters, was the Lord Chamberlain, a position that controlled the printers and the publication of plays. The two brothers were wealthy men who could easily finance the First Folio, a very expensive undertaking far beyond the resources of printers.

Pembroke was also the patron of the poet-playwright Ben Jonson, who contributed the ambiguous portrait poem and eulogy to the First Folio. Jonson also devised and scripted court masques, elaborate tableaus or pageants with courtiers in costumes. Oxford's daughters took roles in several court masques. In 1616, Jonson had taken great care with details of the publication of his own *Works*, also in a big folio volume, and was thus eminently qualified to see the Shakespeare First Folio through the presses. If Oxford's daughters and his wealthy, powerful in-laws had wanted to assure publication of the First Folio, they could hardly have arranged it any better.

His Stage and Audience

Playwrights write for their audiences, and the primary audience for the best playwrights during the reign of Elizabeth I was the queen herself, her court and England's aristocrats. She loved dancing and theatrical entertainments. Early in her reign, she granted a nobleman a license to produce "comedies, tragedies, interludes, [and] stage plays" for the entertainment of her subjects as well as for her "solace and pleasure." E. K. Chambers, one of the most eminent Shakespeare scholars, considers that the success of the theater during her reign was largely due to her appreciation and support. At the beginning of his four-volume work, *The Elizabethan Stage*, he states that she and her court had "a profound effect in helping to determine the character of the Elizabethan play," including, of course, the Shakespeare plays. Elizabeth and her court were the audience that Oxford would have had in mind when writing or revising a play.

Noblemen sponsored acting companies to shelter them from laws that branded itinerant actors as "rogues and vagabonds" and made them subject to arrest. The most prominent companies in the records of that time were the Lord Chamberlain's Men and the Lord Admiral's Men. Oxford was the patron of two acting companies and probably three. (Records for all the acting companies are scant and fragmentary.) In the 1580s, when he was in his thirties, Oxford's Men performed at court and possibly at the first public theater in London, called quite simply The Theatre. They also went on tour in the provinces, as did other acting companies from time to time. More than a decade later, another record mentions that plays were performed by Oxford's Men, which may have been a reorganized acting company of the 1580s company. Oxford also had a troupe of boy actors who performed at court and at Blackfriars, an indoor theater for aristocrats. Two years before he died, Oxford secured the queen's special

8

for patriotism if invasion by Spanish Armada!

permission for his company to perform in the yard of a tavern called the Boar's Head. In the *Henry the Fourth* plays, the Boar's Head Tavern is where Falstaff and Prince Hal drink sherry and indulge in verbal jousting. As it happens, the boar was also Oxford's heraldic emblem.

Another nobleman who sponsored acting companies was the Earl of Sussex. During one Christmas season at court, Sussex's Men staged five of the eleven anonymous plays, now lost, some of which bear titles that sound intriguingly like early versions of Shakespeare plays. Sussex was one of Oxford's closest friends at court and, in the opinion of some, almost a surrogate father.

While the Globe and the other public theaters get most of the attention as the stage for the Shakespeare plays, there are more than twice as many records of performances of Shakespeare plays at court, upscale theaters like the Blackfriars, universities and at manor houses of aristocrats than at the public theaters. As Professor Alvin Kernan of Princeton University summed it up: "Shakespeare had the court and its interests very much in mind when he wrote."

Actors also performed Shakespeare plays at the huge public theaters, which regularly drew thousands of commoners. Oxford was twenty-six when the first two public theaters were built, the Theatre and the Curtain. The Rose, the Swan and other theaters followed. Indeed, though many do not realize it, the famous Globe theater was not built until 1599, just a few years before Elizabeth and Oxford died.

The largest of these partially roofed, open-air theaters could hold two thousand spectators or more. Most of them sat on benches in three balconies for the afternoon performances. The best seats even had cushions. "Groundlings" paid a penny to stand on the ground, which was open to the sky. The covered balconies were two or three times more expensive. The public theaters were so big and the performances so frequent that seeing plays must have been an enormously popular entertainment, and playwrights produced many hundreds of plays. Almost all of them are now lost.

Blackfriars was the most important of the private theaters, so called because they were located in private precincts of London. Blackfriars was a walled precinct that had once been a sizable monastery complex. Its great hall was much smaller than the public theaters, but it provided protection from rain and snow. The price of admission, paid in advance, was much higher than the entry fee charged at the public theaters. Performances were in the evening and were lighted by torches. The fashionable, well-to-do audience watched performances by visiting acting companies and children's companies of choir boys presenting previews of plays before performing them at court. For a short time, Oxford held the lease to the Blackfriars theater, where his troupe of young actors performed. Blackfriars was so popular that the theatergoers' carriages sometimes caused traffic jams in the narrow, winding streets.

Technical term
"Law Schools" = lawyers' "school"

Plays were also performed at the 'Inns' of Court, (legal societies) where students and acting companies staged entertainments. Shakespeare's *Comedy of Errors* and, notably, *Twelfth Night* with its many legal jests, were performed by visiting troupes of actors at two of the four Inns of the Court. The courtyards of taverns like the Boar's Head were also used for theatrical entertainments, but not much is known about them. For a small city of around 150,000 people, London offered many opportunities for acting companies to perform plays before all levels of society, from the tavern yard to the royal court.

The repertory of the acting companies was enormous. At the height of a theater season, an acting company might give a hundred and fifty performances of thirty different plays. There were no long runs of a play on successive days. A leading actor might perform as many as seventy roles, playing different roles day after day. How plays were staged and how the actors managed to memorize so many different roles continues to be a subject of study by scholars of Elizabethan theater.

The Composition and Publication
of the Plays

OX on Avon River
OX died "1603" 2X 100 yrs

The first collection of Shakespeare plays, the principal authority for the canon, was published in London in 1623, almost two decades after Oxford died (and almost a decade after the death of Shakspere of Stratford.) The big, expensive book contained thirty-six plays and was entitled *Mr. Shakespeares Comedies, Histories, & Tragedies*. Later on, editors began to call it the "First Folio," a shorter name derived from the size of the pages.

Half of the plays in the First Folio were seeing print for the first time. Four of them had never before been performed, published or even mentioned in the records. Where these eighteen plays had been or who possessed the manuscripts of them prior to their publication is unknown. The other eighteen plays had appeared earlier in much smaller, separate editions called quartos, most of them during Oxford's lifetime.

The full extent of the Shakespeare canon remains a subject of study and debate. For example, scholars have generally accepted the quarto edition of *Pericles* as canonical, even though it was not included in the First Folio. Opinion is divided about whether *The Two Noble Kinsmen* should be included. It was published in 1634 as by John Fletcher and William Shakespeare. The anonymous *Locrine* is not generally accepted into the canon, although its title page says it was "newly set forth, overseen and corrected by W.S." Later in the 1600s, editions of Shakespeare plays included a half dozen plays that scholars

10

! impossible

[handwritten: or his secretary]

now exclude from the canon, although *Edward the Third* has recently been accepted by many as a Shakespeare play.

What Oxford actually penned is unknown. No manuscripts have survived. Printers of the quartos and the First Folio set type by hand from manuscripts, from actors' prompt-book copies or perhaps from a "memorial reconstruction" by someone who had seen or acted in the play. The typesetters made changes to the First Folio pages even after the printing began. As a result, no two copies are identical in text and layout.

Over the past three centuries, editors of successive editions have modernized the spelling and punctuation, corrected what seem to be printers' errors and offered interpretations of puzzling words and passages. They have also tried to reconcile the considerable differences between the quarto and folio texts of some of the plays. These textual problems have created an enormous industry in the world of Shakespeare scholarship.

When it was that the dramatist wrote each play or in what sequence and how often he revised each play are also subjects of continuing study and debate. No author's notes or other records exist to indicate a year of composition for any play. Still, an approximate chronology of composition dates for some of the Shakespeare plays can be derived from dates of first performance, first publication, or first mention of a play in various records. For example, *Titus Andronicus* and *The Taming of the Shrew* were written sometime before 1594, when records show they were performed. A version of *Hamlet* was performed by 1589, the year Thomas Nashe mentioned in passing "whole *Hamlets*, I should say handfuls of tragical speeches," and it was performed again in 1594 when records list a performance of *Hamlet* in a theater at Newington Butts.

Stratfordian scholarship dates the composition of a dozen or so plays after Oxford's death in 1604 based almost entirely on references or allusions in the plays. The post-1604 dating scheme fails, however, because none of those references and allusions is unique to writings or events that occurred after 1604. Posthumous publication or performance is not at all unusual for playwrights. Oxford could have written and revised the allegedly post-1604 plays many years before he died. [handwritten: plays after] [handwritten: are]

The Question of the Dramatist's Identity

The widely accepted belief is [handwritten: was] that the poet and dramatist was William Shakspere, the Stratford glove-maker's son who went to London in the late 1580s and supposedly became an actor. In Stratford, "Shakspere," or a close variant thereof without the "e" after the "k," was the way all eight official church records spelled his name, from his baptism in 1564 to his death and burial in 1616, including on the monument in the Stratford church. So also did the six

[handwritten: OX went to live on Avon River when the heat of summer in city unbearable]

"Signatures," supposedly by him, including those on his will. In London, the name on the published plays and poems was uniformly Shakespeare. Stratfordian scholars, however, choose to ignore or reject the difference in the spelling of the two names. They assume that almost any reference in the records to Shakspere in whatever spelling also designated the poet-dramatist Shakespeare.

They seek additional support in the front matter of the First Folio of 1623 where Ben Jonson alludes to the dramatist as "Sweet Swan of Avon," and another poet, Leonard Digges, mentions a "Stratford moniment." They cite two dedication letters in the First Folio that appeared over the names of two actors, John Heminge and Henry Condell, who had been added belatedly to Shakspere's will in 1616. And the records show that late in life Shakspere invested in two theaters.

For centuries, no one questioned the identity of the Bard of Avon, and today's monument to "Shakspeare" (no first name) in Holy Trinity Church at Stratford depicts a man holding a quill pen and poised to write on a sheet of paper on a pillow—seemingly a memorial to the Stratford man as a writer, even though no historical evidence from Stratford suggests that he was a writer.

As scholars and theater people in the 1800s and 1900s realized that Shakespeare's works were the greatest literary achievement in Western civilization, they deified him as the Immortal Bard, and the town of Stratford became a virtual shrine to him. The idea of a commoner writing such stupendous creations was appealing to many who espoused new, democratic ideals. Scholars devoted their careers trying to flesh out the meager records of Shakspere's life and searching for historical and literary evidence to try to establish him firmly as the author.

Close examination of the evidence, however, undercuts the case for him as the author. The names "Shakspere" and "Shakespeare" are similar, but they are not the same. Spelling was chaotic, so it is all the more significant that in London the name on the poems and plays was uniformly Shakespeare, while the Stratford man's name was almost always Shakspere, reflecting a pronunciation with a flat "a," as in "shack spur." For several decades in the late 1800s and early 1900s, Stratfordian scholars adopted the "Shakspere" spelling for the author, but then they realized that this would not do, since the works had been published as by William Shakespeare or Shake-speare.

The prefatory matter in the First Folio is central to the Stratfordian belief, but the only biographical evidence that seems to point to Shakspere of Stratford as the author is allusive and deliberately ambiguous. For example, Oxford himself had an estate on the Avon River and lived the last years of his life in a mansion close by a town named Stratford near London (not the Stratford-on-Avon that was a three-day journey from the capital.) Even Stratfordian scholars doubt that the letters that appeared over the names of Heminge and Condell

12

R i v e r

were written by them. Both letters contain ambiguities, patent falsehoods and parallels to the writings of Ben Jonson, a recognized master of ambiguity who probably wrote the letters. The prefatory matter in First Folio cannot be taken at face value and is not reliable evidence for the Stratford man.

Moreover, the effigy in today's Stratford monument that depicts a writer is not the original, which depicted a sack holder. In 1634, the historian William Dugdale visited Stratford, and his sketch of the original monument shows a man with a drooping moustache, arms akimbo, grasping a sack of wool—no paper, pen or writing surface. For almost a century, this sack holder was the image used to depict the Stratford man. In later centuries, however, the effigy in the monument was taken down several times by Stratford civic leaders for repair and beautification, no doubt transforming it into today's effigy of a man with pen and paper poised to write on a pillow. The man commemorated in the original Stratford monument was not a writer.

Shakspere's life does not fit the life of a writer, much less that of the world's greatest poet-dramatist. Nothing is known about what he was doing until he was twenty-eight years old, a writer's most formative years, except that he married and had three children. There is no record that he went to school in the classroom in Stratford, a rural market town of fewer than 250 families, or anywhere else. No records from his lifetime connect him with writing of any kind, much less the Shakespeare plays and poems. No letters he wrote or received have been found. No one in Stratford, including his family and others who must have known him, left any sign that he was an author. His children, whom he left illiterate, never made a claim to any literary legacy of his. His three-page will is the will of a businessman; it contains no mention of books or manuscripts or anything literary. If he owned any books, not one has been found. No theater records during his lifetime list him as an actor, nor is he mentioned anywhere as having acted in any role. He was supposedly buried under a slab that does not even carry his name, and the short inscription on the Stratford monument on the wall nearby says nothing about plays, poems or the theater. No one wrote anything about his passing in 1616, even though the Shakespeare plays and poems were among the most successful in London.

Given the woefully inadequate historical evidence for the Stratford man as the author, what remains is the similarity of name, the weight of centuries of tradition, and the attraction for many for the belief that the great poet-dramatist was an ordinary, unassuming, un-traveled man of no documented education, but an incredible genius.

No one seriously questioned his credentials until the middle of the 1800s when a few Shakespeare scholars noted the lack of anything literary in the life of the Stratford man and proposed Sir Francis Bacon, the philosopher, essayist and statesman, as someone more qualified to have written the works of Shakespeare.

As the search intensified for the true author, Christopher Marlowe, William Stanley sixth Earl of Derby, and others were also put forward as candidates.

Then, in 1920, J. Thomas Looney, an inquisitive and insightful English schoolmaster, published his pioneering book identifying Edward de Vere, the seventeenth Earl of Oxford, as the true author of Shakespeare's works. Since then, more than a dozen books and scores of articles have expanded on the evidence for Oxford. Today, his candidacy has by far the most support among non-Stratfordians. Although "proof positive" that Oxford was Shakespeare may as yet be lacking, the editors of the plays in this series are among the growing number of those who have concluded that the preponderance of evidence convincingly supports Oxford as the author of the Shakespeare canon. That conviction has informed their research, analysis and interpretations for the introductions and line notes in this Oxfordian Shakespeare Series.

Further Reading +Internet

The following works are a selected few from the wide range of scholarship on the seventeenth Earl of Oxford as the author of the plays that appeared under his pseudonym, William Shakespeare. Citations and bibliographies in these works lead to many other works about Oxford and the authorship controversy. For Internet web sites on the issue and for Oxfordian periodicals and conferences, search the Internet for "Shakespeare Oxford."

Anderson, Mark. *Shakespeare by Another Name: A Biography of Edward de Vere, Earl of Oxford, the Man Who Was Shakespeare.* New York: Gotham, 2004.

Chambers, E. K. *The Elizabethan Stage.* 4 vols. Oxford: Clarendon, 1923. For Oxford's acting companies at Court in the 1580s, see 2:99-102.
   "Court Performances Before Queen Elizabeth." *Modern Language Review* 2.1 (October 1906) For Oxford's acting companies in the 1580s.

Clark, Eva Turner. *Hidden Allusions in Shakespeare's Plays: A Study of the Early Court Revels and the Personalities of the Times.* London: Palmer, 1930. 3d ed. Jennings LA: Minos, 1974. Edited with additional material by Ruth Loyd Miller.

Farina, William. *De Vere as Shakespeare: An Oxfordian Reading of the Canon.* Jefferson NC: McFarland, 2006.

Kernan, Alvin. *Shakespeare, the King's Playwright: Theater in the Stuart Court, 1603-1613.* New Haven CT: Yale UP, 1995.

Looney, J. Thomas. *"Shakespeare" Identified in Edward de Vere, the Seventeenth Earl of Oxford.* London: Palmer, 1920.

Miller, Ruth Loyd, ed. *Oxfordian Vistas.* Jennings LA: Minos, 1975. A collection of scores of articles, many by Miller, on Oxfordian matters.

Ogburn, Charlton. *The Mysterious William Shakespeare: The Myth and the Reality.* McLean VA: EPM, 1984.

Ogburn, Dorothy and Charlton. *This Star of England: William Shakespeare, Man of the Renaissance.* New York: Coward-McCann, 1952.

Sobran, Joseph. *Alias Shakespeare: Solving the Greatest Literary Mystery of All Time.* New York: Free Press, 1997.

Whalen, Richard F. *Shakespeare—Who Was He? The Oxford Challenge to the Bard of Avon.* Westport CT: Greenwood-Praeger, 1994.

Ward, B. M. *The Seventeenth Earl of Oxford (1550-1604) from Contemporary Documents.* London: Murray, 1928.

A Note on the Texts

The play texts in these editions are based on the Globe edition of 1864, edited by William George Clark and William Aldis Wright. The Globe edition is considered the earliest reliable edition of the Shakespeare plays along modern lines. It has been digitized as the "Complete Moby Shakespeare" and can be found on the Internet by searching "MIT Shakespeare."

The Globe edition, it must be noted, occasionally diverges from the First Folio text in ways that have been judged to be unnecessary, arbitrary or inappropriate. For example, the Globe editors changed line breaks, revised stage directions, moved a few entrances and exits, put prose passages into verse, and dropped words here and there. In many such cases, therefore, the texts in this series follow the First Folio and/or a more authoritative quarto text rather than the Globe edition. The Globe also used exclamation points and colons excessively, and capitalized speech prefixes but omitted initial capitals for sentences following question marks and exclamation points. These have been modernized, and the Globe's British spelling and punctuation have been changed to American.

As do all editions of the Shakespeare plays, these Oxfordian editions try to strike a balance between respect for the authority of the First Folio of 1623 and/or earlier quarto editions and the need to modernize texts for today's reader. On three counts the editors have been aggressive: spelling, punctuation and scene locations. These editions, like all current editions of Shakespeare, modernize Elizabethan spelling for ease of comprehension. The punctuation of the First Folio and quartos, which is sparse and erratic, has been judiciously regularized. Although no scene locations are given in the original play texts, speeches in a scene usually provide clues to its location. The play texts in these editions give the scene location at the start of the scene, and they try to be clear about where the scene takes place. Inevitably, the editing in this series, as in all Shakespeare editions, is open to challenge.

Line numbering varies from edition to edition in Shakespeare plays because of changes by modern-day editors to the layout of the texts. Although the line numbering in this series may vary by as many as four or five lines, it generally parallels that of other editions.

Acknowledgments

The general editors wish to acknowledge their debt to the many university professors and independent scholars who have contributed so much to the case for Oxford as the true author of the works of Shakespeare. We want to express our gratitude to all of them but must single out for special mention J. Thomas Looney, Bernard M. Ward, Dorothy and Charlton Ogburn, their son Charlton Ogburn, Eva Turner Clark, Charles Wisner Barrell and Ruth Loyd Miller. Without their pioneering work in the twentieth century, this series would not have been possible.

More recently, dozens of Oxfordian scholars, Mark Anderson in particular, have contributed to the evidence in support of Oxford. They are too numerous to list here, but we want to acknowledge our debt to their scholarship, which has appeared and continues to appear both in print and on Internet web sites.

Finally, in what may seem paradoxical but is not, we are grateful to all the Stratfordian scholars who have done so much research into the works of Shakespeare. Not infrequently, their findings have strengthened the case for Oxford. Several Stratfordian professors have graciously engaged us and other Oxfordian researchers, debating the evidence and helping us test our evidence and conclusions.

Richard F. Whalen
Truro, Massachusetts

Daniel L. Wright
Concordia University, Portland, Oregon

Introduction to *Othello*

One of the greatest of the Shakespeare plays, *Othello, the Moor of Venice*, is also one of the plays that offer compelling support for Edward de Vere, the seventeenth Earl of Oxford, as the dramatist. Venice and Cyprus, where Oxford traveled, are described in accurate detail. Othello suspects his wife of infidelity, as did Oxford. Othello is concerned about his honor and reputation, and so was Oxford. The play shows knowledge of works in Italian not yet translated into English. Passing mentions of nautical, military and legal matters and allusions to falconry reflect an aristocratic author, as do the manners and speech of the upper-class characters and how they relate to each other. Generally overlooked is the influence of *commedia dell'arte*, the satiric, improvised theater that was common in Venice when Oxford was there but was almost unknown in England. (There is no historical evidence that the commoner Will Shakspere of Stratford ever left England, suspected his wife of infidelity or knew foreign languages—or that he could write plays like *Othello*.)

Othello is a play of powerful contrasts, complex characters and black humor, yet the basic plot is simple. Othello, a dark-skinned Moor from North Africa and commander of the Venetian military, has eloped with Desdemona, the daughter of a Venetian senator. His ensign, Iago, shamed and resentful at not having been promoted to be Othello's lieutenant, gets revenge by tricking him into believing that Desdemona has cuckolded him. Under Iago's evil influence, Othello changes from a confident, loving husband to a deluded, enraged, avenger who kills his wife and then himself. Characters in the play range from the high-minded to the base, from lovingly romantic to comically cuckold, from perilously naive to cleverly ironic, from murderous to suicidal.

Othello is an experienced and respected military commander hired by the Venetian rulers, but he is an alien, a black mercenary from Islamic North Africa who finds himself among aristocratic whites in Catholic Venice. He is in a difficult, ambiguous position—an outsider in the upper-class society of Venice, a convert to Catholicism who has turned his back on his own people, a middle-aged soldier who elopes with the teenage daughter of an aristocrat in an interracial marriage. Although he says he comes from a royal Islamic family, he is not experienced in the power politics and intrigues of the sophisticated Venetians. In the senators' council, the equivalent of the English court, he overdoes it when he tries to speak their courtly language. As Harold Bloom notes in *The Invention of the Human*, his "acute sense of reputation" leads him to see himself in "grandiose terms," even in his last words before his suicide. (445)

Scholars have suggested several possible sources for Othello's name. It may well derive from "Othman," the founder of the Turkish dynasty and

18

Islamic empire that ruled North Africa, the Middle East and the Balkans almost to Vienna in the mid-1500s. Another influence may have been the name of the Moorish warrior Otuel or Othuell of the medieval French Charlemagne romances. (See Influences and Sources.) The Italian form may hint at Girolamo Otello of Bassano del Grappa, a town in the Venetian republic about sixty miles from Venice. Otello, a notoriously zealous Jesuit, was in his fifties when Oxford was in Italy. In Italian, "Othello" is pronounced "Otello." And there was an Otelo del Moro family in Venice that was involved in various scandals.

Iago is a courtier-like intriguer and a psychopath whose ambitions have been thwarted and who also suspects that he has been cuckolded. At twenty-eight, he is much younger than Othello but much more sophisticated. Although his name is not the title of the play, he has more lines; he drives the plot forward, and from time to time he stands alone on stage and tells the audience with delight how he is manipulating everyone. Iago is the dramatist within the play, creating the action that escalates unstoppably from satiric comedy to a tragic murder-suicide.

Psychologists have noted that he is a classic psychopath—superficially charming, glib and entertaining but cunning and manipulative, a liar, confident in his deceptions who shows no remorse when events overtake him and he loses his power to manipulate people. Ever since Freud's "analysis" of Hamlet (and embrace of Oxford as the author), psychiatrists and psychologists have acclaimed Shakespeare's uncanny studies of his characters. Iago and Othello are two of his masterworks of psychology.

Iago exploits Othello's inexperience in court politics and outsider's self-doubt to turn him against Lieutenant Michael Cassio, who was Iago's rival for the position of Othello's second-in-command. Iago is an ensign, a position in the English army similar to an aide-de-camp. To get revenge for being passed over and to destroy Othello, Iago subtly insinuates into Othello's guileless mind the suspicion that Cassio has slept with Desdemona. If true, Othello would wear the ludicrous and shameful horns of the cuckold. Iago makes him insanely suspicious of Desdemona, driving him into a rage to seek revenge for what he fears will be the loss of his hard-won reputation for courage, integrity and military leadership.

Scheming, lying, manipulating and improvising to take advantage of the unforeseen, Iago "is pleased and amused by his own cleverness in wanton destruction," in the words of David Bevington in *Shakespeare*. (49) E. A. J. Honigmann says in his Arden edition of the play that Iago takes "artistic delight in power and in manipulating" Othello and Cassio, and especially Roderigo, the rich, foolish courtier who is duped into being Iago's confederate. (35) He makes them all dance to his music.

Iago lies to everyone but not to himself and, in soliloquy, not to the audience. As the dramatist within the play he must be believed when, alone on the stage with Othello in the grip of an epileptic seizure Iago has helped trigger, he says "Work on, / My medicine, work! Thus credulous fools are caught." (4.1.40) For the dramatist, whose Iago always tells the truth to the audience, Othello is not a noble, tragic hero but Iago's "credulous fool." For his aristocratic audience, the white actor in burlesque black-face must have seemed cartoonish.

Iago's name is not Italian but Spanish, so he apparently is of Spanish origin. At one point he curses in Spanish with "*Diablo!*". Anything Spanish was ominous for educated Elizabethans, and Spaniards were often demonized. Catholic Spain under Philip II was the most powerful nation in the world, a dangerous maritime rival to Protestant England, with dependencies in the nearby Low Countries and in Italy. Iago's name echoes Sant'Iago, the patron saint of Catholic Spain, who was known as *Matamoros*, the Moor-killer. In the play, Iago the Spanish Catholic destroys Othello the Moor.

Roderigo's name is also Spanish, and even Othello is a quasi-Spaniard. For Elizabethans, "Othello the Moor" would evoke the Moors of Spain, who threatened all of Europe from across the Pyrenees for several centuries until they lost control of the Iberian peninsula and were finally expelled in the 1490s. The dramatist may well have thought of Othello as a descendant of those Moors who fled to Mauretania and other parts of North Africa. In the late 1570s and mid-1580s, when Oxford was probably writing and re-writing the play, a resurgent Catholic Spain was a serious threat; in 1588 the Spanish Armada tried to invade England. Othello is as much the Moor of Spain as the Moor from North Africa. He and Iago evoke Europe's old enemy, Islamic Spain, and England's more immediate enemy, Catholic Spain. The geo-politics of the play would have been recognized and appreciated by the educated, aristocratic audiences for whom the play was written. (+ patriotism of commoners)

The shame of cuckoldry that would ruin his reputation drives Othello to seek revenge. Iago leads him to suspect that the aristocratic Desdemona has cuckolded him with his own subordinate, Cassio, and that he will be made the laughing stock of the military and Venetian society. After Iago hints that Cassio may be sleeping with Desdemona, Othello exclaims, "Arise, black Vengeance from thy hollow hell; / Yield up, O Love, thy crown and hearted throne / to tyrannous Hate." (3.4.447-9) Later, when Othello confronts Desdemona and tells her that she is "false as hell," he says he could tolerate anything except being shamed as a "fixed figure . . . of scorn." (4.2.54) Bevington says that Desdemona "has betrayed and unmanned him . . . his recourse must be to retaliate. She has inflicted upon him the shame of being labeled a cuckold." (171) > public

Although cooler and more calculating, Iago has his own reasons for revenge. He suspects that Othello and Cassio have made him a cuckold. He also is bitterly resentful because Othello didn't promote him to lieutenant.

shame.

with his wife

Both Othello and Iago seek revenge for perceived wrongs done to them, and in one of his early poems (before he wrote as Shakespeare) Oxford explored the emotion of revenge. It begins "Fain would I sing, but fury makes me fret, / And rage hath sworn to seek revenge of wrong." The 18-line poem ends, "Lo, thus in rage of ruthful mind refused, / I rest revenged on whom I'm abused."

Even Lieutenant Cassio fears for his reputation. After Iago tricks him into a drunken street brawl, shameful for a senior officer, Cassio cries out extravagantly:

> Reputation! Reputation! Reputation! O, I have
> lost my reputation. I have lost the immortal
> part of myself—and what remains is bestial.
> My reputation, Iago, my reputation.
> (2.3.233-5)

Othello reflects Oxford's deep concern for his own reputation as the seventeenth in a line of distinguished earls going back to the time of William the Conqueror. In one of the poems of his youth (before he began writing as "Shakespeare"), he bewailed "the shock of shame and infamy. . . . the loss of my good name." His half-sister had accused him in an inheritance dispute of being a bastard. When he was twenty-six, he bitterly rebuked his father-in-law, William Cecil Lord Burghley, for allowing him to be made "the fable of the world" when rumors circulated that he had been cuckolded while he was in Italy. Someone told him that people were rumoring that he was not the father of his wife's daughter, born when he was in Italy and whose date of birth and paternity were uncertain.

Thus, just as Oxford, who married the teenage daughter of Queen Elizabeth's senior adviser, Lord Burghley, suspected for a time that she cuckolded him and rejected her, so does Othello, who marries the teenage daughter of one of the Doge's senior senators, suspect that she cuckolded him and rejects her. Oxford later reconciled with his wife, who had four more children with him. Tragically, Othello only learns after he kills his wife that his suspicions of being cuckolded were totally unfounded. *Othello* is one of several Shakespeare plays, e.g. *Antony and Cleopatra,* that raise the specter of cuckoldry ruining a man's reputation.

"Othello," says Bloom, "sees the world as a theater for his professional reputation; this most valiant of soldiers has no fear of literal death-in-battle, which only would enhance his glory. But to be cuckolded by his own wife, and with his subordinate Cassio as the other offender, would be a greater metaphorical death-in-life, for his reputation would not survive it, particularly in his own view of his mythic renown." (*Invention* 449)

Ewan Fernie argues in *Shame in Shakespeare* that "the soul of Othello's jealousy is shame." In another early poem by Oxford, a forsaken lover vows that if another man "triumphs over" him he will "hide myself from shame, sith [since] that [that] mine eyes do see. . .hath thus tormented me." In the play, Othello is tormented by what his eyes do see, the "ocular" proof he demanded of Desdemona's infidelity. Fernie says that "it is shame, not jealousy, that is the signal and unifying passion of *Othello*." Iago, he adds, "feels shamed and slighted rather than envious," and Desdemona "suffers the shame of accusations of whoredom and adultery from her husband." (136-8)

In his ELH article "Slander and Skepticism in *Othello*," Kenneth Gross situates the dangers of slander in Elizabethan England:

> The seriousness of the problem of slander should not surprise us in a period so obsessed with the protean status of public identity and the uncertain lures of fame, reputation, and honor, in a period in which the resources of insult, invective, curse, or "giving the lie" were so cultivated, and when (in England at least) both church and state authorities felt such a powerful, almost paranoid, need to defend themselves against the often ghostly threat of rumor, scandal, conspiracy, sedition, or heresy. A complex concern with the work of slander is at the center of a number of Shakespeare's plays, most obviously *Measure for Measure*, *Much Ado About Nothing* and *Cymbeline*, but also *Hamlet* and even (more ironically) *Coriolanus*. (821)

Throughout his life, Oxford impetuously put his "fame, reputation and honor" in jeopardy. People remarked on his many talents but also on his impulsive, mercurial, eccentric behavior–the behavior of an outspoken genius but behavior that could draw ridicule and damage his reputation. Bloom sensed the dramatist's anguish: "*Othello* may have been as painful for Shakespeare as he made it for us. Placing the precarious nobility of Othello and the fragile romanticism of Desdemona upon one stage with the sadistic aestheticism of Iago. . .was already an outrageous *coup* of self-wounding on the poet-dramatist's part." (*Invention* 452) Self-wounding behavior marks Oxford's life story.

Commentators often refer to Desdemona as an innocent victim, but that's only partly true. Probably in her late teens, she is a willful girl who had already rejected several suitors, "wealthy, curled darlings" of Venice, before choosing Othello and eloping. She was, as her father Brabantio feared, "half the wooer." Othello knew she loved him for the warrior-adventurer in him. "She loved me for the dangers I had passed," he says, "and I loved her that she did pity them." (1.3.93-5) She was willing to defy her father and accept the opprobrium of marrying down and marrying a man old enough to be her father. Othello could not recognize how marrying above his station might contribute to his downfall. by her.

Far from being innocent and pure, Desdemona willingly engages with Iago in bawdy repartee in act 2. She already has the manners and morals of Venetian woman, generally considered at the time to be witty, sophisticated and worldly but kept at home under guard until married. In some ways mature beyond her years, she is courageous and articulate when defending her elopement before the senators, including her father, whom she has disobeyed, but she is not experienced in the dangerous intrigues of a courtier-soldier such as Iago. That is her tragic flaw. To the very end, she remains loyal to Othello, failing to recognize Iago's subversion of everyone in his orbit and even blaming herself that Othello killed her.

For aristocratic audiences, Othello's father-in-law, Brabantio, would have been seen as a caricature of Lord Burghley, Oxford's father-in-law. Both were in high positions of authority; both were garrulous and rambling in speech; both had aristocratic daughters suspected of sexual improprieties; both had accomplished but troublesome sons-in-law.

No Italian or Spanish source for the name "Brabantio" has been found. Oxford may have had in mind the province of Brabant in the Low Countries and the Duke of Alençon, heir to the French throne and a persistent suitor of Queen Elizabeth. French troops under Alençon were taking control of most of the Low Countries in the early 1580s. Alençon hoped for an easy, victorious entry into the capital of Brabant on his Barbary horse, a horse from North Africa, but it turned into a disastrous defeat. Iago mocks Brabantio by telling him his daughter is coupling with a Barbary horse, that is, with Othello from the Barbary coast.

Lieutenant Michael Cassio, even more so than Iago, is a courter-like character--even to the point of parody. He comes across as a newly commissioned, upper-class officer and new to the power politics of court intrigue. He fails to recognize Iago's skill at manipulating him and everyone else. Behind his back, Iago disparages Cassio as nothing but a bean-counter from Florence, a desk officer not experienced in battle and statecraft. He's easy for Iago to dupe.

Vain, ambitious and foppish, Cassio is a ladies' man, preferring the company of refined ladies to that of rough soldiers. He has courtly, elegant manners and is given to extravagantly ornate language, especially about the well-born Desdemona. His speech shows all the signs of euphuism, an elaborate, affected, high-flown style of language easily imitated and just as easily caricatured. Oxford knew it well. His secretary, John Lyly, published two *Euphues* novels, in 1579 and 1580, that exemplified a radically innovative style of language. The novels appealed to aristocratic ladies with language that was light, witty,

23

artificial and often logically irrational, as if mocking itself. The novels appear to parody certain courtiers' mannered language in Queen Elizabeth's court. The novels and eight excellent comedies that also appeared as by Lyly were popular, accomplished works. Scholars consider them important influences on Shakespeare comedies. It's not impossible, however, that Oxford wrote the works of Lyly, who published nothing before or after he was Oxford's secretary in the 1580s. The title page of the first of the *Euphues* novels says that Lyly "compiled" it, suggesting that someone else wrote it.

In a telling comment, Harold Bloom says, "Cassio shows himself to be a refined gentleman, a courtier in the tradition prescribed by Baldassare Castiglione in his handbook *The Courtier*." (*Othello* 9) Oxford was very familiar with the book. He wrote a Latin preface to a translation of it from Italian into Latin and had it published in London in 1572, three years before he left for Italy.

Emilia and Bianca, two secondary characters, become enmeshed in Iago's deadly schemes, but like Desdemona they remain true and honest. Emilia, Desdemona's outspoken maid or lady-in-waiting, is tricked by Iago, her husband, into stealing Desdemona's handkerchief. Emilia is suspicious but appears to fear Iago and obeys him. Only at the very end of the play does she suddenly realize that Iago duped Othello into killing Desdemona. Outraged, she exposes Iago's deception and Othello's gullibility. Vengeful, Iago kills her. Honigmann writes:

> Emilia repays some attention: her developing relationship with her husband and her developing moral involvement illustrate Shakespeare's remarkable control of detail, which in turn justifies those critics who think it their duty to peer into the recesses of character and motive. (47)

Critics who "peer into the recesses of character and motive" of *all* the characters in *Othello* can hardly escape suspecting that the dramatist was a well-read aristocrat who was knowledgeable about court intrigues, Venice and the eastern Mediterranean, a playwright who drew on his life experience and deepest concerns.

Oxford may well have borrowed the name "Emilia" from Emilia Bassano Lanier, a member of the Bassano family, which had moved to London from the town of Bassano in the Venetian Republic (the same Bassano of Girolamo Otello). The Bassano family were court musicians who performed regularly for Queen Elizabeth. When in her twenties, Emilia was the "Italian courtesan" of the Lord Chamberlain, the patron of the acting company that performed many of the Shakespeare plays. For some Stratfordians she is a strong candidate as the inspiration for the "Dark Lady" of the Sonnets. She was the first woman in England to publish a book of her poems. Her name was special for Oxford; "Emilia" was his favorite name for non-historical women in his Shakespeare plays.

Bianca is a Venetian courtesan who loves Cassio. Oxford almost certainly named her after Bianca Cappello, a famous, upper-class courtesan from a rich and noble Venetian family. Oxford could hardly have missed her sensational life and may have known her. When she was fifteen, she eloped with a clerk, outraging her father and the Venetian senators. A great beauty, she then became the mistress of the heir to the Medici dukedom. They later married, and both died by poisoning in the 1580s when Oxford probably was re-writing *Othello*.

The upper-class courtesans were cultured and richly dressed. They were held in high esteem in society and usually had rich merchants and noblemen as their patrons. Oxford consorted with a Venetian courtesan named Virginia Padoana. Her neighbor, an English traveler, wrote home playfully that she "honoreth all our nation for my Lord of Oxfords sake."

The name of Lodovico, an emissary from the Venetian senate, may have been inspired by Ludovico Beccadelli. In the play, Lodovico is the voice of reason and authority. He brings a letter from the Duke appointing Cassio as governor of Cyprus and, since the military campaign was finished, ordering Othello and his forces to return to Venice. In the last scene, he arrests Iago and Othello.

Although Ludovico (or Lodovico) Beccadelli died three years before Oxford arrived in Venice, he had been significant figure in political and cultural life there. A bishop, humanist and reformer, he was secretary to Cardinal Contarini of Venice, who was his patron. Contarini's book on Venice may have influenced *Othello*. Ludivico Beccadelli had also been the Pope's representative to Venice and was a close friend of Michelangelo. A biographer of Michelangelo called Ludovico a "clever, cultivated and enormously experienced cleric" who studied law, literature and the classical world." He published a biography of Petrarch, who wrote the first sonnet cycle, in the fourteenth century. Oxford could hardly have missed hearing about Ludovico Beccadelli.

Oxford spent almost fifteen months on the Continent, mostly in Venice and northern Italy and probably traveling the Adriatic and Mediterranean seas. On his way to Italy, he had stopped in Paris for several weeks, where the Venetian ambassador to the French king gave him letters of introduction to the ambassador's relatives in Venice and to the Doge. As Lord Great Chamberlain in Queen Elizabeth's court, Oxford would have met and been entertained by Venetian senators and aristocrats while he was living there.

Sixteenth-century Venice was the richest city in Europe, exotic and sophisticated, a center of trade between East and West and a center of painting, music and theater, especially the *commedia dell'arte*. Oxford spent about five months in Venice, and act 1 of *Othello* reflects his first-hand knowledge of

Venice in general and in particular, from the unusual oligarchy government to Othello's lodgings on a street called (in English) Sagittary, a street that can be found today. (See line note 1.1.153.)

Act 1 also shows that he knew about a detail of Middle Eastern history. The Venetian senate hears reports about a Turkish fleet of two hundred ships heading towards Rhodes but then turning towards Cyprus. The Duke orders Othello to sail for Cyprus and defend it against invasion by the Turks.

It is an historical fact that in June 1570, five years before Oxford arrived in Italy, a Turkish fleet of two hundred ships headed towards Rhodes but then turned toward Cyprus, Venice's most valuable colony and closest to the Middle East. Although the Turks did in fact invade Cyprus in July 1570, they landed at the western end of the island, a hundred miles from the fortified port-city of Famagusta, which they did not take until August of the following year. During the action of the play, the Moorish invaders are off-stage and far away, a distant, ominous, unstated threat to Famagusta, the setting for most of *Othello* and still in Venetian hands but not for long.

Act 2 contains evidence that Oxford may have visited Famagusta during the summer of 1575. He had written home from Paris that he hoped to take two months to sail to Constantinople and Greece. He arrived in Venice in May, and letters and other records indicate where he was most of the time. No records, however, tell where he was from around mid-May to mid-September, suggesting that he did indeed go on a sea voyage.

He no doubt sailed across the Adriatic to Ragusa (today's Dubrovnik), a setting for *Twelfth Night,* and then down to Sicily, the setting for *Much Ado About Nothing* , and probably on to Cyprus, the setting for most of *Othello*. Sea travel from Venice was on galleys, two-masted ships propelled by both sails and oarsmen. Scores of such galleys were based in the port of Venice, which had a major shipbuilding industry. A rich nobleman from England would have no difficulty chartering a fast galley for his exclusive use.

As act 2 opens, Montano, the Venetian governor of Cyprus, and others are waiting for the Venetian fleet and Othello to arrive at Famagusta harbor. Famagusta is not named in the play, but it is the island's only well-protected, fortified seaport. It is also only a hundred miles from the trading city of Aleppo in Syria. Othello evokes Aleppo just before he kills himself, and a witch mentions Aleppo in *Macbeth* (1.3.6).

The topography of the battlements directly above the wharf at Famagusta harbor is implied in the dialogue no fewer than twelve times in scene 1 of act 2 (lines 1-210). Montano and others are standing on the battlements, and each time it's clear from what they say that from the battlements they cannot see the harbor wharf directly below. At one point, for example, Montano says, "Let's to the seaside . . . to see the vessel that's come in." (2.1.36-7) This unusual topography, mentioned so often in the play, reflects precisely the unusual topography of Famagusta, the fortified port, where the battlements tower directly above the harbor's wharf. Unless the dramatist had stood on the battlements where he has Montano and others waiting as the Venetian fleet arrives, it's difficult to understand why he would put into the play such an accurate yet casual insistence on the topography. (It's very difficult, if not impossible, to believe that Will Shakspere of Stratford could have known about the Famagusta topography.)

Modern-day editors of *Othello* do not identify the port, although it was identified as Famagusta by Edmund Malone in his 1790 edition of the plays, and then by a few other editors. Nor have any editors or commentators until now recognized that the dramatist's description of the port and its fortifications is accurately conveyed in the dialogue—a description that has gone unremarked for the entire three centuries of Shakespeare scholarship. (See Appendices.)

Othello may also be seen as subtle commentary on the religio-geopolitics of Ottoman Islam, Roman Catholic Spain, the other Catholic countries, the Papacy and Protestant England under Queen Elizabeth.

In the background of the play but very much in the foreground for the aristocratic and court audiences in the 1570s and 1580s was the superpower Spain. By the mid-1500s, the Spanish empire had expanded to Latin America, the Philippines and the Low Countries (the Netherlands and parts of Belgium) and to Sicily. Spain also controlled two of the most important city-states of Italy, Milan and Naples. Spain was the most powerful country in the world; and Iago, Roderigo and even Othello are quasi-Spaniards.

A few Stratfordian scholars have sensed the geopolitics of *Othello*. For example, Lilian Winstanley of University College of Wales entitled her 1924 book, "Othello" *as the Tragedy of Italy*. In it, she argues, as her full title states, that "Shakespeare's Italian contemporaries interpreted the story of the Moor and the Lady of Venice as symbolizing the tragedy of their country in the grip of Spain."

In 1575, the year Oxford arrived in Italy with plans to go to Constantinople, England's first diplomatic-trade mission arrived in that city, the capital of the Ottoman empire, and British ships began trading in the eastern Mediterranean. Historian Kenneth R. Andrews called the year 1575 the beginning of "England's main breakthrough into the Turkey trade." Oxford was on the scene, and although no records have him playing a role in opening diplomatic relations with Constantinople, he had hoped to go there and may have been on a semi-diplomatic mission during the four summer months of 1575 when his whereabouts and doings are unrecorded. The coincidence in timing is quite suggestive. What his unofficial mission may have been is unknown, but when he returned to Venice by way of Genoa after four months incommunicado, his "success and good disposition in this, his travel" were reported to Lord Burghley by an Italian banker. And at the end of his stay in Venice that city-state named its first ambassador to England.

In the late 1570s and in the 1580s, London strengthened relations with Constantinople as a counterforce to expansionist Spain. Elizabeth sent a diplomatic representative to Constantinople, and Sultan Murad III sent a letter of friendship to her, an unprecedented communication for a sultan, especially to a ruler who was a woman. In her reply, Elizabeth suggested that Islam and Protestant England had in common their worship of "One True God" without the Roman Catholic icons and pictures of God that Islam also rejected.

The queen and the sultan had in common a concern about Spain's intentions. In 1583, she named an ambassador to Constantinople, and Sir Francis Walsingham, her chief administrator and spymaster, told him to ask the sultan for naval assistance to divert the resources of the Spanish, whose navy threatened England and would try to invade England in 1588. It was during these years, while events were fresh in mind, that Oxford was probably writing and re-writing *Othello* about a Moor who defected from Ottoman Islam, converted to Roman Catholicism, signed on as commander for Catholic Venice to fight the Ottoman Turks—and even married a Catholic, Venetian aristocrat. These complex, nuanced geopolitical realities mirrored in the play would have struck a chord with Queen Elizabeth and her court.

Influences and Sources

The barebones plot for *Othello* came from stories by two Italian writers, Giovanni Giraldi, known as Cinthio, and to a lesser but still significant extent an earlier tale by Matteo Bandello. Cinthio's *Hecatommithi (A Hundred Tales)* was published in Venice in 1565, just ten years before Oxford arrived. One of the stories in the "Third Decade," which is on marital infidelity, tells about a "valiant Moor" soldier who is married to a "virtuous lady of Venice" who insists on traveling to Cyprus with him. Oxford adopted several plot lines and character traits from Cinthio, including, for example, themes of sexual jealousy and revenge, the trickery of the Moor's ensign and the handkerchief device. He also made important additions and changes. Act 1, set in the streets of Venice and the senate, is not in Cinthio, nor are Brabantio, the Duke or the courtier-soldier Roderigo.

Cinthio was not translated into English until 1735. Although a French translation was published in 1583, Michael Neill says in his edition of *Othello* that the dramatist "almost certainly read [Cinthio] in the original." (22) He cites among others Honigmann, who says that "details that point to his [the dramatist's] acquaintance with the Italian text consist of unusual words or phrases not replicated" in the French translation, and he lists several of them. (*Othello* 368) Oxford could have read Cinthio in the Italian in Venice or in London in the extensive library of books of Lord Burghley, his guardian and then his father-in-law. That would explain the unusual words and phrases from the original Italian that are found in *Othello*.

The sole source for details of Othello's murder of Desdemona is a story in Bandello's multi-volume *Novelle* (1554, 1573) about a wife-murder. The details include Desdemona's reviving and exonerating Othello, Emilia's cry for help and the arrival of help. Naseeb Shaheen points out in *Shakespeare Survey* 47 (2002) that these details are found only in the original Italian of Bandello, not in the French or English translations, which were quite loose. "The murder scene in Bandello" he says, "is the strongest evidence that Shakespeare read Bandello in the original Italian." He also cites several verbal parallels that "reinforce the conclusion that Shakespeare could read Italian" and that show that his "knowledge of Italian was hardly superficial." (164-6) Oxford owned at least three books in Italian, including *La Historia d'Italia* (1565) and had every opportunity in London to learn Italian and to become even more proficient when he was in Italy.

Works by Pliny the Elder, Leo Africanus and Cardinal Gasparo Contarini of Venice may also have influenced Oxford. Two of them were first published in Venice and the third was by the Cardinal of Venice, a worldly aristocratic churchman from a distinguished Venetian family and a ducal councillor. All three works were readily accessible to Oxford in Venice, if not in London, by the 1570s. Pliny's *Naturalis Historia* was published in 1469 in Venice. *Cosmographia dell'Africa* by Leo Africanus, a Moor who was born in Spain and grew up in North Africa, was published in 1550, also in Venice. Cardinal Contarini's *De Magistratibus et Republica Venetorum* was first published in Latin in 1543, then the following year in Italian and French editions. (Stratfordian commentators cite English translations of the three works in 1601, 1600 and 1599, especially Lewis Lewkenor's of Contarini, as important sources for Will Shakspere, their candidate for Shakespeare, but the works were all accessible for Oxford much earlier in Venice.)

As do many of the plays, *Othello* reflects Oxford's military experience. He served in his youth for several months as an adjutant in the English campaigns at the Scottish border and in 1585 for about a month or two in the Low Countries with command of several thousand soldiers and officers in the campaign against the French and Spanish. Two cousins and best friends were renowned generals in campaigns in the Low Countries, and Oxford tried several times to have the queen assign him to serve with the military.

At the start of *Othello*, for example, Iago's complaint about an inexperienced theoretician, Cassio, receiving preferential treatment echoes a complaint in 1578 by Barnaby Googe, a poet and protege of Burghley, about the appointment of officers who were inexperienced in battle. The play is also accurate concerning responsibility for the watch. Henry J. Webb notes that "while there were, in Elizabethan times, all sorts of subordinate officers in charge of the watch . . . the final responsibility for the watch rested with the general's second-in-command, which is the position Cassio holds." Bloom notes that the dramatist depicts Othello accurately as a skilled professional officer whose military judgment is clearly sound. The dramatist understood details of military rank and the role of officers. (See the Appendices.)

The comedy in the tragedy of *Othello* is not just "comic relief," as in the Porter scene in *Macbeth;* it is integral to the play and essential to understanding Iago the psychopathic entertainer. A powerful motif of the play is fear of the gleeful, sniggering ridicule of cuckoldry that is no laughing matter for a proud, insecure husband who thinks he is the cuckold. W. H. Auden in his essay "The Joker in the Pack" calls Iago "a practical joker of a peculiarly appalling kind." (256) In his Arden edition of *Othello*, M. R. Ridley says that in Iago's soliloquy ("And what's he then. . .") near the end of act 2 "we sense not only his delight at the prospect of revenge, but his sheer intellectual pleasure in a subtle and finished piece of black artistry." (86) *Othello* might well be considered a semi-satirical, black-humor comedy masquerading as a tragedy.

A major influence on the play was *commedia dell'arte* with its stock characters and their improvised skits that were often bawdy and satiric. It was at the peak of its popularity in Venice in the 1570s when Oxford was there. The players performed in the squares, hired halls and in the palaces of aristocrats.

Performances of *commedia dell'arte* did not follow an author's script. The performers themselves had a store of stock situations, such as disgraceful love intrigues, swindling schemes, mistaken identities, servants conning their masters, foolish old men being deceived, husbands being cuckolded. They improvised clever repartee and comic bits of theater based on their stock scenarios. Improvisation was the hallmark of *commedia dell'arte*, and in *Othello*, as Harold Bloom notes, "Improvisation by Iago constitutes the tragedy's heart and center." (*Invention* 454)

Commedia dell'arte, however, was virtually unknown in England when Will Shakspere was supposed to be writing the Shakespeare plays. Shakespeare scholars recognize this but have difficulty reconciling it with what they see as the influence of *commedia dell'arte* in some of the plays. In their 1990 book on *commedia,* Kenneth and Laura Richards reluctantly conclude that "the Italian acting companies quite failed to penetrate the English market." (264) In her book, *Italian Drama in Shakespeare's Time* (1989), Louise George Clubb concludes that "it cannot be proved that Shakespeare [of Stratford] read Italian plays, or saw *commedia dell'arte* troupes or Italian amateurs perform *commedia grave* at Elizabeth's court, or heard about them from a friend." (63) The only book-length study of *commedia* by a Shakespeare scholar is *The World of Harlequin* (1963) by Allardyce Nicoll, who was chair of the English department at the University of Birmingham. He finds traces of *commedia dell'arte* in ten plays (although not in *Othello*) and concludes: "Whether Shakespeare [of Stratford] actually witnessed any performances given by the Italians we cannot say with certainty . . . but with assurance we can declare that the inner spirit of his early comedies closely approaches that of *commedia* scenarios, and we can reasonably guess that *commedia dell'arte* performances would have appealed to him" (223). These Stratfordian scholars, and others who have addressed the issue, offer no suggestions to explain how Will Shakspere knew about Italian *commedia dell'arte* that influenced a dozen Shakespeare plays.

A few troupes of Italian players were in England in the 1570s when Will Shakspere was not yet out of his early teens and, with one brief exception, not again until he was long dead. Records of payments to "Italian players" appear in court records in the 1570s. These performances were probably tumbling, slapstick fighting and pantomimes without much dialogue, which would have been in Venetian, Neapolitan or other Italian dialects and almost impossible for the English to understand. Scholars have found no records of *commedia dell'arte* performances in England for a century after the 1570s, except for a single performance by Italians at court for Queen Elizabeth in 1602. Arthur

Kinney of UMass-Amherst calls *commedia dell'arte* "a contemporary form of comedy in Italy—but one posterior to Shakespeare in England."

Othello is rarely considered by *commedia* scholars, probably because it is classed as a tragedy. In their book, the Richards do recognize that in *The Merchant of Venice* and *Othello* "some details [of *commedia* influence] are indeed striking," but they cite none and then dismiss any significance to them. (264) The characters in *Othello* do indeed show strikingly that the dramatist was very familiar with *commedia dell-arte*. All the principal characters derive from some of the stock characters of *commedia dell'arte*. The *Zanni* (Iago) was a trusted servant but a cunning scoundrel who has a love of mischief for its own sake and deceives others with elaborate schemes for his advancement but gets his comeuppance at the end. The sub-*Zanni* (Roderigo) was a witless buffoon. *Pantalone* (Brabantio) was a foolish, talkative, old man, usually a rich Venetian merchant, who is duped by his wife or daughter. The *Capitano* (Othello) was a boastful, swashbuckling mercenary, often a Spaniard, who tells tall tales about his military exploits, especially against the Turks. *Pedrolino* (Cassio, Othello's lieutenant) was a naïve servant who was often personable and charming but sometimes to excess. The female lead (Desdemona), played by a woman, was sweet, charming and usually an unwitting foil in the *Zanni*'s intrigues; she was an innocent, but sometimes was eloquent. The maid (Emilia) was always a bold, outspoken truth-teller.

Act 1 opens as pure *commedia dell'arte* that could be played for laughs and probably should be. Iago (the scheming *Zanni*) and Roderigo (the witless, rejected suitor) wake up Brabantio (the foolish, old *Pantalone*) to taunt him with lewd suggestions that his daughter, Desdemona (the innocent), is having sex with Othello (an upgraded mercenary, semi-Spanish *Capitano*) in a bestial way after they eloped. As the play begins, Iago is gulling Roderigo into joining him in a scene of raucous, obscene comedy.

Ren Draya
Richard F. Whalen

Othello,

the Moor of Venice

The Principal Characters

Othello, a Moorish general

Desdemona, Othello's bride

Brabantio, a Venetian senator and father of Desdemona

Iago, Othello's ancient (ensign)

Emilia, wife to Iago and waiting-woman to Desdemona

Roderigo, a young gentleman of Venice

Cassio, lieutenant to Othello

Bianca, a courtesan and mistress to Cassio

The Duke (the Doge) of Venice

Senators of Venice

Montano, Governor of Cyprus

Gentlemen of Cyprus

Lodovico and Gratiano, two noble Venetians and kinsmen to Brabantio

A Clown, a messenger, a herald, officers, sailors, musicians, and assorted attendants

Locations: Venice (act 1), then Famagusta on Cyprus (acts 2-5)

7-9 Three great ones...Off-capped to him: These are *savvy grandi,* three of the senior ministers, aristocrats who ruled Venice. Oxford lived for five months in Venice, and, as a noble man, would have been well-informed about the complex structure of the Venetian governing body of ministers. Iago claims, probably lying, that he had the support of three of the senior ministers, who urged Othello to make Iago his lieutenant, tipping their hats, "off-capping" to Othello as a sign of respect.

8 lieutenant: from the French *lieu tennant* ("place" and "holding"), thus one holding a superior's place in his absence. It was a new military rank, its first use as such in 1578 (OED), two years after Oxford returned from Italy, and probably designating a lieutenant general, not today's much lower rank. Oxford had military experience. (See Appendices.)

10 place: Michael Neill argues in his edition that "place," i.e. rank, social standing, "is a more important dimension in *Othello* than 'race.'"

17 a great arithmetician: someone whose skill is in the behind-the-lines arithmetic of military strategy and who has not been a warrior, an important distinction in the military in Elizabethan times.

19 almost damned in a fair wife: M. R. Ridley cites an Italian proverb: *"L'hai tolta bella?Tuo danno* ("You have married a fair wife? You are damned.") Oxford would have noted it in Italy, esp. given his troubles with his wife. Cassio is not married, so the line probably means he "almost" entered into a marriage that would have been "damned," not blessed.

22 spinster: someone who spins wool (OED original meaning).

28 be-leed: to be put in the lee of another ship that blocks the wind during the maneuvering of ships in close quarters. (OED obsolete, a Shakespeare coinage) Oxford made several sea voyages.

29 countercaster: a sarcastic label for a bookkeeper. (OED obsolete, a Shakespeare coinage) "Casters" were disks used in counting. (OED obsolete) In Italy, men from Florence were known for their expertise in trade, not war.

31 moorship's ancient: Moorship is a coinage, sneeringly from "worship." An ancient, or ensign, was the standard bearer or flag bearer for a military officer, a much lower position than lieutenant; in today's parlance an aide-de-camp.

ACT 1

Scene 1. Venice. A street. Enter Roderigo and Iago.

Roderigo
  Never tell me! I take it much unkindly
  That thou, Iago, who hast had my purse
  As if the strings were thine, shouldst know of this.
Iago
  But you will not hear me. If ever I
  Did dream of such a matter, abhor me.   5
Roderigo
  Thou told'st me thou didst hold him in thy hate.
Iago
  Despise me if I do not. Three great ones of the city,
  In personal suit to make me his lieutenant,
  Off-capped to him; and, by the faith of man,
  I know my price, I am worth no worse a place.   10
  But he, as loving his own pride and purposes,
  Evades them, with a bombast circumstance
  Horribly stuffed with epithets of war,
  Nonsuits my mediators. For, "Certes," says he,
  "I have already chose my officer."   15
  And what was he?
  Forsooth, a great arithmetician,
  One Michael Cassio, a Florentine
  (A fellow almost damned in a fair wife)
  That never set a squadron in the field   20
  Nor the division of a battle knows
  More than a spinster—unless the bookish theoric,
  Wherein the toga'd consuls can propose
  As masterly as he. Mere prattle without practice
  Is all his soldiership. But he, sir, had the election. 25
  And I (of whom his eyes had seen the proof
  At Rhodes, at Cyprus, and on other grounds
  Christian and heathen) must be be-leed and calmed
  By debitor and creditor. This countercaster,
  He, in good time, must his lieutenant be,   30
  And I—God bless the mark!—his moorship's ancient.

37

38 affined: bound by any tie. (OED)

46 cashiered: discharged from military service, originally from the French. The term probably dates to the English campaign in the Netherlands of 1585. (OED) Oxford was an officer with English forces in the Netherlands in 1585 and probably used it in a revision of *Othello* on his return. The term's first use in English was in *Othello* and *The Merry Wives of Windsor* (1.1.184)

47 Whip me. . .knaves: that is, whip them for me.

51 lined their coats: that is, taken what they need for themselves. Iago approves of self-interest and identifies himself that way. As a courtier, Oxford was well aware of corrupt practices of wily officials.

53 Do themselves homage: sarcastically, pay themselves the money or tribute ("homage") that under feudal law was supposed to be paid by vassals to their king or lord as formal acknowledgment of allegiance. (OED)

55 Were I the Moor. . .Iago: probably meaning, if I were Othello, I would not have to be the scheming, hypocritical Iago that I am.

59-63 For when my outward action . . . daws to peck at: that is, if my behavior were to correspond with my actual feelings, it would be as if I was wearing my heart on my sleeve for birds (jackdaws, considered foolish) to peck at.

64 I am not what I am: "I am not inwardly what I seem to be." Iago's self-revelatory line echoes two striking thoughts in Oxford's writings. One is the opening line of a pre-Shakespeare poem by the youthful Oxford: "I am not as I seem to be." Appearance vs. reality is a major theme in *Othello* and throughout the Shakespeare works. The second, a reversal, is Oxford's defiant "I am that I am" in a 1584 letter to Lord Burghley, his father-in-law and principal adviser to Queen Elizabeth, and then equally defiant in his Shakespeare sonnet 121. The exclamation is from St. Paul's first letter to the Corinthians. (15.10)

65 If he can carry it thus: if he can carry off this elopement.

Roderigo
By heaven, I rather would have been his hangman.
Iago
Why, there's no remedy. 'Tis the curse of service;
Preferment goes by letter and affection,
And not by old gradation, where each second   35
Stood heir to the first. Now, sir, be judge yourself
Whether I in any just term am affined
To love the Moor.
Roderigo
I would not follow him then.
Iago
O, sir, content you.
I follow him to serve my turn upon him.   40
We cannot all be masters, nor all masters
Cannot be truly followed. You shall mark
Many a duteous and knee-crooking knave
That, doting on his own obsequious bondage,
Wears out his time, much like his master's ass,   45
For nought but provender, and when he's old, cashiered.
Whip me such honest knaves. Others there are
Who, trimmed in forms and visages of duty,
Keep yet their hearts attending on themselves,
And, throwing but shows of service on their lords,   50
Do well thrive by them and when they have lined their coats
Do themselves homage. These fellows have some soul,
And such a one do I profess myself. For, sir,
It is as sure as you are Roderigo,
Were I the Moor I would not be Iago.   55
In following him, I follow but myself—
Heaven is my judge, not I for love and duty,
But seeming so, for my peculiar end.
For when my outward action doth demonstrate
The native act and figure of my heart   60
In compliment extern, 'tis not long after
But I will wear my heart upon my sleeve
For daws to peck at. I am not what I am.
Roderigo
What a full fortune does the thick-lips owe
If he can carry it thus!   65

72 timorous accent: "Timorous" here no doubt means causing fear or dread (OED obsolete), the opposite of today's meaning; and "accent" here is the way something is said, expressing feeling (OED, which cites this line in the play.) Iago is telling Roderigo to disguise his voice, for Brabantio does not recognize it at first. Iago no doubt disguises his voice, too; Brabantio never does identify Iago as one of the two troublemakers. This scene, with the two of them shouting at Brabantio in false voices in the dark of night, is typical of *commedia dell'arte.*

76-8 Awake!. . .thieves: As the manipulative *Zanni,* Iago hides his own identity from Brabantio, gulls Roderigo into taking the blame for the raucous obscenities, and enjoys every minute of it. Oxford would have seen *commedia dell'arte,* which was especially popular in Venice when he was there but was virtually unknown in England after the 1570s (when Will Shakspere was not yet into his teens.)

78 What. . . terrible summons: Brabantio, Desdemona's father, is modeled on *Pantalone* in *commedia dell'arte.* The *Pantalone* character is often deceived by disgraceful love affairs of his wife or daughter, and here Brabantio has been deceived by his daughter and unwillingly become Othello's father-in-law. Similar to Polonius in *Hamlet,* Brabantio is likely Oxford's satiric dig at his own father-in-law, William Cecil Lord Burghley.

82 gown: the robe or uniform of a Venetian senator, who was required to wear it in public. The custom was unique to Venice, probably unknown in England.

84-5 Even now . . . white ewe: that is, an older black man (Othello) is copulating with your white daughter (Desdemona).

86 snorting citizens: people asleep, snoring.

89 do you know my voice?: a foolish question by the foolish Roderigo, since Brabantio has not recognized his "timorous accent" (LN 72).

Iago

Call up her father.
Rouse him, make after him, poison his delight,
Proclaim him in the streets; incense her kinsmen,
And, though he in a fertile climate dwell,
Plague him with flies. Though that his joy be joy,
Yet throw such changes of vexation on it   70
As it may lose some color.

Roderigo

Here is her father's house. I'll call aloud.

Iago

Do, with like timorous accent and dire yell
As when, by night and negligence, the fire
Is spied in populous cities.

Roderigo

What ho, Brabantio! Signor Brabantio, ho!   75

Iago

Awake! What ho, Brabantio! Thieves, thieves!
Look to your house, your daughter, and your bags!
Thieves, thieves!

                 Brabantio [appears above] at a window.

Brabantio

What is the reason of this terrible summons?41
What is the matter there?

Roderigo

Signor, is all your family within?   80

Iago

Are your doors locked?

Brabantio

Why, wherefore ask you this?

Iago

Sir, you're robbed. For shame, put on your gown!
Your heart is burst; you have lost half your soul.
Even now, now, very now, an old black ram
Is tupping your white ewe. Arise, arise!   85
Awake the snorting citizens with the bell,
Or else the devil will make a grandsire of you.
Arise, I say!

Brabantio

What, have you lost your wits?

95 Being full of supper: Because of the yelling and bawdy language he has heard, Brabantio assumes the men have been out feasting and drinking.

97 start my quiet: startle me out of a quiet sleep.

101 grange: an isolated farmhouse, in contrast to Brabantio's palace in cosmopolitan Venice.

104-7 Because...germans. that is, you're treating us as if we're hoodlums when actually we're helping you out; by ignoring our warning, you'll end up with half-breed grandchildren. The "Barbary horse" is another insulting reference to the Moor from Barbary on the coast of North Africa; "coursers" are racehorses; "jennets" are small Spanish horses. Oxford's travels and noble status would have given him familiarity with these terms. "Germans" are closely related kin. "Covered" is a bestial coupling, a taunting barnyard reference to counter Brabantio's assertion that his house is not a grange.

110 beast with two backs: a saying in Italian and French describing obscenely the human sexual act; first usage in English here, probably from Oxford's time in Italy and/or from Rabelais' *Gargantua and Pantagruel* (1532-4).

112 You are a senator!: Iago's sarcastic retort to Brabantio's "Thou are a villain!" implying that a senator is worse than a villain and playing it for laughs.

113 This thou shalt answer: probably, "You'll answer for this."   **I know thee Roderigo:** But it's Iago who has been shouting at him in a disguised voice for eight lines.

Roderigo

Most reverend signor, do you know my voice?

Brabantio

Not I. What are you?   90

Roderigo

My name is Roderigo.

Brabantio

The worser welcome.

I have charged thee not to haunt about my doors.

In honest plainness thou hast heard me say

My daughter is not for thee. And now, in madness,

Being full of supper and distempering drafts,   95

Upon malicious bravery, dost thou come

To start my quiet.

Roderigo

Sir, sir, sir—

Brabantio

But thou must needs be sure, my spirit and my place have in

their power to make this bitter to thee.

Roderigo

Patience, good sir.   100

Brabantio

What tell'st thou me of robbing? This is Venice; My house is

not a grange

Roderigo

Most grave Brabantio, in simple and pure soul I come to you

Iago

Sir, you are one of those that will not serve God if the devil

bid you. Because we come to do you service and you think

we are ruffians, you'll have your daughter covered with a   105

Barbary horse; you'll have your nephews neigh to you; you'll

have coursers for cousins and jennets for germans.

Brabantio

What profane wretch art thou?

Iago

I am one, sir, that comes to tell you your daughter and the

Moor are now making the beast with two backs.   110

Brabantio

Thou art a villain.

Iago

You are—a senator.

116 Odd-even and dull watch of the night: an in-between time of night, perhaps one or two in the morning. "Watch" conveys a military connotation, as if something or someone needs to be guarded.

118 gondolier: Although this term is familiar today, Oxford's contemporaries, and especially commoners, probably would only have known it if they had been to Italy. (Cf. "gundello" at 4.1.38 in *As You Like It.*) Oxford probably introduced the word into English.

120 allowance: approval, permission.

121 saucy: impudent, insolent.

129 wheeling stranger: someone traveling far from his home.

130 Straight satisfy yourself: Go see for yourself right away.

134-5 Strike on the tinder . . . a taper: Make a spark, give me a candle.

140 not meet, nor wholesome to my place: that is, not good for me.

143 gall. . .check: to make sore ("gall") by reining in ("check"), as of a horse (OED), showing the dramatist's knowledge of horsemanship. Or possibly to annoy ("gall") by stopping or checking temporarily, from chess, a game of aristocrats. Or both, in imaginative wordplay. Iago knows that official Venice considers Othello too valuable to dismiss him.

147 fathom: grasp, ability. (OED)

Brabantio
This thou shalt answer. I know thee, Roderigo.
Roderigo
Sir, I will answer anything. But I beseech you,
If it be your pleasure and most wise consent—
As partly I find it is—that your fair daughter, 115
At this odd-even and dull watch of the night,
Transported with no worse nor better guard
But with a knave of common hire, a gondolier,
To the gross clasps of a lascivious Moor—
If this be known to you and your allowance 120
We then have done you bold and saucy wrongs.
But if you know not this, my manners tell me
We have your wrong rebuke. Do not believe
That, from the sense of all civility,
I thus would play and trifle with your reverence. 125
Your daughter (if you have not given her leave)
I say again, hath made a gross revolt,
Tying her duty, beauty, wit, and fortunes
In an extravagant and wheeling stranger
Of here and everywhere. Straight satisfy yourself. 130
If she be in her chamber or your house,
Let loose on me the justice of the state
For thus deluding you.
Brabantio
Strike on the tinder, ho!
Give me a taper! Call up all my people! 135
This accident is not unlike my dream.
Belief of it oppresses me already.
Light! I say, light!

Exit.

Iago
Farewell, for I must leave you.
It seems not meet nor wholesome to my place 140
To be produced—as, if I stay, I shall—
Against the Moor. For, I do know the state,
However this may gall him with some check,
Cannot with safety cast him, for he's embarked
With such loud reason to the Cyprus wars, 145
Which even now stands in act, that, for their souls,
Another of his fathom they have none

45

153 the Sagittary: a street in Venice, and probably designating a district (as does "Broadway" and "Wall Street.") This off-hand reference shows that the dramatist had first-hand knowledge of the Venetian streets. For whatever reason, he had Desdemona and Othello, who had just eloped, staying in a townhouse on a street known as *Frezzeria* and, in Latin, *sagittarius*. Both *frezza* and *sagitta* referred to arrow- makers, who had their ateliers on the street. That "the Sagittary" was not an inn or a boat or the Arsenal or the Hall of Justice, as various commentators have suggested, is clear because both Brabantio and Othello refer to a "house." (Jeffery article and Richard Roe via private communication) Oxford almost certainly walked the street in Venice that he put into English as "the Sagittary."

156 despised time: unhappy life.

166 charms: Brabantio suspects that his daughter is under some kind of spell because she hasn't acted in a normal way. **Property**: the quality or nature of a person. (OED obsolete)

178 special officers of night: the Venetian security forces patrolling at night. Another indication that the dramatist had first-hand knowledge of Venice.

179 deserve your pains: repay you for the trouble you've taken.

To lead their business. In which regard,
Though I do hate him as I do hell-pains,
Yet for necessity of present life   150
I must show out a flag and sign of love,
Which is indeed but sign. That you shall surely find him,
Lead to the Sagittary the raised search,
And there will I be with him. So farewell.

Exit Iago.

Enter Brabantio with servants and torches.

Brabantio
It is too true an evil. Gone she is;   155
And what's to come of my despised time
Is nought but bitterness. Now, Roderigo,
Where didst thou see her? O unhappy girl—
With the Moor, sayst thou?—Who would be a father!—
How didst thou know 'twas she? O she deceives me   160
Past thought—What said she to you?—Get more tapers.
Raise all my kindred.—Are they married, think you?
Roderigo
Truly, I think they are.
Brabantio
O heaven! How got she out? O treason of the blood!
Fathers, from hence trust not your daughters' minds   165
By what you see them act. Is there not charms
By which the property of youth and maidhood
May be abused? Have you not read, Roderigo,
Of some such thing?
Roderigo
Yes, sir, I have indeed.   170
Brabantio
Call up my brother.—O, would you had had her!—
Some one way, some another.—Do you know
Where we may apprehend her and the Moor?
Roderigo
I think I can discover him, if you please
To get good guard and go along with me.   175
Brabantio
Pray you, lead on. At every house I'll call;
I may command at most.—Get weapons, ho!
And raise some special officers of night.--
On, good Roderigo, I'll deserve your pains.

47

Enter. . . with torches: Lighting with torches indicates that act 1 takes place at night and was written to be staged indoors, and thus written for aristocrats and nobility who would see it performed for Queen Elizabeth and courtiers or at the indoor Blackfriars theater. The public theaters, like the Globe, where performances were in the afternoon, were open to the sky.

6 he prated: chattered on and on. Iago is lying about an unnamed slanderer, probably Roderigo, but it was Iago himself who spoke maliciously about Othello and Desdemona to Brabantio. With this lie, he deflects in advance any blame. His malicious plotting closely resembles the worst of power politics in a court such as Queen Elizabeth's, which only an insider such as Oxford would know about. (Cf. the Thane of Ross in the Oxfordian edition of *Macbeth*.)

12 the magnifico: referring sarcastically to Brabantio. "Magnifico" was an honorific for the leading noblemen of Venice, but in the world of *commedia dell'arte* it was also satirically another name for the *Pantalone* character, the foolish rich old man.

13-14 voice. . .double as the Duke's: the "great ones" could have power equal to or even greater than the Duke's; a reference to the unusual checks-and-balances government of Venice that only a dramatist who had been there would be likely to know and use in the play.

17 give him cable: give him scope, allow him. A nautical term reflecting an easy familiarity with how ships are anchored. More scope or "cable" allows a ship at anchor to swing more freely and securely on a longer anchor line. Oxford made several sea voyages.

22 royal siege: noble ancestry in the Ottoman empire. **demerits:** meritorious actions, a meaning contrary to today's and now obsolete. (OED)

23 unbonneted: probably not having to do with headgear, but from "bonnet," an additional piece of canvas laced to the foot or top of a sail in order to catch more wind. (OED) Thus, unbonneted here means without addition or amplification; that is, Othello needs no additional merit to be worthy of Desdemona. Oxford used an unusual nautical term to make his point.

28 what lights come yond?: This is the first of several occasions, some crucial to the plot, when Othello apparently cannot see who's coming or what's happening and Iago provides the information. Othello's seemingly weak eyesight may be a metaphor for his weak understanding; Iago sees all and understands all.

They exit.

Scene 2. Another street in Venice.
Enter Othello, Iago, attendants with torches.

Iago
 Though in the trade of war I have slain men,
 Yet do I hold it very stuff of the conscience
 To do no contrived murder. I lack iniquity
 Sometimes to do me service. Nine or ten times
 I had thought to have yerked him here under the ribs.   5
Othello
 'Tis better as it is.
Iago
 Nay, but he prated,
 And spoke such scurvy and provoking terms
 Against your honor
 That, with the little godliness I have,
 I did full hard forbear him. But, I pray you, sir,   10
 Are you fast married? Be assured of this,
 That the magnifico is much beloved,
 And hath in his effect a voice potential
 As double as the Duke's. He will divorce you,
 Or put upon you what restraint or grievance   15
 The law, with all his might to enforce it on,
 Will give him cable.
Othello
 Let him do his spite.
 My services which I have done the signorie
 Shall out-tongue his complaints. 'Tis yet to know,
 Which, when I know that boasting is an honor,   20
 I shall promulgate. I fetch my life and being
 From men of royal siege, and my demerits
 May speak unbonneted to as proud a fortune
 As this that I have reached. For know, Iago,
 But that I love the gentle Desdemona,   25
 I would not my unhoused free condition
 Put into circumscription and confine
 For the sea's worth. But, look, what lights come yond?

29 raised father: Brabantio, who has been awakened ("raised") from sleep.

31-32 my parts: my personal qualities and standing will show who I am.

33 Janus: Ancient Italian god for January: Janus faces back and forward, thus is two-faced.

40 heat: importance, urgency. **galleys:** a term for sailing ships still used in Venice in the 16th century but not in England.

43 consuls: government officials.

50 carrack: a large cargo ship used primarily by the Portuguese and Spanish in their East Indies ventures and often carrying valuable shipments or treasure. Iago, whose name is Spanish, compares Desdemona (a "land carrack") to a Spanish treasure ship that Othello has boarded and seized, a bawdy metaphor for a sexual conquest. "Carrack" is yet another example of Oxford's ready knowledge of sailing ships in the Mediterranean.

Enter Cassio and officers with torches.

Iago
  Those are the raised father and his friends.
  You were best go in.
Othello
  Not I. I must be found.   30
  My parts, my title, and my perfect soul
  Shall manifest me rightly. Is it they?
Iago
  By Janus, I think no.
Othello
  The servants of the duke? And my lieutenant?
  The goodness of the night upon you, friends!   35
  What is the news?
Cassio
  The Duke does greet you, General,
  And he requires your haste-post-haste appearance
  Even on the instant.
Othello
  What is the matter, think you?
Cassio
  Something from Cyprus, as I may divine.
  It is a business of some heat. The galleys   40
  Have sent a dozen sequent messengers
  This very night at one another's heels,
  And many of the consuls, raised and met,
  Are at the Duke's already. You have been hotly called for;
  When, being not at your lodging to be found,   45
  The senate hath sent about three several quests
  To search you out.
Othello
  'Tis well I am found by you.
  I will but spend a word here in the house,
  And go with you.

                                                      Exit Othello.

Cassio
  Ancient, what makes he here?
Iago
  Faith, he tonight hath boarded a land carrack.   50

54 Marry: a mild oath, a version of "by the Virgin Mary."

58 Come, sir: In a sham, Iago pretends Roderigo is his enemy and challenges him to fight, thus hiding the fact that Roderigo is his co-conspirator and setting him up for even more serious mischief later. The episode is typical of *commedia dell'arte* in which the *Zanni* would turn on his erstwhile friend, a baffled "sub-*Zanni*," and beat him. Roderigo's bafflement could be played for laughs.

59-61 Keep up....swords: Othello, the military commander, instinctively takes charge to head off a rash duel in the street between his ancient and Roderigo. Commentators have noted the dramatist's ready and accurate knowledge of the military. (See Appendices.)

62-81 O thou. . . .peril: Brabantio's long harangue about his daughter's scandalous eloping with Othello may well be the dramatist's not so subtle mockery of William Cecil Lord Burghley, his father-in-law, who was famous for being garrulous and who rambled on in memos to himself about a paternity scandal involving his daughter Anne and Oxford. (Cf. Polonius in *Hamlet*.)

63 damned as thou art: most likely a reference to Othello's dark skin, at a time when a dark complexion suggested black devils and damnation.

If it prove lawful prize, he's made forever.

Cassio

I do not understand.

Iago

He's married.

Cassio

To who?

Enter Othello.

Iago

Marry, to—Come, Captain, will you go?

Othello

Have with you.

Cassio

Here comes another troop to seek for you.

Enter Brabantio, Roderigo, with officers and torches.

Iago

It is Brabantio. General, be advised.   55

He comes to bad intent.

Othello

Holla! Stand there!

Roderigo

Signor, it is the Moor.

Brabantio

Down with him, thief!

Iago

You, Roderigo! Come, sir, I am for you.

Othello

Keep up your bright swords, for the dew will rust them.

Good signor, you shall more command with years   60

Than with your weapons.

Brabantio

O thou foul thief, where hast thou stowed my daughter?

Damned as thou art, thou hast enchanted her.

For I'll refer me to all things of sense,

If she in chains of magic were not bound   65

Whether a maid so tender, fair, and happy,

So opposite to marriage that she shunned

69 to incur a general mock: to cause people to mock her.

70 sooty bosom: an insulting reference to Othello's dark skin.

75 motion: an inward prompting or impulse. (OED obsolete). Brabantio seems to refer to what he believes should be his daughter's innate virtue and restraint.

77 attach thee: "arrest you," a sixteenth-century legal term. Oxford's first tutor, Sir Thomas Smith, was one of England's greatest scholars of law; and Oxford attended Gray's Inn at the Inns of Court. This is one of several references and allusions to the law in the play.

79 arts inhibited: prohibited black magic. **out of warrant:** not sanctioned, illegal.

86 direct session: a judicial trial or investigation, an Elizabethan legal term now obsolete.

93 How? The duke. . . in council: Brabantio seems not to have been invited to the emergency senate meeting, although in the Venetian government he may not have been needed for a quorum at this midnight meeting.

The wealthy curled darlings of our nation,
Would ever have, to incur a general mock,
Run from her guardage to the sooty bosom   70
Of such a thing as thou—to fear, not to delight.
Judge me the world if 'tis not gross in sense
That thou hast practiced on her with foul charms,
Abused her delicate youth with drugs or minerals
That weakens motion. I'll have it disputed on;   75
'Tis probable and palpable to thinking.
I therefore apprehend and do attach thee
For an abuser of the world, a practicer
Of arts inhibited and out of warrant.—
Lay hold upon him! If he do resist,   80
Subdue him at his peril.

Othello

Hold your hands,
Both you of my inclining, and the rest.
Were it my cue to fight, I should have known it
Without a prompter.—Whither will you that I go
To answer this your charge?

Brabantio

To prison, till fit time   85
Of law and course of direct session
Call thee to answer.

Othello

What if I do obey?
How may the Duke be therewith satisfied,
Whose messengers are here about my side
Upon some present business of the state   90
To bring me to him?

Officer

'Tis true, most worthy signor.
The Duke's in council, and your noble self,
I am sure, is sent for.

Brabantio

How? The Duke in council?
In this time of the night? Bring him away.
Mine's not an idle cause. The Duke himself,   95
Or any of my brothers of the state,
Cannot but feel this wrong as it were their own;
For if such actions may have passage free,

55

98-9 Bond-slaves. . . statesmen be: probably a slighting allusion to Othello in the past having been sold into slavery, and in Brabantio's view a heathen. He is saying, "If Othello can get away with enchanting and abducting my daughter, then Venetian noblemen might as well be the slaves of our slaves."

Scene 3 . . Officers: The quarto gives *"Enter Duke and Senators, seated at a table, with lights, Officers, and attendants."* Candles and torches would have been the "lights," again indicating a play written for indoor performance at court or Blackfriars.

1 no composition: no consistency (OED obsolete.)

5 jump not: probably, do not agree (OED obsolete.)

6 aim: estimate or guess. (OED) In his Arden edition, E. A. J. Honigmann notes that "before modern methods of communication were invented the movements of foreign armies and navies were reported to the Privy Council (or guessed at) exactly as here: cf. HMC, Hatfield House, Part 12 (1602), 386." The commoner from Stratford, unlike Oxford, would hardly have heard about, much less seen, such reports to the Privy Council.

8 A Turkish fleet. . . to Cyprus. The play is set in 1571 when a Turkish fleet did in fact move on Cyprus, which at that time was ruled by Venice.

14 the Turkish . . . Rhodes: that is, the Turkish ships, prepared for battle, are now headed for Rhodes, an island ten miles off the coast of Turkey where the Aegean Sea meets the Mediterranean.

16 Signior Angelo: Geoffrey Bullough suggests that Angelo was Angelus Soriano, a Venetian military leader who, with his galley, was sent to meet the Venetian ambassador. If so, only a dramatist, like Oxford, who had been to Venice in the mid-1570s, could have picked up this obscure detail.

Bond-slaves and pagans shall our statesmen be.

Exit.

Scene 3. Enter Duke, Senators and Officers.

Duke
  There is no composition in these news
  That gives them credit.
First Senator
  Indeed, they are disproportioned.
  My letters say a hundred and seven galleys.
Duke
  And mine, a hundred and forty.
Second Senator
  And mine, two hundred.
  But though they jump not on a just account   5
  (As in these cases, where the aim reports
  'Tis oft with difference) yet do they all confirm
  A Turkish fleet, and bearing up to Cyprus.
Duke
  Nay, it is possible enough to judgment.
  I do not so secure me in the error   10
  But the main article I do approve
  In fearful sense.
Sailor
  (Within) What ho, what ho, what, ho!

Enter Sailor

Officer
  A messenger from the galleys.
Duke
  Now, what's the business?
Sailor
  The Turkish preparation makes for Rhodes.
  So was I bid report here to the state   15
  By Signior Angelo.
Duke
  How say you by this change?

18-40 This cannot be. . . toward Cyprus: Only a dramatist who was in Venice not long after the early 1570s would have been likely to write so accurately about the details of this moment in Venetian history—the importance to the Turks of Cyprus; the Venetian island not heavily defended; Rhodes' strong defenses ("abilities / That Rhodes is dressed in"); and the rendezvous of the two Turkish fleets. Oxford was in Italy in 1575-6.

20 gaze: probably an allusion to gaze-hounds that hunt by sight, not scent. (OED) Hunting with hounds was an aristocratic sport.

34 The Ottomites: people of the Ottoman Empire, here synonymous with Turks, although the powerful Ottoman Empire, with its capital at Constantinople, extended far beyond Turkey.

36-40 injointed with an after fleet. . .toward Cyprus: joined with a fleet following after the first. This is historically accurate. Honigmann notes, "In 1570 a Turkish fleet sailed toward Rhodes, then joined another fleet to attack Cyprus, as here [in the play]. Shakespeare must have known this." (See also the Variorum edition.) It would seem, however, unlikely that Will Shakspere of Stratford would have acquired this information.

40 Montano: the Venetian governor of Cyprus.

43 believe: Most text editors suspect a typographical error and change this to "relieve," although "believe" seems quite possible.

45 Marcus Luccicos: Although this is the only mention of him in the play, he was almost certainly someone Oxford knew or heard about in Italy in the 1570s. Otherwise why bother to put him in the play? Possibly a Cypriot of Roman and Greek ancestry, but his historical identity has not been discovered.

First Senator
  This cannot be
  By no assay of reason. 'Tis a pageant
  To keep us in false gaze. When we consider   20
  The importancy of Cyprus to the Turk,
  And let ourselves again but understand
  That, as it more concerns the Turk than Rhodes,
  So may he with more facile question bear it,
  For that it stands not in such warlike brace,   25
  But altogether lacks the abilities
  That Rhodes is dressed in. If we make thought of this,
  We must not think the Turk is so unskillful
  To leave that latest which concerns him first,
  Neglecting an attempt of ease and gain   30
  To wake and wage a danger profitless.
Duke
  Nay, in all confidence, he's not for Rhodes.
First Officer
  Here is more news.

Enter a Messenger

Messenger
  The Ottomites, reverend and gracious,
  Steering with due course towards the isle of Rhodes,   35
  Have there injointed them with an after fleet.
First Senator
  Ay, so I thought. How many, as you guess?
Messenger
  Of thirty sail; and now they do re-stem
  Their backward course, bearing with frank appearance
  Their purposes toward Cyprus. Signor Montano,   40
  Your trusty and most valiant servitor,
  With his free duty recommends you thus,
  And prays you to believe him.
Duke
  'Tis certain then for Cyprus.
  Marcus Luccicos, is not he in town?   45
First Senator
  He's now in Florence.

51-2 I did not see you. . .help tonight: The Duke's diplomatic greeting to Brabantio suggests that the old senator had not been invited to this emergency council session, or that he forgot to attend, adding to the portrait of Brabantio as a foolish and confused old man in the tradition of a *Pantalone* character.

51 gentle: well-born, noble; the earliest meaning of the word. (OED)

57 floodgate: the lower gate of a canal lock that holds the water in the lock, as distinguished from the upper gate, the sluice-gate. (OED) If the floodgate were opened when the lock was full, the water in the lock would flood downstream, as from a burst dam. Northern Italy from Venice west was laced with canals and locks. Anyone of means traveling in northern Italy, like Oxford, would travel by canals and through their locks. Here, by rhetorical extension, Brabantio compares his grief with the water pouring through a floodgate and swamping his other sorrows.

58 engluts: gulps down.

61 abused: wronged, deceived.

62 spells and medicines: probably a phrase from Venetian law. (Variorum) **mountebanks:** rascals, con artists. Cosmopolitan Venice had more than its share of such entertaining but unsavory quacks.

68 bloody book of law: Under Venetian law, giving love potions was a criminal offense and witchcraft was a capital crime. The dramatist knew such details of Venetian law. "Bloody" probably had the sense of decreeing bloodshed if the law is violated. (OED)

69-71 You shall. . . action: that is, Brabantio can choose to interpret the law in the most severe manner even if the offending man turns out to be the Duke's son in Brabantio's lawsuit ("action").

Duke
Write from us to him, post-post-haste. Dispatch.
First Senator
Here comes Brabantio and the valiant Moor.

Enter Brabantio, Othello, Cassio, Iago, Roderigo, and officers.

Duke
Valiant Othello, we must straight employ you
Against the general enemy Ottoman. 50
[To Brabantio.] I did not see you; welcome, gentle signor.
We lacked your counsel and your help tonight.
Brabantio
So did I yours. Good Your Grace, pardon me.
Neither my place nor aught I heard of business
Hath raised me from my bed, nor doth the general care 55
Take hold on me, for my particular grief
Is of so floodgate and overbearing nature
That it engluts and swallows other sorrows
And it is still itself.
Duke
Why, what's the matter?
Brabantio
My daughter! O, my daughter!
Duke and Senators
Dead?
Brabantio
Ay, to me. 60
She is abused, stolen from me, and corrupted
By spells and medicines bought of mountebanks.
For nature, so preposterously to err,
(Being not deficient, blind, or lame of sense)
Sans witchcraft could not. 65
Duke
Whoever he be that in this foul proceeding
Hath thus beguiled your daughter of herself,
And you of her, the bloody book of law
You shall yourself read in the bitter letter
After your own sense—yea, though our proper son 70
Stood in your action.

61

78 approved: men who have proved themselves.

82-94 Rude am I in my speech. . . .his daughter : In this opening statement, Othello the soldier concedes that normally his speech is "rude," not polished. Nevertheless, here and later in the play he tries to speak in the courtly language of the Venetian council chambers by using orotund language and colorful figures of speech. Kenneth Gross notes that Othello's language "is full of odd, gorgeous, self-conscious excesses of ornament." Aristocratic playgoers at court or private theaters in London would recognize an outsider straining to speak what he thinks is the language of courtiers and sounding a bit ridiculous, like the *Capitano* in *commedia dell'arte*.

84 seven years' pith: apparently meaning he had the strength or power of arms to join the military in some capacity when he was seven years old.

85 nine moons wasted: Othello apparently is saying, with regret, that it's been nine months since he'd been in battle.

86 dearest: most important or valuable.

96 motion: interior feelings or desires. (OED)

98 credit: reputation.

Brabantio
Humbly I thank Your Grace.
Here is the man, this Moor, whom now it seems
Your special mandate for the state affairs
Hath hither brought.
All
We are very sorry for it.
Duke
[To Othello] What, in your own part, can you say to this? 75
Brabantio
Nothing, but this is so.
Othello
Most potent, grave, and reverend signors,
My very noble and approved good masters:
That I have taken away this old man's daughter,
It is most true; true, I have married her. 80
The very head and front of my offending
Hath this extent, no more. Rude am I in my speech,
And little blessed with the soft phrase of peace;
For since these arms of mine had seven years' pith,
Till now some nine moons wasted, they have used 85
Their dearest action in the tented field;
And little of this great world can I speak
More than pertains to feats of broil and battle,
And therefore little shall I grace my cause
In speaking for myself. Yet, by your gracious patience, 90
I will a round unvarnished tale deliver
Of my whole course of love—what drugs, what charms,
What conjuration, and what mighty magic,
For such proceeding I am charged withal,
I won his daughter.
Brabantio
A maiden, never bold; 95
Of spirit so still and quiet that her motion
Blushed at herself; and she, in spite of nature,
Of years, of country, credit, everything,
To fall in love with what she feared to look on!
It is a judgment maimed and most imperfect 100
That will confess perfection so could err
Against all rules of nature, and must be driven
To find out practices of cunning hell

105 blood: supposedly the seat of emotions, including passions. (OED)

108 To vouch. . .proof: The Duke, the person of highest authority, knows that merely to claim something is not to prove it–a point introduced early in the play that will be a contrast to Othello's later behavior, when he seeks to obtain ocular proof of Desdemona's supposed infidelity.

109 thin habits: trivial, external appearances.

114 Or came it by request: The senator asks if Othello gained Desdemona's affection through an open exchange of questions and answers. **fair:** Because the word appears throughout the play, both as a noun and as an adjective, it may well underscore the racial tensions.

117 Sagittary: See 1.1.153n.

122 you best know the place: indicating again that Sagittary is a street where Othello has taken a house, not a landmark location. Iago knows the street and the house on it; others may not.

124 vices: faults, tendencies. (OED)

128-170 Her father. . .witness it: a long, quite pompous, speech in which Othello strains to impress the senators with his military adventures and triumphs, as would the *Capitano* in *commedia del-arte*.

129 Still questioned me: often questioned me.

Why this should be. I therefore vouch again
That with some mixtures powerful over the blood, 105
Or with some dram conjured to this effect,
He wrought upon her.

Duke

To vouch this is no proof,
Without more wider and more overt test
Than these thin habits and poor likelihoods
Of modern seeming do prefer against him. 110

First Senator

But Othello, speak.
Did you by indirect and forced courses
Subdue and poison this young maid's affections?
Or came it by request and such fair question
As soul to soul affordeth?

Othello

I do beseech you, 115
Send for the lady to the Sagittary
And let her speak of me before her father.
If you do find me foul in her report,
The trust, the office I do hold of you
Not only take away, but let your sentence 120
Even fall upon my life.

Duke

Fetch Desdemona hither.

Othello

Ancient, conduct them. You best know the place.

Exit Iago and attendants.

And, till she come, as truly as to heaven
I do confess the vices of my blood,
So justly to your grave ears I'll present 125
How I did thrive in this fair lady's love,
And she in mine.

Duke

Say it, Othello.

Othello

Her father loved me, oft invited me,
Still questioned me the story of my life
From year to year—the battles, sieges, fortunes 130

135 moving: that is, emotionally moving.

137 insolent: cruel, bullying.

139 portance: bearing or effect on. (OED) **travailous:** from Old French for laborious, wearisome.

140 antars: caverns, lairs. From Greek and Latin, probably by way of poetic French, *antre*, which carries a connotation of dangerous wild animals within. (OED) Oxford was fluent in Latin and French.

145 The Anthropophagi: from Pliny's *Natural History* and perhaps also Ptolemy's *Geographia Universalis*, which included sketches of "anthropophagi and men whose heads do grow beneath their shoulders." Oxford had access to these books and to various travel accounts. There is no indication that Shakspere of Stratford owned any books or had access to the only significant collections of books, the libraries of noblemen, such as William Cecil Lord Burghley, Oxford's guardian in his teenage years and then his father-in-law.

155 intentively: earnestly attentive. (OED)

159 sighs: Although the First Folio gives "kisses," most editors use "sighs" from the Quarto edition as more demure and appropriate for a teenage girl. Kisses on the cheek, however, could be quite commonplace in Elizabethan times.

168 pity them: something that arouses tender compassion (OED)

169 This only is. .witchcraft: Probably an allusion to Pliny who tells about a slave accused of using sorcery to get rich. The slave answered that his farm tools were the only "sorceries" and "enchantments" that he used.

That I have passed.
I ran it through, even from my boyish days
To the very moment that he bade me tell it,
Wherein I spoke of most disastrous chances,
Of moving accidents by flood and field,   135
Of hair-breadth scapes in the imminent deadly breach,
Of being taken by the insolent foe
And sold to slavery, of my redemption thence,
And portance in my travels' history,
Wherein of antars vast and deserts idle,   140
Rough quarries, rocks, and hills whose heads touch heaven,
It was my hint to speak. Such was the process,
And of the Cannibals that each other eat,
The Anthropophagi, and men whose heads   145
Do grow beneath their shoulders. These things to hear
Would Desdemona seriously incline;
But still the house affairs would draw her thence,
Which ever as she could with haste dispatch
She'd come again, and with a greedy ear
Devour up my discourse. Which I, observing,   150
Took once a pliant hour, and found good means
To draw from her a prayer of earnest heart
That I would all my pilgrimage dilate,
Whereof by parcels she had something heard,
But not intentively. I did consent,   155
And often did beguile her of her tears,
When I did speak of some distressful stroke
That my youth suffered. My story being done,
She gave me for my pains a world of kisses.
She swore, in faith, 'twas strange, 'twas passing strange,   160
'Twas pitiful, 'twas wondrous pitiful.
She wished she had not heard it, yet she wished
That heaven had made her such a man. She thanked me,
And bade me, if I had a friend that loved her,
I should but teach him how to tell my story,   165
And that would woo her. Upon this hint I spoke.
She loved me for the dangers I had passed,
And I loved her that she did pity them.
This only is the witchcraft I have used.
Here comes the lady: Let her witness it.   170

175 If she. . . half the wooer: The line echoes the gossip in London in 1571 about Oxford's engagement to Anne Cecil, daughter of William Cecil, who would become Lord Burghley. A Lord St. John wrote to the Earl of Rutland, who was in Paris, "The Earl of Oxford hath gotten himself a wife—or at the least a wife hath caught him; this is Mistress Anne Cecil, whereunto the Queen hath given her consent." (Quoted in Ward 61)

187 so much I challenge: that is, so much I claim as my right.

188 the Moor: Characters in the play often refer to "the Moor," rather than to "Othello," emphasizing his position as an outsider for the aristocratic Venetians. Oxford himself was something of an "outsider,' an eccentric, difficult earl for the Elizabethan establishment.

197 To hang clogs: Clogs in England were wooden blocks attached to the legs or necks of animals or persons to prevent them from moving freely or escaping. (OED) Brabantio is saying that if he had other girls he would keep them under even closer control. Clogs in England were also wooden-soled shoes, and "clogs" here may be a slight, passing allusion to the clogs or "chopines" worn in Venice by aristocratic wives--and courtesans--to raise them above the puddles and mud of the streets (OED) These chopines became decorated fashion accessories, symbols of feminine beauty and height, and today are museum pieces. Some were more than a foot high. In this passage, "clogs" may be unintentional irony by Brabantio.

198-207 Let me speak. . .grief: The Duke says he will deliver a decision ("lay a sentence") to resolve the issues, and he does so in rhyming couplets, as if to reinforce the wisdom of his formal opinion.

199 grise: a variant spelling of "grece," a step or stairway. (OED)

Enter Desdemona, Iago, and attendants.

Duke
I think this tale would win my daughter too.
Good Brabantio,
Take up this mangled matter at the best.
Men do their broken weapons rather use
Than their bare hands.

Brabantio
I pray you, hear her speak.
If she confess that she was half the wooer,   175
Destruction on my head if my bad blame
Light on the man.—Come hither, gentle mistress.
Do you perceive in all this noble company
Where most you owe obedience?

Desdemona
My noble father,
I do perceive here a divided duty.   180
To you I am bound for life and education;
My life and education both do learn me
How to respect you. You are the lord of duty,
I am hitherto your daughter. But here's my husband,
And so much duty as my mother showed   185
To you, preferring you before her father,
So much I challenge that I may profess
Due to the Moor my lord.

Brabantio
God be with you! I have done.
Please it Your Grace, on to the state affairs.
I had rather to adopt a child than get it.   190
Come hither, Moor.
I here do give thee that with all my heart
Which, but thou hast already, with all my heart
I would keep from thee.—For your sake, jewel,
I am glad at soul I have no other child,   195
For thy escape would teach me tyranny,
To hang clogs on them.—I have done, my lord.

Duke
Let me speak like yourself, and lay a sentence
Which, as a grise or step, may help these lovers.
When remedies are past, the griefs are ended   200

208-19 So let the Turk. . . the ear: Brabantio responds to the Duke's decision seemingly with resignation and thinly veiled sarcasm, also in rhymed couplets. "Words are words," he says, nothing more, and the Duke's words can be easily borne although Brabantio's heart is broken ("bruised"). Ironically, words in this play, principally those of Iago, will cause a great deal of pain that cannot be borne.

219-27 The Turk. . .expedition: It's back to affairs of state, and the Duke shifts to prose.

220 fortitude: physical or structural strength. (OED obsolete).

221 a substitute: a stand-in, deputy, probably referring to Montano.

223 slubber: darken or stain. (OED)

227 agnize: recognize or acknowledge. (OED obsolete)

234 accommodation: lodgings. (OED and apparently the first use of this word in this sense.) **besort:** probably, suitable company. (OED cites the word only here and in *King Lear* at 1.4.272.)

By seeing the worst, which late on hopes depended.
To mourn a mischief that is past and gone
Is the next way to draw new mischief on.
What cannot be preserved when Fortune takes,
Patience, her injury a mockery makes. 205
The robbed that smiles steals something from the thief;
He robs himself that spends a bootless grief.

Brabantio

So let the Turk of Cyprus us beguile,
We lose it not, so long as we can smile.
He bears the sentence well that nothing bears 210
But the free comfort which from thence he hears,
But he bears both the sentence and the sorrow
That, to pay grief, must of poor patience borrow.
These sentences, to sugar or to gall,
Being strong on both sides, are equivocal. 215
But words are words I never yet did hear:
That the bruised heart was pierced through the ear.
I humbly beseech you, proceed to the affairs of state.

Duke

The Turk with a most mighty preparation makes for Cyprus.
Othello, the fortitude of the place is best known to you. And 220
though we have there a substitute of most allowed sufficiency,
yet opinion, a sovereign mistress of effects, throws a more
safer voice on you. You must therefore be content to slubber
the gloss of your new fortunes with this more stubborn and
boisterous expedition.

Othello

The tyrant custom, most grave senators, 225
Hath made the flinty and steel couch of war
My thrice-driven bed of down. I do agnize
A natural and prompt alacrity
I find in hardness, and do undertake
These present wars against the Ottomites. 230
Most humbly therefore bending to your state,
I crave fit disposition for my wife,
Due reference of place and exhibition,
With such accommodation and besort
As levels with her breeding. 235

Duke

Why, at her father's.

239 in his eye: within sight. Eyes and sight are recurring themes in the play. Later, Othello will demand "ocular proof" of Desdemona's supposed infidelity.

240 prosperous ear: favorable, sympathetic ear.

241 charter: authorization, permission.

252-55 A moth of peace. . . .dear absence: Desdemona is probably saying that instead of being a moth "at peace" in the dark of a clothes closet, she is someone who would rather "go to the war" with Othello, as a moth in flight is drawn to a burning candle or torch. Ironically, she does not realize that her metaphor is double-edged: Just as there is danger for a moth near a torch, she will be in mortal danger with Othello (and Iago) on Cyprus.

256-70 Let her have. . . .estimation: another orotund speech by Othello, the outsider-soldier trying to speak the language of the Duke and his Venetian court, using faintly ridiculous rhetoric.

259 please the palate: Othello's calm assurances that he is not driven by passion stand as an ironic measure of how little he understands himself or the power of love.

264 light-winged toys: probably Cupid's arrows. In five lines, Othello strains to impress the senators with inflated oratory linking Cupid, euphuistic talk for "eyes," falconry and a kitchen skillet; lines typical of the pompous pedant *Doctore* in *commedia dell'arte*.

265 seel: a term from falconry, in which the eyelids of the falcon are sewn shut during training. As a nobleman, Oxford was experienced in falconry.

266 speculative and officed instruments: eyes, in an over-elegant Latinism.

267 disports: (sexual) amusements. (OED archaic)

Brabantio
  I will not have it so.
Othello
  Nor I.
Desdemona
  Nor I. I would not there reside,
  To put my father in impatient thoughts
  By being in his eye. Most gracious Duke,
  To my unfolding lend your prosperous ear,   240
  And let me find a charter in your voice,
  To assist my simpleness.
Duke
  What would you, Desdemona?
Desdemona
  That I did love the Moor to live with him,
  My downright violence and storm of fortunes   245
  May trumpet to the world. My heart's subdued
  Even to the very quality of my lord.
  I saw Othello's visage in his mind,
  And to his honors and his valiant parts
  Did I my soul and fortunes consecrate.   250
  So that, dear lords, if I be left behind
  A moth of peace, and he go to the war,
  The rites for why I love him are bereft me,
  And I a heavy interim shall support
  By his dear absence. Let me go with him.   255
Othello
  Let her have your voice.
  Vouch with me, heaven, I therefore beg it not
  To please the palate of my appetite,
  Nor to comply with heat—the young affects
  In me defunct—and proper satisfaction   260
  But to be free and bounteous to her mind.
  And heaven defend your good souls that you think
  I will your serious and great business scant
  When she is with me. No, when light-winged toys
  Of feathered Cupid seel with wanton dullness   265
  My speculative and officed instruments,
  That my disports corrupt and taint my business,
  Let housewives make a skillet of my helm,
  And all indign and base adversities

269 indign: shameful.

270 Make head. . .estimation: that is, attack my reputation, my being esteemed. (OED obsolete) The Quarto gives "reputation."

280 honesty and trust: Othello's unquestioning trust in Iago because he is a comrade in arms is a fatal weakness. Unused to political power struggles like those in court Othello the warrior doesn't understand that the shame of being passed order for promotion, as was Iago, can generate a desire for revenge.

286 Your son-in-law is far more fair than black: A pun on "fair" that could mean light-skinned and also virtuous. (OED) This may also be word-play on "fair," which sounds like "Vere," Oxford's surname. Othello is the "more fair" son-in-law of a troubled Brabantio, just as de Vere was the son-in-law of Lord Burghley in a troubled marriage. Wordplay on "Vere" is found throughout the Shakespeare works.

289 She has deceived . . .may thee: In Brabantio's last words in the play, he steps out of his *commedia dell'arte* role as *Pantalone* and delivers a short, sober and ominous warning that Othello may find (falsely, as it turns out) that Desdemona has deceived him, too. This mirrors quite closely Oxford's learning when he returned to England from Italy about rumors, which may not have been not true, that his wife had deceived him.

Make head against my estimation!　　　　　　　270
Duke
　Be it as you shall privately determine,
　Either for her stay or going. The affair cries haste,
　And speed must answer it.
A Senator
　You must away tonight.
Desdemona
　Tonight, my lord?
Duke
　This night.
Othello
　With all my heart.
Duke
　At nine in the morning here we'll meet again.　　　275
　Othello, leave some officer behind,
　And he shall our commission bring to you,
　With such things else of quality and respect
　As doth import you.
Othello
　So please Your Grace, my ancient;
　A man he is of honest and trust.　　　　　　　280
　To his conveyance I assign my wife,
　With what else needful Your Good Grace shall think
　To be sent after me.
Duke
　Let it be so.
　Good night to everyone. And, noble signior,
　If virtue no delighted beauty lack,　　　　　　285
　Your son-in-law is far more fair than black.
First Senator
　Adieu, brave Moor. Use Desdemona well.
Brabantio
　Look to her, Moor, if thou hast eyes to see.
　She has deceived her father, and may thee.

　　　　　Exit Duke, Brabantio, Cassio, Senators, and officers.

Othello
　My life upon her faith! Honest Iago,　　　　　290
　My Desdemona must I leave to thee.

290 Honest: "a vague epithet of appreciation or praise, esp. as used in a patronizing way to an inferior." (OED) Unsophisticated, Othello does not understand that Iago may resent this salutation.

292 thy wife: Naively, Othello assigns Iago's wife to be Desdemona's companion and servant, further demeaning Iago.

293 best advantage: most favorable opportunity.

294 I have but an hour: Scholars and audiences have debated when or if Othello and Desdemona ever consummate their marriage. Here, Othello says that he has only an hour to spend with his bride and also get ready for their voyage.

297 noble heart: probably sarcastic to the point of contempt, which the dull Roderigo fails to catch.

298 incontinently: immediately. (OED archaic)

305 guinea hen...baboon: Guinea-hen was probably slang for a loose woman. (OED, but first recorded in this play). Iago speaks with contempt at the thought of being upset because of true love for such a woman, thus insulting Desdemona. If that were to happen, he'd shun his "humanity" to be a lecherous baboon. Iago is a witty, jesting villain, the *Zanni*, throughout most of the play.

308 A fig: an expression of contempt. Iago may also be making the Italian obscene gesture of contempt using the thumb and two fingers, called "fig," (OED) hardly a gesture seen very often in London.

I prithee, let thy wife attend on her,
And bring them after in the best advantage.
Come, Desdemona. I have but an hour
Of love, of worldly matters and direction,   295
To spend with thee. We must obey the time.

Exit with Desdemona.

Roderigo
  Iago—
Iago
  What say'st thou, noble heart?
Roderigo
  What will I do, think'st thou?
Iago
  Why, go to bed and sleep.
Roderigo
  I will incontinently drown myself.
Iago
  If thou dost, I shall never love thee after. Why, thou silly
  gentleman?
Roderigo
  It is silliness to live when to live is torment; and then have we
  a prescription to die when death is our physician.   300
Iago
  O villainous! I have looked upon the world for four times
  seven years, and, since I could distinguish betwixt a benefit
  and an injury, I never found man that knew how to love
  himself. Ere I would say I would drown myself for the love of
  a guinea hen, I would change my humanity with a baboon.   305
Roderigo
  What should I do? I confess it is my shame to be so fond, but
  it is not in my virtue to amend it.
Iago
  Virtue? A fig! 'Tis in ourselves that we are thus or thus. Our
  bodies are our gardens, to the which our wills are gardeners.
  So that if we will plant nettles or sow lettuce, set hyssop and   310
  weed up thyme, supply it with one gender of herbs or distract
  it with many, either to have it sterile with idleness or manured
  with industry—why, the power and corrigible authority of
  this lies in our wills. If the beam of our lives had not one
  scale of reason to poise another of sensuality, the blood and   315

318 unbitted: unbridled, unrestrained. (OED)

319 scion: a shoot or sucker usually from the base or root of a tree (OED obsolete), thus figuratively referring to the withdrawal of nourishment from the parent stem. (OED, citing a 1591 usage) Iago may be comparing Roderigo's foolish "love" of Desdemona that is uncontrolled by "reason" to the Family of Love, a "sect, or scion" that threatened to sap the power of the Anglican Church in the late 1570s before being outlawed. Lord Burghley, Oxford's father-in-law, branded the religious sect a "brain-sick heresy," in 1578. Bishops complained about its growing success, and in 1580 Queen Elizabeth ordered its books burned and imprisonment of members of the "dangerous and damnable sect. . . . to defend Christ's church, to root them out from further infecting of her realm." From 1578 to 1581, when Oxford was writing *Othello*, the Family of Love sect was considered a serious threat.

325 stead thee: act in your stead, on your behalf.

325 Put money in thy purse: a strange exhortation interjected ten more times in this passage. Iago wants Roderigo to raise money, perhaps to help carry out their scheme in some way. Roderigo, as was Oxford throughout his life, is land-rich and cash-poor. (See line note 358 below.)

326 usurped beard: perhaps a slur that the young Roderigo does not yet have a beard, thus lacks manliness and will have to borrow ("usurp") a beard.

331 sequestration: separation, putting aside.

334 luscious as locusts: not the insect but probably the sweet fruit of the carob tree.

335 acerb as coloquintida: a bitter apple, often used as a medicine.

340 sanctimony: perhaps a pretended holiness, as in sanctimonious.

349 hearted: firm in my heart, absolute. **conjunctive:** together, united.

baseness of our natures would conduct us to most
preposterous conclusions. But we have reason to cool our
raging motions, our carnal stings, our unbitted lusts, whereof I
take this that you call love to be a sect or scion.

Roderigo

It cannot be. 320

Iago

It is merely a lust of the blood and a permission of the will.
Come, be a man. Drown thyself? Drown cats and blind
puppies. I have professed me thy friend and I confess me knit
to thy deserving with cables of perdurable toughness. I could
never better stead thee than now. Put money in thy purse. 325
Follow thou the wars; defeat thy favor with an usurped beard.
I say, put money in thy purse. It cannot be long that
Desdemona should continue her love to the Moor—put
money in thy purse—nor he his to her. It was a violent
commencement in her, and thou shall see an answerable 330
sequestration—put money in thy purse. These Moors are
changeable in their wills—fill thy purse with money. The
food that to him now is as luscious as locusts shall be to him
shortly as bitter as coloquintida. She must change for youth; 335
when she is sated with his body, she will find the error of her
choice. She must have change, she must. Therefore
put money in thy purse. If thou wilt needs damn thyself,
do it a more delicate way than drowning. Make all the money
thou canst. If sanctimony and a frail vow betwixt an erring 340
barbarian and a supersubtle Venetian be not too hard for my
wits and all the tribe of hell, thou shalt enjoy her. Therefore
make money. A pox of drowning thyself! It is clean out of
the way. Seek thou rather to be hanged in compassing thy joy
than to be drowned and go without her. 345

Roderigo

Wilt thou be fast to my hopes, if I depend on the issue?

Iago

Thou art sure of me. Go, make money. I have told thee often,
and I retell thee again and again, I hate the Moor. My cause is
hearted; thine hath no less reason. Let us be conjunctive in
our revenge against him. If thou canst cuckold him, thou dost 350
thyself a pleasure, me a sport. There are many events in the
womb of time which will be delivered. Traverse, go, provide
thy money. We will have more of this tomorrow. Adieu.

350-1 cuckold. . .sport : Iago's scheme and "sport" will be to revenge himself by making Othello think he has been cuckolded by Cassio and Desdemona, but here, playfully, Iago leads the foolish Roderigo, who courted Desdemona, to think that he will be the one to seduce Desdemona and make Othello the victim of her adultery. Iago probably knows that what Othello fears most is the loss of his reputation and being made a laughing stock.

353 Traverse: probably, mount up; that is, let's go. (OED)

355 Go to: An all-purpose Elizabethan exclamation, here similar to today's "Oh, come on."

358 I'll sell all my land: that is to put money in his purse, as Iago was urging. (See lines 325 ff.) Oxford was notorious for selling his inherited properties in order to raise cash for his travels, retainers, clothes, extravagant spectacles for the queen, and what all. In a letter from Padua in November 1575, he enjoined Burghley "to make no stay of the sales of my land." The following January he wrote Burghley from Sienna authorizing him to complete the sale of lands and stating that "I have determined to continue my travel." The same concern to turn land into cash for expenses appears in other Shakespeare plays. In *As You Like It*, Rosalind exclaims, "A traveler!. . .I fear you have sold your own lands to see other men's." (4.1.21-5) Oxford sold his own lands to see Italy. In *Timon of Athens*, to raise cash the spendthrift Timon says, "Let all my lands be sold." (2.1.834)

359 Thus do I: Iago begins the first of several soliloquies in the play, probably to be spoken directly to the audience, taking them into his confidence as he plots his revenge. Oxford, the courtier-dramatist, allows his audience to understand the reasoning of Iago, his courtier-villain, but leaves them to judge Othello the general and outsider almost entirely by his actions and conversations.*

361 snipe: a gullible fool. The snipe is a long-billed bird allied to the woodcock, which could be easily trapped for food. Iago sees Roderigo as someone he can trap and use. (OED, the first such usage of the word.)

368 proper man: good-looking, respectable, genteel. (OED); that is, a man whom Othello could be made to suspect as his aristocratic wife's lover, a more appropriate match for her than a black soldier like himself.

373 dispose: disposition, bearing.

Roderigo
Where shall we meet in the morning?
Iago
At my lodging.
Roderigo
I'll be with thee betimes.
Iago
Go to, farewell.—Do you hear, Roderigo? 355
Roderigo
What say you?
Iago
No more of drowning, do you hear?
Roderigo
I am changed.
Iago
Go to, farewell. Put money enough in your purse.
Roderigo
I'll sell all my land.

Exit.

Iago

Thus do I ever make my fool my purse;
For I mine own gained knowledge should profane 360
If I would time expend with such a snipe
But for my sport and profit. I hate the Moor;
And it is thought abroad that twixt my sheets
He's done my office. I know not if it be true;
But I, for mere suspicion in that kind, 365
Will do as if for surety. He holds me well;
The better shall my purpose work on him.
Cassio's a proper man. Let me see now:
To get his place and to plume up my will
In double knavery. How, how? Let's see: 370
After some time, to abuse Othello's ear
That he is too familiar with his wife.
He hath a person and a smooth dispose
To be suspected, framed to make women false.
The Moor is of a free and open nature, 375
That thinks men honest that but seem to be so,
And will as tenderly be led by the nose

1.3

*In his introduction to the play, M. R. Ridley takes issue with Coleridge's famous assignment to Iago of "motiveless malignity" and expands on a line note for this passage: "It is sometimes argued that Iago's revenge is so disproportionate to the injury received that only an incarnate fiend could have conceived it. This is to misjudge and exaggerate both Iago's powers of far-sighted planning and his 'malignity'. . . .We know so well the catastrophe in which Iago's plot results that we are apt carelessly to assume that he intended this result from the outset. He intended nothing of the kind. He is not a long term strategist, but a superbly skillful and opportunist tactician. And the moment we realize this, his progress becomes immeasurably more exciting. His plot develops as it goes along, and some moves in it, so far from being intended, are forced on him." (lxi-ii) Ridley's perception of Iago as a gifted improviser (as in *commedia dell'arte*) complements other commentators' views of Iago as a clever (and witty) psychopath and evil practical joker.

As asses are.
I have it. It is engendered. Hell and night
Must bring this monstrous birth to the world's light.

Exit.

Montano: arriving to join the two gentlemen on the cape.

1 cape: the end of a promontory that juts out above the sea. (OED) Montano and the gentlemen are standing on the battlements directly above the harbor. What they describe in some detail in the lines that follow suggests that the dramatist had first-hand knowledge of the aftermath of a storm at sea as seen from a fort above a harbor, something Oxford might well have experienced (but not Will Shakspere.) The three men, safe and dry on the battlements, can see the remnants of the storm but not the wharf directly below. This is an accurate description of Famagusta (not named in the play), the only well-protected, deep-water harbor on Cyprus and the harbor used by the Venetians. Its battlements and citadel are on the heights directly above the harbor wharf. While on his Italian travels, Oxford could have stopped at Famagusta. He had written home that he hoped to see Greece and Constantinople, which are not that far from Cyprus. It's difficult to understand how or why the dramatist could have, or would have, included repeatedly in these conversations such an off-hand but accurate description of Famagusta's fort and battlements directly above the wharf--unless he'd been there. Today there is an "Othello tower" at the fort, but the naming of it dates to recent centuries. (See Appendices.)

8-9 mountains melt. . .mortise: when ocean swells crash over wooden ships and break the joints holding the frame secure.

10 segregation: splitting up, dispersal, the first usage in this sense. (OED)

11 stand. . .shore: that is, if you stand below on the shoreline you'll see how high the waves send spray into the air.

12 pelt the clouds. . .pole: echoing a passage in Arthur Golding's translation of Ovid's *Metamorphoses*. Golding was Oxford's uncle and "receiver," and Oxford may have done the translation that was published as by Golding, whose other writings are quite prosaic and staid compared to the racy translation of *Metamorphoses*.

14-15 burning Bear. . . the guards: the constellation Ursa Minor (or Little Bear) and two stars in it that, along with the "ever-fixed" Pole star, were important for navigation. Many of the Shakespeare plays show an in-depth knowledge of astronomy and navigation.

16 like molestation: that is, such turmoil or trouble. A unique coinage derived from Cinthio's tale in the Italian, not in a translation of it.

ACT 2

Scene 1.The battlements above the port of Famagusta on Cyprus.
Enter Montano and two gentlemen.

Montano
  What from the cape can you discern at sea?
First Gentleman
  Nothing at all. It is a high-wrought flood.
  I cannot, twixt the heaven and the main,
  Descry a sail.
Montano
  Methinks the wind hath spoke aloud at land;   5
  A fuller blast never shook our battlements.
  If it hath ruffianed so upon the sea,
  What ribs of oak, when mountains melt on them,
  Can hold the mortise? What shall we hear of this?
Second Gentleman
  A segregation of the Turkish fleet.   10
  For do but stand upon the foaming shore,
  The chidden billow seems to pelt the clouds;
  The wind-shaked surge, with high and monstrous mane,
  Seems to cast water on the burning Bear
  And quench the guards of the ever-fixed pole.   15
  I never did like molestation view
  On the enchafed flood.
Montano
  If that the Turkish fleet
  Be not ensheltered and embayed, they are drowned;
  It is impossible they bear it out.

Enter a Third Gentleman.

Third Gentleman
  News, lads! Our wars are done.   20
  The desperate tempest hath so banged the Turks
  That their designment halts. A noble ship of Venice
  Hath seen a grievous wreck and sufferance
  On most part of their fleet.

26 Verennessa: either a type of ship called a *verrinessa* in Italian, perhaps similar to a cutter, or a ship from Verona, an inland city in the Venetian state. (Variorum) Either way, the passing mention suggests that only someone like Oxford who had been there would know the obscure type of an Italian ship or know that Verona was linked to Venice and the Adriatic by canals and even had its own seagoing ships. Verona had ships at the battle of Lepanto a year after Othello arrives on Cyprus. (An untraveled English commoner like Shakspere would hardly have known about Veronese ships to put such an incidental mention in the play.)

29 in full commission: referring to Othello's commission to rule as military governor of Cyprus.

32 sadly: seriously, gravely.

35-6 commands like a full soldier: Montano testifies to Othello's reputation as a general who knows the military rules of command, obedience and loyalty. This will be in contrast to Othello's almost pathetic vulnerability to the lies and manipulations of his "honest Iago," a disloyal, courtier-like figure who takes advantage of Othello's naiveté about marriage, adultery and jealousy.

36 to the seaside: one of a dozen indications in this scene that the men are not at the harbor wharf but on the battlements directly above it. This is the topography of the harbor and fort at Famagusta. See line note 2.1.1.

48 bark: from *barca longa*, a large Spanish ship having two or three masts, seen mostly in the Mediterranean. *Barca longa* is from the Portuguese or Old Spanish. (OED) The play has many such incidental references to matters Mediterranean, indicating the dramatist's first-hand knowledge of the area.

49 allowance: acknowledgment. (OED, now obsolete.)

Montano
  How? Is this true?
Third Gentleman
  The ship is here put in,   25
  A Verennessa. Michael Cassio,
  Lieutenant to the warlike Moor, Othello,
  Is come on shore; the Moor himself at sea,
  And is in full commission here for Cyprus.
Montano
  I am glad on it. 'Tis a worthy governor.   30
Third Gentleman
  But this same Cassio, though he speak of comfort
  Touching the Turkish loss, yet he looks sadly
  And prays the Moor be safe, for they were parted
  With foul and violent tempest.
Montano
  Pray heavens he be,
  For I have served him, and the man commands   35
  Like a full soldier. Let's to the seaside, ho!
  As well to see the vessel that's come in
  As to throw out our eyes for brave Othello,
  Even till we make the main and the aerial blue
  An indistinct regard.
Third Gentleman
  Come, let's do so;   40
  For every minute is expectancy
  Of more arrivance.

Enter Cassio.

Cassio
  Thanks, you the valiant of this warlike isle,
  That so approve the Moor! O, let the heavens
  Give him defense against the elements,   45
  For I have lost him on a dangerous sea.
Montano
  Is he well shipped?
Cassio
  His bark is stoutly timbered, his pilot
  Of very expert and approved allowance;
  Therefore my hopes, not surfeited to death,   50
  Stand in bold cure.

2.1

50-1 my hopes. . .bold cure: that is, perhaps, therefore my hopes are not overblown, and I'm confident they will be cured or satisfied. Ridley says "Cassio is throwing off a conceit, a verbal bubble that disappears if one examines it too closely."

54 brow of the sea: the projecting edge of a cliff overlooking the sea below. (OED)

55 shot of courtesy: a single cannon shot from a warship to indicate that it arrives as friend, not foe. The dramatist was familiar with this custom for ships arriving at fortified sea ports.

61 achieved: obtained, acquired.

62 paragons: surpasses. (OED, which gives this line as the first and only usage with this meaning.)

62-4 One that excels. . . ingeniuer: an obscure passage, possibly meaning that Desdemona excels what poets might write about her and that her nature ("vesture of creation") challenges the skill of her Creator (ingeniuer = engineer?). Throughout the play, Cassio speaks the high-flown language of the courtier in the late 1570s, called euphuism. (Shakspere was in his teens in Stratford.) See the Introduction for the source of Cassio's euphuistic language.

69 guttered rocks and congregated sands: a description of the ledges enclosing the harbor of Famagusta and its narrow entrance, an exact, nautical detail that would remain in the memory of a writer who had sailed into the harbor.

Cassio
  What noise?
A Gentleman
  The town is empty. On the brow of the sea
  Stand ranks of people, and they cry "A sail!"
Cassio
  My hopes do shape him for the governor.
Second Gentlemen
  They do discharge their shot of courtesy;   55
  Our friends, at least.
Cassio
  I pray you, sir, go forth,
  And give us truth who 'tis that is arrived.
Second Gentleman
  I shall.

                                                          Exit.

Montano
  But, good Lieutenant, is your general wived?   60
Cassio
  Most fortunately. He hath achieved a maid
  That paragons description and wild fame,
  One that excels the quirks of blazoning pens,
  And in the essential vesture of creation
  Does tire the ingeniuer.

                Enter Second Gentlemen.

  How now? Who has put in?   65
Second Gentleman
  'Tis one Iago, ancient to the general.
Cassio
  He's had most favorable and happy speed.
  Tempests themselves, high seas, and howling winds,
  The guttered rocks and congregated sands—
  Traitors ensteeped to clog the guiltless keel—   70
  As having sense of beauty, do omit
  Their mortal natures, letting go safely by
  The divine Desdemona.
Montano
  What is she?

                          89

77 sennight speed: that is, a week speedier or earlier than expected. The dramatist knew that storms at sea, although dangerous, could have favorable winds that would drive a ship faster to its destination. **Great Jove. . .powerful breath:** Probably a reference to sixteenth century maps that showed Jove blowing ships across the seas, maps that Oxford would have seen in private libraries and the offices of court officials.

80 love's quick pants: possibly during sexual intercourse, but Cassio always shows a courtly respect for Desdemona, so more likely figuratively for the excitement of loving hearts reunited after their separate and dangerous voyages. Or both. Cassio is trying to be personable and charming, as does *Pedrolino* of *commedia dell'arte*. Oxford may have been making fun of Cassio's overblown rhetoric with this double-meaning phrase.

86-7 Before. . .round: Honigmann asks, "Could Shakespeare have known Donne's (unpublished) Elegy 19, 'Going to bed'? [with the lines] 'License my roving hands, and let them go / Before, behind, between, above, below.'?" This is a striking similarity of thought, although it's not clear who may have inspired whom; and Cassio, ever proper, invokes God ("grace of heaven") as the agent instead of Donne's lover. Oxford and Donne moved in the same literary and court circles.

96 See for the news: Cassio, on the battlements directly above the harbor wharf, sends a gentleman down to the wharf to see who has arrived.

Cassio
She that I spake of, our great captain's captain,
Left in the conduct of the bold Iago,   75
Whose footing here anticipates our thoughts
A sennight's speed. Great Jove, Othello guard
And swell his sail with thine own powerful breath,
That he may bless this bay with his tall ship,
Make love's quick pants in Desdemona's arms,   80
Give renewed fire to our extincted spirits.

Enter Desdemona, Iago, Roderigo, and Emilia.

O, behold,
The riches of the ship is come on shore!
You men of Cyprus, let her have your knees.
Hail to thee, lady! And the grace of heaven   85
Before, behind thee, and on every hand
Enwheel thee round!
Desdemona
I thank you, valiant Cassio.
What tidings can you tell me of my lord?
Cassio
He is not yet arrived, nor know I aught
But that he's well and will be shortly here.   90
Desdemona
O, but I fear—How lost you company?
Cassio
The great contention of the sea and skies
Parted our fellowship.

Within, "A sail! A sail!" *A shot.*

But hark. A sail!
Second Gentleman
They give their greeting to the citadel.   95
This likewise is a friend.
Cassio
See for the news.

Exit Second Gentleman.

Good Ancient, you are welcome.
Welcome, mistress.

91

97 Welcome mistress.: Given the remarks that follow, Cassio probably kisses Emilia—either flirting or being especially courtly. Or both.

98-9 breeding. . .bold show of courtesy: behavior befitting an aristocratic courtier. As the *Pedrolino* of *commedia dell'arte*, Cassio is trying to be personable and charming, but he overdoes it in kissing Emilia, the maid. His flowery language is in sharp contrast to that of the blunt Iago.

100 her lips. . . her tongue: suggesting Emilia's kisses and her speech, a sarcastic gibe at his wife, accusing her of being a scold and perhaps wanton in her kissing.

100-66 Sir, would she. . .the scholar.: Iago's bawdy banter with Desdemona is very much in the manner of *commedia dell'arte*. As the *Zanni,* he is skilled at witty improvisation. He plays the truth-telling jester to Desdemona, the aristocratic Venetian who is adept at sexual innuendo and sophisticated, witty repartee. Oxford was considered a court wit, quick with a riposte.

104 list: a wish, desire.

Let it not gall your patience, good Iago,
That I extend my manners. 'Tis my breeding
That gives me this bold show of courtesy.
Iago
  Sir, would she give you so much of her lips   100
  As of her tongue she oft bestows on me,
  You would have enough.
Desdemona
  Alas, she has no speech!
Iago
  In faith, too much.
  I find it still, when I have list to sleep.
  Marry, before your ladyship, I grant,   105
  She puts her tongue a little in her heart
  And chides with thinking.
Emilia
  You have little cause to say so.
Iago
  Come on, come on. You are pictures out of doors,
  Bells in your parlors, wildcats in your kitchens,   110
  Saints in your injuries, devils being offended,
  Players in your housewifery, and housewives in your beds.
Desdemona
  O, fie upon thee, slanderer!
Iago
  Nay, it is true, or else I am a Turk.
  You rise to play, and go to bed to work.   115
Emilia
  You shall not write my praise.
Iago
  No, let me not.
Desdemona
  What wouldst write of me, if thou shouldst praise me?
Iago
  O gentle lady, do not put me to it.
  For I am nothing if not critical.
Desdemona
  Come on assay. There's one gone to the harbor?   120
Iago
  Ay, madam.

121 beguile: here, disguise or divert attention from. (OED)

121-22 I am not merry. . seeming otherwise: an echo of the first two lines of one of Oxford's early, teenage poems: "I am not as I seem to be / For when I smile I am not glad." Even with Desdemona, the dramatist is concerned with appearance vs. reality. Iago put it more bluntly: "I am not what I am." (1.1.64.)

126 frieze: coarse woolen fabric.

129-31 wit. . .witty: Not necessarily humorous, but intelligent, sensible, having good judgment. (OED obsolete)

137 an heir: All the jesting about a woman's sexual behavior underscores the fact that Oxford believed his first wife to be unfaithful. For some time, he did not accept her first daughter as his own "heir."

138 fond: foolish; the earliest OED meaning, often found in Shakespeare.

141 foul pranks: sexual pranks.

145 put on the vouch: probably, challenge or assert. In effect, Desdemona asks, "What about a woman who is so confident of her own virtue that she can ask 'malice' to be a witness?"

Desdemona
  I am not merry, but I do beguile
  The thing I am, by seeming otherwise.
  Come, how wouldst thou praise me?
Iago
  I am about it, but indeed my invention   125
  Comes from my pate as birdlime does from frieze—
  It plucks out brains and all. But my Muse labors,
  And thus she is delivered:
  If she be fair and wise, fairness and wit,
  The one's for use, the other useth it.   130
Desdemona
  Well praised! How if she be black and witty?
Iago
  If she be black, and thereto have a wit,
  She'll find a white that shall her blackness fit.
Desdemona
  Worse and worse.
Emilia
  How if fair and foolish?   135
Iago
  She never yet was foolish that was fair,
   For even her folly helped her to an heir.
Desdemona
  These are old fond paradoxes to make fools
  laugh in the alehouse. What miserable praise hast thou
  for her that's foul and foolish?   140
Iago
  There's none so foul and foolish thereunto,
   But does foul pranks which fair and wise ones do.
Desdemona
  O heavy ignorance! Thou praisest the worst best. But what   145
  praise couldst thou bestow on a deserving woman indeed, one
  that, in the authority of her merit, did justly put on the vouch
  of very malice itself?
Iago
  She that was ever fair and never proud,
   Had tongue at will and yet was never loud,
  Never lacked gold and yet went never gay,   150
  Fled from her wish and yet said, 'Now I may,'
  She that being angered, her revenge being nigh,

2.1

155 cod's head. . .salmon's tail: Iago's witty answers have been getting more and more sexual, and this line is quite obscene. Here, paraphrasing the Roman Pliny, he's saying that a wise woman would not exchange a cod's head, that is, a man's penis, with a salmon's tail, a woman's pudenda. Iago dares to try to shock Desdemona.

158 wight: either a human being, or an unearthly, preternatural being. (OED) Here, Iago probably means an exceptional person.

160 chronicle small beer: probably, to be concerned with trivial matters.

163 liberal: free-spoken to the point of being licentious.

164 He speaks home: to the point, on target; a fencing term.

169 gyve: chain, shackle.

174 courtesy: elegant courtly behavior. (OED)

175 clyster pipes: tubes used for enemas or douches. OED cites this usage as the first. Iago's vulgar images show that he can take an innocent action (Cassio's courtesy toward Desdemona) and twist it to his own uses.

Bade her wrong stay and her displeasure fly,
She that in wisdom never was so frail
To change the cod's head for the salmon's tail, 155
She that could think and never disclose her mind,
See suitors following and not look behind,
She was a wight, if ever such wight were—
Desdemona
To do what?
Iago
To suckle fools and chronicle small beer. 160
Desdemona
O most lame and impotent conclusion! Do not learn of him,
Emilia, though he be thy husband. How say you, Cassio? Is he
not a most profane and liberal counselor?
Cassio
He speaks home, madam. You may relish him more in the 165
soldier than in the scholar.
Iago
[Aside] He takes her by the palm. Ay, well said, whisper.
With as little a web as this will I ensnare as great a fly as
Cassio. Ay, smile upon her, do; I will gyve thee in thine own
courtship. You say true; 'tis so, indeed. If such tricks as these 170
strip you out of your lieutenantry, it had been better you had
not kissed your three fingers so oft, which now again you are
most apt to play the sir in. Very good; well kissed! An
excellent courtesy! 'Tis so, indeed. Yet again your fingers to
your lips? Would they were clyster pipes for your sake! 175

Trumpet within.

The Moor! I know his trumpet.
Cassio
'Tis truly so.
Desdemona
Let's meet him and receive him.
Cassio
Lo, where he comes!
Enter Othello and Attendants
Othello
O my fair warrior!
Desdemona
My dear Othello! 180

2.1

189 content: capacity to contain. (OED) Classical writers often referred to death at moments of supreme happiness. Othello's flowery speech began with the other use of "content" as satisfied. He repeats the word again on line 194.

197-8 well-tuned. . . set down the pegs: In this aside, Iago is saying that Othello and Desdemona are in harmony ("well-tuned"), but he'll loosen the pegs that tune the strings and ruin their music, or perhaps make them change their tune. Or both. He plays off Othello's forced metaphor of kisses as "discords" two lines earlier and in effect declares that he is the musician in control of the music. Oxford was well-acquainted with this detail of string instruments from his aristocratic upbringing. (See the Appendices.)

202 old acquaintance: old friends, that is Montano and perhaps the throng of Cyprians. The phrase may well be from a poem attributed to the court poet Robert Ayton, a Scotsman, diplomat and court official who was the same age as Oxford. He wrote poems in Latin, Greek and English. His poem, *Old Long Syne* opens, "Should auld acquaintance be forgot." His poem probably also inspired the Robert Burns poem with the same first line that is well-known today.

207 Go the bay. . .coffers: Unthinking, Othello treats Iago, a military staff officer of some standing, as a mere baggage ("coffers") handler. Here in this scene is also another of the dozen indications that Othello, Iago and the others are not at the harbor but on the battlements directly above, which is the topography of Famagusta.

210 challenge: rightly claim. (OED, archaic)

Othello

It gives me wonder great as my content
To see you here before me. O my soul's joy,
If after every tempest come such calms,
May the winds blow till they have wakened death,
And let the laboring bark climb hills of seas   185
Olympus-high, and duck again as low
As hell's from heaven! If it were now to die,
'Twere now to be most happy, for I fear
My soul hath her content so absolute
That not another comfort like to this   190
Succeeds in unknown fate.

Desdemona

The heavens forbid
But that our loves and comforts should increase
Even as our days do grow!

Othello

Amen to that, sweet powers!
I cannot speak enough of this content.
It stops me here; it is too much of joy.   195
And this, and this, the greatest discords be
That ever our hearts shall make!

Iago

[Aside] O, you are well tuned now!
But I'll set down the pegs that make this music,
As honest as I am.

Othello

Come, let us to the castle.   200
News, friends! Our wars are done, the Turks are drowned.
How does my old acquaintance of this isle? —
Honey, you shall be well desired in Cyprus;
I have found great love amongst them. O my sweet,
I prattle out of fashion, and I dote   205
In mine own comforts.—I prithee, good Iago,
Go to the bay and disembark my coffers.
Bring thou the master to the citadel;
He is a good one, and his worthiness
Does challenge much respect.—Come, Desdemona;   210
Once more, well met at Cyprus!

Exit Othello and Desdemona .

99

2.1

215 court of guard: guardhouse or watchtower.

218 but for bragging: that is, only for his bragging. fantastical lies: exaggeration, mere story-telling.

220 the devil: that is, Othello. For Elizabethans, black was the devil's color.

228 pregnant: weighty, compelling. (OED)

230 very voluble: fluent or glib. (OED, first usage in this sense) With a connotation of inconstant, changeable; perhaps referring disparagingly to Cassio's naïve, euphuistic manner of speaking.

234 slipper: shifty, unreliable. (OED)

238 folly and green minds: that is, Desdemona, whom Iago describes as foolish and immature.

Iago

(*To an attendant*] Do thou meet me presently at the harbor.
(To Roderigo)Come hither. If thou be'st valiant,—as, they say,
Base men being in love have then a nobility in their natures
More than is native to them—list me. The lieutenant tonight watches
On the court of guard. First, I must tell thee this: 215
Desdemona is directly in love with him.

Roderigo

With him? Why, 'tis not possible.

Iago

Lay thy finger thus, and let thy soul be instructed. Mark me
With what violence she first loved the Moor, but for bragging
And telling her fantastical lies. To love him still for prating?
Let not thy discreet heart think it. Her eye must be fed; and
What delight shall she have to look on the devil? When the   220
Blood is made dull with the act of sport, there should be, again
To inflame it and to give satiety a fresh appetite, loveliness in
Favor, sympathy in years, manners and beauties—all which
The Moor is defective in. Now, for want of these required
Conveniences, her delicate tenderness will find itself abused,
Begin to heave the gorge, disrelish and abhor the Moor. Very   225
Nature will instruct her in it and compel her to some second
Choice. Now, sir, this granted—as it is a most pregnant and
Unforced position—who stands so eminent in the degree of
This fortune as Cassio does? A knave very voluble, no
Further conscionable than in putting on the mere form of civil   230
And humane seeming for the better compassing of his salt and
Most hidden loose affection. Why, none, why, none. A slippery
And subtle knave, a finder out of occasions, that has an eye
Can stamp and counterfeit advantages, though true advantage
Never present itself; a devilish knave. Besides, the knave is   235
Handsome, young, and hath all those requisites in him that
Folly and green minds look after. A pestilent complete knave,
And the woman hath found him already.

Roderigo

I cannot believe that in her. She's full of most blessed
condition.   240

Iago

Blessed fig's end! The wine she drinks is made of grapes. If
she had been blessed, she would never have loved the Moor.
Blessed pudding! Didst thou not see her paddle with the palm

241 Blessed fig's end!: Iago again refers to the Italian hand gesture simulating copulation. Cf. 1.3.308.

243 paddle: fondle, caress. The OED cites a sixteenth century Scots word ("padle" or "pattle") meaning to rub; to paddle the palm is to rub or pat it with the fingers, a practice considered a sexual invitation. Oxford may have heard it when he was in Scotland.

245 courtesy: not just politeness but elegant, courtly behavior. (OED)

246 index: here, an indication or sign of.

249 mutualities: intimate actions; here, preludes to sexual union. (OED) The young and impressionable Roderigo is easily led to believe that Cassio and Desdemona have slept together.

258 choler: anger.

264 impediment: that is, Cassio.

267 necessaries: baggage.

of his hand? Didst not mark that?

Roderigo

  Yes, that I did; but that was but courtesy.   245

Iago

  Lechery, by this hand. An index and obscure prologue to
The history of lust and foul thoughts. They met so near
With their lips that their breaths embraced together.
Villanous thoughts, Roderigo! When these mutualities so
Marshal the way, hard at hand comes the master and main   250
Exercise, the incorporate conclusion. Pish! But, sir, be you
Ruled by me: I have brought you from Venice. Watch you
Tonight; for the command, I'll lay it upon you. Cassio
knows you not. I'll not be far from you. Do you find
some occasion to anger Cassio, either by speaking too   255
loud, or tainting his discipline, or from what other course
you please, which the time shall more favorably minister.

Roderigo

  Well.

Iago

  Sir, he's rash and very sudden in choler, and haply may
Strike at you. Provoke him, that he may, for even out of
That will I cause these of Cyprus to mutiny, whose   260
Qualification shall come into no true taste again but by the
Displanting of Cassio. So shall you have a shorter journey
To your desires, by the means I shall then have to prefer
Them, and the impediment most profitably removed,
Without the which there were no expectation of our prosperity.   265

Roderigo

  I will do this, if I can bring it to any opportunity.

Iago

  I warrant thee. Meet me by and by at the citadel.
I must fetch his necessaries ashore. Farewell.

Roderigo

  Adieu.

     Exit.

Iago

  That Cassio loves her, I do well believe it;
That she loves him, 'tis apt and of great credit.   270
The Moor, howbeit that I endure him not,
Is of a constant, loving, noble nature,
And I dare think he'll prove to Desdemona

270 great credit: completely credible, believable.

271 endure him not: cannot tolerate him.

275 absolute lust: pure and simple lust. **peradventure:** as it happens, as a matter of chance.

279 my seat: Iago suspects Othello of sleeping with Emilia. Thus, Iago has several motives: revenge because Othello did not make him his lieutenant, desire to oust Cassio from the position, suspicion that Othello has cuckolded him, and the sheer pleasure of exercising his power to make trouble for everyone.

282 wife for wife: Iago's parody of the Old Testament phrase "an eye for an eye. . . ."

286 poor trash. . .trace. . .quick hunting: "Poor trash" is Iago's contemptuous term for the well-born but naive Roderigo. **trace:** some editors suggest that "trace' is a mis-transcription in the First Folio for a second use of "trash," a hunting term for holding back a hound from "quick hunting." (OED) Hunting with hounds was an aristocratic sport. Or if "trace" in the First Folio is correct, it could mean to pursue, keep after or dog (OED), alluding to the aristocratic sport of falconry, with Iago keeping after Roderigo as a falconer keeps a falcon hungry so it will hunt more eagerly. Either way, the word points to aristocratic activities.

288 on the hip: that is, at a disadvantage, from wrestling.

289 rank garb: offensive or lascivious manner. (OED)

290 my nightcap. . .madness: Iago extends his unfounded jealousy and implies with dark humor that Cassio, too, may have slept with Iago's wife Emilia, and done so ludicrously in Iago's "night cap." Iago delights in the power to manipulate men "even to madness."

294 but yet confused: Iago is still working out his intricate revenge plot.

2 mere: pure or total. (OED obsolete).

3 perdition: utter destruction.

8 offices: rooms used for domestic service such as kitchens, pantries, etc.

A most dear husband. Now, I do love her too,
Not out of absolute lust—though peradventure   275
I stand accountant for as great a sin—
But partly led to diet my revenge,
For that I do suspect the lusty Moor
Hath leaped into my seat. The thought whereof
Doth, like a poisonous mineral, gnaw my inwards;   280
And nothing can or shall content my soul
Till I am evened with him, wife for wife,
Or failing so, yet that I put the Moor
At least into a jealousy so strong
That judgment cannot cure. Which thing to do,   285
If this poor trash of Venice, whom I trace
For his quick hunting, stand the putting on,
I'll have our Michael Cassio on the hip,
Abuse him to the Moor in the rank garb
(For I fear Cassio with my nightcap too)   290
Make the Moor thank me, love me, and reward me.
For making him egregiously an ass
And practicing upon his peace and quiet
Even to madness. 'Tis here, but yet confused.
Knavery's plain face is never seen till used.   295

Exit.

Scene 2, enter Othello's Herald with a proclamation.

Herald
It is Othello's pleasure, our noble and valiant general, that
Upon certain tidings now arrived, importing the mere
Perdition of the Turkish fleet, every man put himself into
Triumph: some to dance, some to make bonfires, each man
To what sport and revels his addiction leads him. For,   5
Besides these beneficial news, it is the celebration of his
Nuptial. So much was his pleasure should be proclaimed.
All offices are open, and there is full liberty of feasting
From this present hour of five till the bell have told eleven.
Heaven bless the isle of Cyprus and our noble general   10
Othello!

Exit.

2.3.1 guard: A major duty of a lieutenant was commanding the watch.

2 stop: pause for consideration before proceeding. (OED obsolete)

3 outsport: probably, to go beyond customary bounds. (OED, only use cited)

9 purchase made: advantage gained. (OED obsolete)

10 profit's: If "profit" means the consummation of their marriage, then Othello and Desdemona have not had time together until this night in Cyprus. But some scholars think that "profit" here suggests a more generalized enjoyment of being together, a fulfillment of love.

16 Jove: In classical literature, Jove was often a womanizer. With a series of ribald comments, Iago will mock Cassio's decorous remarks about Desdemona.

19 game: probably, a willingness to indulge in sensual sport.

Scene 3. Enter Othello, Desdemona, Cassio, and attendants.

Othello
Good Michael, look you to the guard tonight.
Let's teach ourselves that honorable stop
Not to outsport discretion.
Cassio
Iago hath direction what to do,
But notwithstanding, with my personal eye   5
Will I look to it.
Othello
Iago is most honest.
Michael, good night. Tomorrow with your earliest
Let me have speech with you.
[To Desdemona.] Come, my dear love,
The purchase made, the fruits are to ensue;
That profit's yet to come 'tween me and you.—   10
Good night.

Exit [Othello, with Desdemona and attendants].

Enter Iago

Cassio
Welcome, Iago. We must to the watch.
Iago
Not this hour, lieutenant; 'tis not yet ten o' the clock. Our
general cast us thus early for the love of his Desdemona; who
let us not therefore blame. He hath not yet made wanton the   15
night with her; and she is sport for Jove.
Cassio
She's a most exquisite lady.
Iago
And, I'll warrant her, full of game.
Cassio
Indeed, she's a most fresh and delicate creature.   20
Iago
What an eye she has! Methinks it sounds a parley to
provocation.
Cassio
An inviting eye, and yet methinks right modest.

2.3

24 alarum to love: a call to action.

27 stoup: tankard or flagon. **brace:** a pair

29 unhappy: bothersome, unfortunate.

35 qualified: To qualify a liquid was to modify its strength. (OED) Cassio probably means "diluted."

40 it dislikes me: I don't like what alcohol does to me.

Iago
And when she speaks, is it not an alarum to love?
Cassio
She is indeed perfection.   25
Iago
Well, happiness to their sheets! Come, Lieutenant, I have a
stoup of wine, and here without are a brace of Cyprus gallants
that would fain have a measure to the health of black Othello.
Cassio
Not tonight, good Iago. I have very poor and unhappy brains
for drinking. I could well wish courtesy would invent some   30
other custom of entertainment.
Iago
O, they are our friends. But one cup. I'll drink for you.
Cassio
I have drunk but one cup tonight, and that was craftily
qualified, too, and behold what innovation it makes here. I am   35
unfortunate in the infirmity and dare not task my weakness
with any more.
Iago
What, man? 'Tis a night of revels. The gallants desire it.
Cassio
Where are they?
Iago
Here at the door. I pray you, call them in.
Cassio
I'll do it, but it dislikes me.   40

                                                        Exit.

Iago
If I can fasten but one cup upon him,
With that which he hath drunk tonight already,
He'll be as full of quarrel and offence
As my young mistress' dog. Now, my sick fool Roderigo,
Whom love hath turned almost the wrong side out,   45
To Desdemona hath tonight caroused
Potations pottle-deep; and he's to watch.
Three else of Cyprus, noble swelling spirits,
(That hold their honors in a wary distance,
The very elements of this warlike isle)   50
Have I tonight flustered with flowing cups,

47 Potations pottle-deep: liquids reaching the depth of a half gallon. (OED)

48 else: others.

56-7 if consequence. . .stream: that is, if events turn out the way I hope, it will all be smooth sailing for me.

58 rouse: a big drink. (OED)

61 cannikin: a little drinking can or cup. The song is probably a traditional drinking song. Counting trumpet fanfares, Iago's song is the first of nine pieces of music in the play. Oxford was known for his knowledge and appreciation of music. (See Appendices.)

72 Almain: German. (OED obsolete)

And they watch too.
Now, amongst this flock of drunkards,
Am I to put our Cassio in some action
That may offend the isle.—But here they come.   55

Enter Cassio, Montano, and gentlemen.

If consequence do but approve my dream,
My boat sails freely both with wind and stream.
Cassio
'Fore God, they have given me a rouse already.
Montano
Good faith, a little one; not past a pint, as I am a soldier.
Iago
Some wine, ho!   60
      And let me the cannikin clink, clink,
      And let me the cannikin clink.
      A soldier's a man,
      O, man's life's but a span;
      Why, then, let a soldier drink.
Some wine, boys!   65
Cassio
'Fore God, an excellent song.
Iago
I learned it in England, where indeed they are most potent in
potting. Your Dane, your German, and your swag-bellied
Hollander—drink, ho!—are nothing to your English.
Cassio
Is your Englishman so exquisite in his drinking?   70
Iago
Why, he drinks you, with facility, your Dane dead drunk; he
Sweats not to overthrow your Almain; he gives your Hollander
A vomit, ere the next bottle can be filled.
Cassio
To the health of our general!
Montano
I am for it, Lieutenant, and I'll do you justice.   75
Iago
O sweet England!
      King Stephen was an a worthy peer,
      His breeches cost him but a crown;

76-83 King Stephen. . .about thee: a song based on a traditional ballad about pride and the expense of dressing above one's station.

79 lown: a variant spelling for loon, a lowborn, base fellow. (OED)

93-4 the lieutenant. . .ancient: Drunk, Cassio unwittingly reminds Iago again that he now outranks him.

He held them sixpence all too dear,
With that he called the tailor lown.
He was a wight of high renown, 80
And thou art but of low degree,
'Tis pride that pulls the country down;
Then take thy auld cloak about thee.

Some wine, ho!

Cassio

'Fore God, this is a more exquisite song than the other.

Iago

Will you hear it again? 85

Cassio

No, for I hold him to be unworthy of his place that does
Those things. Well, heaven's above all; and there be souls must
Be saved, and there be souls must not be saved.

Iago

It's true, good Lieutenant.

Cassio

For mine own part—no offence to the general, nor any man 90
of quality—I hope to be saved.

Iago

And so do I too, Lieutenant.

Cassio

Ay, but, by your leave, not before me; the lieutenant is to be
Saved before the ancient. Let's have no more of this; let's to
Our affairs.—God forgive us our sins!—Gentlemen, let's
Look to our business. Do not think, gentlemen, I am drunk.
This is my ancient; this is my right hand, and this is my left. 95
I am not drunk now. I can stand well enough, and I speak
Well enough.

Gentlemen

Excellent well.

Cassio

Why, very well then; you must not think then that I am
drunk.

Exit.

Montano

To the platform, masters. Come, let's set the watch.

Exit Gentlemen.

99 platform: a gun platform or part of the citadel ramparts.

103 just equinox: probably, a precise counterbalance. Iago is pretending to praise Cassio as worthy of standing next to Caesar, but he also insinuates that the lieutenant's "vice" (drunkenness) will have dire consequences.

109 horologue: a clock. Again, Iago disparages Cassio's mental abilities, saying that Cassio could stay awake for two revolutions of the clock ("a double set") if it weren't for his drinking.

117 ingraft: firmly implanted, ingrained.

Iago

You see this fellow that is gone before.   100
He is a soldier fit to stand by Caesar
And give direction; and do but see his vice.
'Tis to his virtue a just equinox,
The one as long as the other. 'Tis pity of him.
I fear the trust Othello puts him in,   105
On some odd time of his infirmity,
Will shake this island.

Montano

But is he often thus?

Iago

'Tis evermore the prologue to his sleep.
He'll watch the horologe a double set,
If drink rock not his cradle.   110

Montano

It were well
The General were put in mind of it.
Perhaps he sees it not, or his good nature
Prizes the virtue that appears in Cassio
And looks not on his evils. Is not this true?

Enter Roderigo.

Iago

[Aside] How now, Roderigo? I pray you, after the   115
Lieutenant. Go.

Exit Roderigo.

Montano

And 'tis great pity that the noble Moor should hazard such a
Place as his own second with one of an ingraft infirmity.
It were an honest action to say so to the Moor.

Iago

Not I, for this fair island.
I do love Cassio well and would do much   120
To cure him of this evil.
But, hark! What noise?

Enter Cassio, pursuing Roderigo.

Cassio

You rogue! You rascal!

Enter Cassio, pursuing Roderigo: The drunken courtier-soldier chasing and fighting a foolish fop of a courtier in the lines that follow is typical of *commedia dell'arte*. The dramatist leaves it to the actors to improvise the fight scene, which is not detailed in the stage directions and could be improvised slapstick. Iago, the *Zanni*, has instigated the fighting, but as soon as it starts he immediately seizes the opportunity for more mischief. He pulls his sidekick Roderigo out of the fighting and tells him to "go cry a mutiny," thus summoning Othello and others to see the drunken, brawling Cassio and advance Iago's scheme to get him demoted.

124 I'll beat. . . .twiggen bottle: that is, whip him so hard that his skin will look like the wicker on a bottle of wine. "Twiggen" means made of twigs, resembling a wicker pattern.

129 mazard: a slang term for the head or skull. (OED)

132 sir: Iago cynically addresses both Cassio and Montano as "sir" to reinforce what they assume is his respect for their leadership positions. In the confusion of the moment, no one realizes that Iago himself has engineered the fight.

135 the bell: an alarm bell.   **Diablo:** Spanish for devil. Iago's name is Spanish, as is Roderigo's.

139 He dies: probably meaning that "I, Montano, will kill him."

Montano
 What's the matter, Lieutenant?
Cassio
 A knave teach me my duty? I'll beat the knave into a twiggen
 Bottle.
Roderigo
 Beat me? 125
Cassio
 Dost thou prate, rogue?
Montano
 Nay, good Lieutenant.
 I pray you, sir, hold your hand.
Cassio
 Let me go, sir, or I'll knock you over the mazard.
Montano
 Come, come, you're drunk.
Cassio
 Drunk? 130
Iago [Aside to Roderigo]
 Away, I say. Go out, and cry a mutiny.

 Exit Roderigo.

Nay, good Lieutenant—Alas, gentlemen—
 Help, ho!—Lieutenant—sir—Montano—sir—
 Help, masters!—Here's a goodly watch indeed!
 Who's that which rings the bell?—Diablo, ho! 135
 The town will rise. Fie, fie, Lieutenant, hold!
 You'll be ashamed forever.

 Enter Othello and attendants.

Othello
 What is the matter here?
Montano
 I bleed still.
 I am hurt to the death. He dies!
Othello
 Hold, for your lives!
Iago
 Hold, ho! Lieutenant—sir—Montano—gentlemen— 140
 Have you forgot all sense of place and duty?

117

141 place: probably, the importance and dignity of your positions (not "here at Famagusta").

144-5 Are we turned Turks...Ottomites: The religion of the Turks, the Islamic "Ottomites," was thought to forbid fighting among themselves. So Othello is rebuking the brawlers for turning into men like the Venetians' enemies. With this rebuke, Othello seems to take advantage of the situation to remind Montano and the others that he has rejected his Islamic origins and turned Christian.

145 heaven: perhaps an allusion to the storm (sent by heaven) that caused the destruction of the Turkish fleet.

146 For Christian shame: Although it's not explicit in the play, Othello must have converted from Islam to Christianity at some time in the past.

154 quarter: relations with or conduct toward one another. (OED obsolete.)

155 devesting them for bed: taking off their clothes. Ironically, the brawl fomented by Iago has interrupted Othello's first night on Cyprus with Desdemona, and Iago can't resist mentioning it.

168 unlace: undo or destroy, perhaps with a connotation from hunting of carving up the kill. (OED obsolete)

Hold! The General speaks to you. Hold, for shame!
Othello
Why, how now, ho! From whence ariseth this?
Are we turned Turks, and to ourselves do that
Which heaven hath forbid the Ottomites? 145
For Christian shame, put by this barbarous brawl!
He that stirs next to carve for his own rage
Holds his soul light; he dies upon his motion.
Silence that dreadful bell. It frights the isle
From her propriety. What is the matter, masters? 150
Honest Iago, that looks dead with grieving,
Speak. Who began this? On thy love, I charge thee.
Iago
I do not know. Friends all but now, even now,
In quarter and in terms like bride and groom
Devesting them for bed; and then, but now— 155
As if some planet had unwitted men—
Swords out, and tilting one at others' breasts
In opposition bloody. I cannot speak
Any beginning to this peevish odds;
And would in action glorious I had lost 160
Those legs that brought me to a part of it!
Othello
How comes it, Michael, you are thus forgot?
Cassio
I pray you, pardon me. I cannot speak.
Othello
Worthy Montano, you were wont be civil;
The gravity and stillness of your youth 165
The world hath noted, and your name is great
In mouths of wisest censure. What's the matter
That you unlace your reputation thus
And spend your rich opinion for the name
Of a night-brawler? Give me answer to it. 170
Montano
Worthy Othello, I am hurt to danger.
Your officer, Iago, can inform you—
While I spare speech, which something now offends me.
Of all that I do know; nor know I aught
By me that's said or done amiss this night, 175
Unless self-charity be sometimes a vice,

173 something: probably, somewhat.

180 collied: probably, darkened or besmirched. Origin unknown; perhaps from coal. First used in this play and in *A Midsummer Night's Dream.* (OED)

189 To manage: to conduct or carry on. (OED)

192 partially affined: favorably connected to (Cassio). (OED)

202 execute: use a weapon against. (OED)

And to defend ourselves it be a sin
When violence assails us.
Othello
Now, by heaven,
My blood begins my safer guides to rule,
And passion, having my best judgment collied,   180
Assays to lead the way. If I stir,
Or do but lift this arm, the best of you
Shall sink in my rebuke. Give me to know
How this foul rout began, who set it on;
And he that is approved in this offence,   185
Though he had twinned with me, both at a birth,
Shall lose me. What? In a town of war
Yet wild, the people's hearts brimful of fear,
To manage private and domestic quarrel?
In night, and on the court and guard of safety?   190
'Tis monstrous. Iago, who began it?
Montano
If partially affined, or leagued in office,
Thou dost deliver more or less than truth,
Thou art no soldier.
Iago
Touch me not so near.
I had rather have this tongue cut from my mouth   195
Than it should do offence to Michael Cassio;
Yet, I persuade myself, to speak the truth
Shall nothing wrong him. Thus it is, General.
Montano and myself being in speech,
There comes a fellow crying out for help,   200
And Cassio following him with determined sword
To execute upon him. Sir, this gentleman *[indicating Montano]*
Steps in to Cassio and entreats his pause.
Myself the crying fellow did pursue,
Lest by his clamor—as it so fell out—   205
The town might fall in fright. He, swift of foot,
Outran my purpose, and I returned the rather
For that I heard the clink and fall of swords
And Cassio high in oath, which till tonight
I never might say before. When I came back—   210
For this was brief—I found them close together
At blow and thrust, even as again they were

209 high in oath: probably, loud curses.

219 indignity: insult.

220 pass: overlook, pass over.

221: mince: to extenuate or make little of. (OED)

222 thee: In stripping Cassio of his rank, Othello addresses him as "thee," a term that conveys familiarity and affection but also Cassio's loss of status.

223 raised up: awakened.

227 myself: Either Othello will make sure Montano's wounds are treated or perhaps will treat Montano himself.

When you yourself did part them.
More of this matter cannot I report.
But men are men; the best sometimes forget.   215
Though Cassio did some little wrong to him,
As men in rage strike those that wish them best,
Yet surely Cassio, I believe, received
From him that fled some strange indignity,
Which patience could not pass.   220
Othello
I know, Iago, thy honesty and love doth mince this matter,
Making it light to Cassio. Cassio, I love thee, but never more
Be officer of mine.

Enter Desdemona, attended.

Look, if my gentle love be not raised up. I'll make thee an
Example.
Desdemona
  What's the matter, dear?   225
Othello
All's well now, sweeting.
Come away to bed. *[To Montano.]* Sir, for your hurts,
Myself will be your surgeon—Lead him off.
Iago, look with care about the town
And silence those whom this vile brawl distracted.
Come Desdemona. 'Tis the soldiers' life
To have their balmy slumbers waked with strife.   230

Exeunt [all but Iago and Cassio]

Iago
  What, are you hurt, Lieutenant?
Cassio
  Ay, past all surgery.
Iago
  Marry, God forbid!
Cassio
  Reputation! Reputation! Reputation! O, I have lost my
  Reputation! I have lost the immortal part of myself, and what
  Remains is bestial. My reputation, Iago, my reputation!   235
Iago
  As I am an honest man, I thought you had received some

233 Reputation: Cassio's concern echoes Oxford's own concern about his reputation. For example, in a letter to Burghley he complained that Burghley had made him "a fable of the world" by being indiscreet about Oxford's rejection of his wife and daughter when he returned from Italy. And one of his early, pre-Shakespeare poems is entitled "His good name being blemished, he bewailith." The last line says, "To wail the loss of my good name, as of these griefs the ground."

239-40 You have lost. . .loser: a sentence echoing the thought in the works of three Greek writers--Plutarch, Epictetus, and Marcus Antoninus. (Variorum) Oxford had easy access to the works of all three writers.

242 cast: that is, cast off.

244 one would beat. . .imperious lion: thought to be from a French proverb about beating a dog to make a show of force and frighten a lion, hence some act that is not very genuine or effective. Thus, Othello probably reluctantly had to fire "offenseless" Cassio as good military "policy." The lion reference may be a glance at Venice's heraldic badge featuring a winged "imperious" lion.

249 fustian: a coarse and heavy cloth, but figuratively, inflated, turgid or inappropriately lofty language. (OED)

254 enemy: alcohol.

bodily wound; there is more sense in that than in reputation.
Reputation is an idle and most false imposition, oft got
without merit, and lost without deserving. You have lost no
reputation at all, unless you repute yourself such a loser. 240
What, man, there are ways to recover the General again.
You are but now cast in his mood—a punishment more in
policy than in malice, even so as one would beat his
offenseless dog to affright an imperious lion. Sue to him
again and he's yours. 245

Cassio
I will rather sue to be despised than to deceive so good a
commander with so slight, so drunken, and so indiscreet an
officer. Drunk? And speak parrot? And squabble? Swagger?
Swear? And discourse fustian with one's own shadow? O
thou invisible spirit of wine, if thou hast no name to be known 250
by, let us call thee devil!

Iago
What was he that you followed with your sword? What had
he done to you?

Cassio
I know not.

Iago
Is it possible?

Cassio
I remember a mass of things, but nothing distinctly; a quarrel,
but nothing wherefore. O God, that men should put an enemy
in their mouths to steal away their brains! That we should, 255
with joy, pleasance, revel, and applause transform ourselves
into beasts!

Iago
Why, but you are now well enough. How came you thus
recovered?

Cassio
It hath pleased the devil drunkenness to give place to the devil
wrath. One unperfectness shows me another, to make me
frankly despise myself. 260

Iago
Come, you are too severe a moraler. As the time, the place,
and the condition of this country stands, I could heartily
wish this had not befallen; but since it is as it is, mend it for

2.3

261 moraler: one who moralizers (a term unique to Shakespeare).

264-8 I will ask...a devil.: Improvising, Iago will seize on Cassio's reluctance here to ask Othello to restore his lieutenancy and will urge him (lines 272-82) to ask Desdemona to intercede with Othello on his behalf.

265 Hydra: from Greek mythology, a many-headed monster. Allusions to myths and legends of monsters are a unifying feature of this play.

272 approved: proven, affirmed.

273-82 You or any man...was before.: Iago will use Cassio to get revenge for what he perceives is his damaged reputation.

280 to splinter: apply splints to or mend.

281 lay: wager. (OED)

285 betimes: before the customary time, early.

your own good.

Cassio

I will ask him for my place again; he shall tell me I am a
drunkard! Had I as many mouths as Hydra, such an answer   265
would stop them all. To be now a sensible man, by and by a
fool, and presently a beast! O strange! Every inordinate cup
is unblessed, and the ingredient is a devil.

Iago

Come, come: good wine is a good familiar creature, if it be
well used. Exclaim no more against it. And, good lieutenant,   270
I think you think I love you.

Cassio

I have well approved it, sir. I drunk?

Iago

You or any man living may be drunk at a time, man.
I'll tell you what you shall do. Our general's wife is
Now the general. I may say so in this respect, for that
He hath devoted and given up himself to the contemplation,
Mark, and denotement of her parts and graces. Confess   275
Yourself freely to her; importune her help to put you in your
Place again. She is of so free, so kind, so apt, so blessed a
Disposition, she holds it a vice in her goodness not to do more
Than she is requested. This broken joint between you and her
Husband entreat her to splinter; and my fortunes against any   280
Lay worth naming, this crack of your love shall grow stronger
Than it was before.

Cassio

You advise me well.

Iago

I protest, in the sincerity of love and honest kindness.

Cassio

I think it freely. And betimes in the morning I will beseech the 285
Virtuous desdemona to undertake for me. I am desperate of
My fortunes if they check me here.

Iago

You are in the right. Good night, Lieutenant. I must to the
watch.

Cassio

Good night, honest Iago.   290

Exit Cassio.

291-318 And what's he then. . .enmesh them all.: Alone on stage, Iago tells the audience how his plot will "enmesh them all." To a large extent, his plotting creates the plot of the play. And as Ridley says, "We sense not only his delight at the prospect of revenge, but his sheer intellectual pleasure in a subtle and finished piece of black artistry."

294 probal: likely, probable; according to the OED, first used here.

297 framed as fruitful: fashioned to be generous. Iago may intend a subtle double meaning that she is promiscuous.

304 weak function: probably, his weakness for Desdemona.

305 parallel course: the scheme that Iago is devising.

308 When devils. . . as I do now: Iago returns to the theme of "I am not what I am."

316-18 pitch: black, foul tar that will ensnare Othello and everybody else.

320 cry: the pack of hounds. (OED) Hunting with hounds was an aristocratic sport, and here the dramatist shows that he knows that there are hounds that track the scent and those that merely run with the pack, filling up the "cry."

Iago
  And what's he then that says I play the villain,
  When this advice is free I give and honest,
  Probal to thinking, and indeed the course
  To win the Moor again? For 'tis most easy   295
  The inclining Desdemona to subdue
  In any honest suit; she's framed as fruitful
  As the free elements. And then for her
  To win the Moor—were it to renounce his baptism,
  All seals and symbols of redeemed sin—   300
  His soul is so enfettered to her love
  That she may make, unmake, do what she list,
  Even as her appetite shall play the god
  With his weak function. How am I then a villain,
  To counsel Cassio to this parallel course   305
  Directly to his good? Divinity of hell!
  When devils will the blackest sins put on,
  They do suggest at first with heavenly shows,
  As I do now. For whiles this honest fool
  Plies Desdemona to repair his fortune,   310
  And she for him pleads strongly to the Moor,
  I'll pour this pestilence into his ear,
  That she repeals him for her body's lust;
  And by how much she strives to do him good,
  She shall undo her credit with the Moor.   315
  So will I turn her virtue into pitch,
  And out of her own goodness make the net
  That shall enmesh them all.

Enter Roderigo.

  How now, Roderigo?
Roderigo
  I do follow here in the chase, not like a hound that hunts, but
  One that fills up the cry. My money is almost spent; I have   320
  Been tonight exceedingly well cudgeled; and I think the issue
  Will be I shall have so much experience for my pains, and so,
  With no money at all and a little more wit, return again to
  Venice.
Iago
  How poor are they that have not patience!   325
  What wound did ever heal but by degrees?

321 cudgeled: beaten up.

322-323 I shall have...to Venice: reflecting Oxford's travels (his "experience") in Italy from his base in Venice, the wisdom he gained ("wit" per OED) from his travels and his need for money, which led him to write to his father-in-law, Lord Burghley, authorizing him to sell some land to raise cash.

330 cashiered: dismissed, discharged from his duties. See line note 1.1.46.

335 billeted: a military term for lodging.

340 jump: exactly, precisely. (OED obsolete)

342 device: an ingenious scheme by an evil character, with a connotation of it being a pleasurable undertaking. (OED)

Thou know'st we work by wit, and not by witchcraft,
And wit depends on dilatory time.
Does it not go well? Cassio hath beaten thee.
And thou, by that small hurt, hast cashiered Cassio.   330
Though other things grow fair against the sun,
Yet fruits that blossom first will first be ripe.
Content thyself awhile. In troth, 'tis morning!
Pleasure and action make the hours seem short.
Retire thee; go where thou art billeted.   335
Away, I say. Thou shalt know more hereafter.
Nay, get thee gone.

Exit Roderigo.

Two things are to be done.
My wife must move for Cassio to her mistress;
I'll set her on myself, the while, to draw the Moor apart
And bring him jump when he may Cassio find   340
Soliciting his wife. Ay, that's the way.
Dull not device by coldness and delay.

Exit.

3.1.2 "Good morrow, General": The courtly Cassio has musicians play a morning song, a traditional *aubade* to wake the newly married couple. The vulgar Clown, however, insults their playing and sends them away with obscene jibes. He knows (but Cassio does not) that real soldiers don't like morning music. This episode echoes the raucous awakening of Brabantio in act 1. It also suggests an aborted attempt at the French charivari, noisy, rough music played outside a newlyweds' bedroom house to protest an inappropriate marriage or to mock a cuckold husband. See Michael Bristol's article noted in the bibliography.

3-4 Naples. . .nose thus?: that is, have a nasal sound such as one hears in Naples. In Italy, the Neapolitans had a reputation for their accent, a drawling nasal twang, which Oxford probably heard or heard about. The Clown may also be alluding to syphilis, which sometimes attacks the nose. The Venetians called syphilis the Neapolitan disease. In *commedia dell'arte*, the *Pulcinella* character, a Neapolitan clown, often wore a half-mask with a big nose and spoke in a nasal twang. Honigmann suggests a bilingual pun with *nez*, French for nose, plus "pulls" illustrated "by the clown's pulling his own nose to make his speech sound comically nasal, or possibly tweaking the nose of his interlocutor." Oxford was multilingual.

9 hangs a tale. . .wind instrument: a ribald pun on "tale" for "tail," that is, a person's bottom, and "wind," as in breaking wind.

16-17 the General. . .not greatly care.: Honigmann notes that the passage "resonates. . .with Castiglione's portrait of the early modern professional soldier as one who eschews music as effeminate artifice." Oxford wrote the preface to Castiglione's work, *The Courtier*, and had it published in 1572 before he went to Italy.

17 none such: perhaps a pun, "Nonesuch" being the name of a popular tune.

Act 3

Scene 1. Enter Cassio, Musicians, and Clown.

Cassio
  Masters, play here—I will content your pains—
  Something that's brief, and bid "Good morrow, General."
Clown
  Why, masters, have your instruments been in Naples, that
  they speak in the nose thus?
First Musician
  How, sir, how?   5
Clown
  Are these, I pray you, wind instruments?
First Musician
  Ay, marry, are they, sir.
Clown
  O, thereby hangs a tail.
First Musician
  Whereby hangs a tale, sir?
Clown
  Marry, sir, by many a wind-instrument that I know. But,   10
  Masters, here's money for you. And the General so likes
  Your music that he desires you, for love's sake, to make no
  More noise with it.
First Musician
  Well, sir, we will not.
Clown
  If you have any music that may not be heard, to it again;   15
  But, as they say, to hear music the General does not greatly
  Care.
First Musician
  We have none such, sir.
Clown
  Then put up your pipes in your bag, for I'll away. Go, vanish
  Into air, away!
                                                      Exit Musicians.
Cassio
  Dost thou hear, mine honest friend?   20

22 keep up: desist, refrain. **quillets:** verbal niceties, quibbles. (OED obsolete).

27 stirring: possibly a pun; that is, awakening and (sexually) aroused. (OED obsolete)

28 seem to notify unto her: The Clown's overly formal phrasing mocks Cassio's overly mannered way of speaking, with perhaps a voyeur's pun on the earliest meaning of "notify," to observe. (OED obsolete)

30 In happy time: from the French *a la bonne heure*, early.

37 a mean: an opportunity. (OED obsolete)

40 Florentine: Cassio, a Florentine, is saying that not even in Florence did he know anyone more kind and honest than Iago.

41 good lieutenant: Emilia calls him lieutenant as a sign of respect and support even though she knows he has lost that position. **displeasure:** trouble or injury. (OED obsolete)

Clown

No, I hear not your honest friend; I hear you.

Cassio

Prithee, keep up thy quillets. There's a poor
piece of gold for thee. If the gentle-
woman that attends the General's wife be stirring, tell
her there's one Cassio entreats her a little favor of   25
speech. Wilt thou do this?

Clown

She is stirring, sir. If she will stir hither, I shall
seem to notify unto her.

Cassio

Do, good my friend.

Exit Clown.

Enter Iago.

In happy time, Iago.   30

Iago

You have not been abed, then?

Cassio

Why, no. The day had broke
Before we parted. I have made bold, Iago,
To send in to your wife. My suit to her
Is that she will to virtuous Desdemona
Procure me some access.   35

Iago

I'll send her to you presently;
And I'll devise a mean to draw the Moor
Out of the way, that your converse and business
May be more free.

Cassio

I humbly thank you for it.

Exit Iago.

I never knew a Florentine more kind and honest.   40

Enter Emilia.

Emilia

Good morrow, good Lieutenant. I am sorry
For your displeasure, but all will sure be well.
The General and his wife are talking of it,

45 he: Montano, governor of Cyprus.

46 affinity: kinship, connections with a number of people.   **wholesome wisdom:** that is, what's best for Cyprus.

49 To take the safest occasion by the front: to seize the opportune moment before it is lost. The "front" is the forehead (OED) and, by extension, the forelock. The line is an allusion to *Kairos*, the Greek god or spirit of opportunity who could be caught by his forelock of long hair only as he approached, not if he had passed by.

52 Desdemon: an affectionate diminutive of her name.

53 bestow you: place you.

55 I am much bound to you: Ironically, the usually florid Cassio extends a simple, direct avowal, which will have terrible consequences for both of them.

3.2.

1 letters: presumably military reports to be sent by ship to the Venetian Senate.

3 works: castle fortifications.

4 Repair there to me: report to me there.

And she speaks for you stoutly. The Moor replies
That he you hurt is of great fame in Cyprus   45
And great affinity, and that in wholesome wisdom
He might not but refuse you. But he protests he loves you
And needs no other suitor but his likings
To take the safest occasion by the front
To bring you in again.
Cassio
Yet, I beseech you,   50
If you think fit, or that it may be done,
Give me advantage of some brief discourse
With Desdemon alone. .
Emilia
Pray you, come in.
I will bestow you where you shall have time
To speak your bosom freely.
Cassio
I am much bound to you.   55

Exeunt.

Scene 2. Enter Othello, Iago, and Gentlemen.
Othello
These letters give, Iago, to the pilot,
And by him do my duties to the Senate.
That done, I will be walking on the works;
Repair there to me.
Iago
Well, my good lord, I'll do it.
Othello
This fortification, gentlemen, shall we see it?   5
Gentleman
We'll wait upon your lordship.

Exeunt.

Scene 3. Enter Desdemona, Cassio, and Emilia.
Desdemona
Be thou assured, good Cassio, I will do
All my abilities in thy behalf.
Emilia
Good madam, do. I warrant it grieves my husband

5 honest: Even Desdemona calls Iago honest, a central irony of the play.

9 servant: not only someone who is obligated to serve a master or mistress but a professed lover, one who is devoted to the service of a lady. (OED obsolete) Cassio, the excessively charming *Pedrolino* of *commedia dell'arte*, switches to high-flown courtly gallantry in Desdemona's presence.

12 in strangeness: estranged.

13 politic: judicious, prudent, tactful.

14 policy: course of action.

15 nice: thin.

19 doubt: fear.

23 watch him tame: keep him awake until he's obedient to commands; from hawking, a pastime of the aristocracy and nobility.

24 shrift: the confessional.

27-8 thy solicitor. . .cause way: Desdemona here winds up a series of legalisms—"warrant. . .last article. . .bed-board. . .suit. . .solicitor. . . cause"— that seems natural for someone, like Oxford, who had matriculated at Gray's Inn, the law school. **rather die:** Desdemona, the solicitor, ironically will in fact die because she will take up Cassio's cause and argue it, as does a solicitor in a court of equity.

As if the cause were his.
Desdemona
  O, that's an honest fellow. Do not doubt, Cassio,   5
  But I will have my lord and you again
  As friendly as you were.
Cassio
  Bounteous madam,
  Whatever shall become of Michael Cassio,
  He's never anything but your true servant.
Desdemona
  I know it; I thank you. You do love my lord;   10
  You have known him long, and be you well assured
  He shall in strangeness stand no further off
  Than in a politic distance.
Cassio
  Ay, but, lady,
  That policy may either last so long,
  Or feed upon such nice and waterish diet,   15
  Or breed itself so out of circumstance,
  That, I being absent and my place supplied,
  My general will forget my love and service.
Desdemona
  Do not doubt that. Before Emilia here
  I give thee warrant of thy place. Assure thee,   20
  If I do vow a friendship I'll perform it
  To the last article. My lord shall never rest.
  I'll watch him tame and talk him out of patience;
  His bed shall seem a school, his board a shrift;
  I'll intermingle everything he does   25
  With Cassio's suit. Therefore be merry, Cassio,
  For thy solicitor shall rather die
  Than give thy cause away.

Enter Othello and Iago at a distance.

Emilia
  Madam, here comes my lord.
Cassio
  Madam, I'll take my leave.
Desdemona
  Why, stay, and hear me speak.

42 suitor: Cassio, who has a suit to plead.

43 languishes: suffers with drooping spirits.

45 your lieutenant: Unwittingly and innocently, Desdemona refers to Cassio as Othello's lieutenant, although Othello has stripped him of that rank. A general, such as Othello, knows the importance of rank and command in the military. The teenage Desdemona does not, highlighting the fact that husband and wife are from different worlds.

46 grace: quality pleasing to you.

Cassio
  Madam, not now. I am very ill at ease,   30
  Unfit for mine own purposes.

Desdemona
  Well, do your discretion.

Enter Othello and Iago.

Iago
  Ha? I like not that.
Othello
  What dost thou say?
Iago
  Nothing, my lord; or if—I know not what.   35
Othello
  Was not that Cassio parted from my wife?
Iago
  Cassio, my lord? No, sure, I cannot think it,
  That he would steal away so guilty-like,
  Seeing you coming.
Othello
  I do believe 'twas he.   40
Desdemona
  How now, my lord?
  I have been talking with a suitor here,
  A man that languishes in your displeasure.
Othello
  Who is it you mean?
Desdemona
  Why, your lieutenant, Cassio. Good my lord,   45
  If I have any grace or power to move you,
  His present reconciliation take;
  For if he be not one that truly loves you,
  That errs in ignorance and not in cunning,
  I have no judgment in an honest face.   50
  I prithee, call him back.
Othello
  Went he hence now?

58 dinner: the mid-day meal.

60 citadel: the fortress within the fortifications.

64 in faith: truly.

65 trespass: misdeed.

68 check: reprimand.

71 mammering: vacillating, wavering (OED obsolete), here probably with a connotation of stammering hesitation. Desdemona apparently refers to Othello's repeated reluctance to discuss Cassio's "trespass." Honigmann notes that "it echoes *Euphues* [by John Lyly], 'neither stand in mammering whether it be best to depart or not.' (Lyly I.253)" John Lyly was Oxford's secretary for a decade and his associate in one of his acting companies. There is some evidence that Oxford may have written the works that appeared as by Lyly. (See Dating the Play.)

77 not a boon: not a favor. Here, and in the nine lines that follow, Desdemona compares her simple request to the difficult challenges that the feudal mistress of a chivalric knight would give him to perform for her to prove his love.

Desdemona
  Yes, faith, so humbled
  That he hath left part of his grief with me
  To suffer with him. Good love, call him back.   55
Othello
  Not now, sweet Desdemon. Some other time.
Desdemona
  But shall it be shortly?
Othello
  The sooner, sweet, for you.
Desdemona
  Shall it be tonight at supper?
Othello
  No, not tonight.
Desdemona
  Tomorrow dinner, then?
Othello
  I shall not dine at home.
  I meet the captains at the citadel.   60
Desdemona
  Why, then, tomorrow night; or Tuesday morn,
  Or Tuesday noon, or night, or Wednesday morn.
  I prithee, name the time, but let it not
  Exceed three days. In faith, he's penitent;
  And yet his trespass, in our common reason   65
  (Save that, they say, the wars must make example
  Out of her best) is not almost a fault
  To incur a private check. When shall he come?
  Tell me, Othello. I wonder in my soul
  What you would ask me, that I should deny,   70
  Or stand so mammering on. What? Michael Cassio,
  That came a-wooing with you, and so many a time,
  When I have spoke of you dispraisingly,
  Hath taken your part—to have so much to do
  To bring him in! Trust me, I could do much—   75
Othello
  Prithee, no more. Let him come when he will;
  I will deny thee nothing.
Desdemona
  Why, this is not a boon.
  'Tis as I should entreat you wear your gloves,

83 poise: weighty, important. (OED obsolete)

88 straight: right away.

91 wretch: a little creature, in playful depreciation (OED), here a term of endearment. **perdition:** damnation.

92-3 Chaos: perhaps today's meaning of total disorder but more likely from classical mythology referring to the vast, dark void out of which the universe evolved, the earliest OED definition; hence total emptiness. Iago immediately takes advantage of Othello's moment of doubt about his love for Desdemona to sow the first seed of suspicion in Othello's mind and launch his campaign of slander against Desdemona to get revenge on Othello.

Or feed on nourishing dishes, or keep you warm,
Or sue to you to do a peculiar profit   80
To your own person. Nay, when I have a suit
Wherein I mean to touch your love indeed,
It shall be full of poise and difficult weight,
And fearful to be granted.

Othello
I will deny thee nothing.
Whereon, I do beseech thee, grant me this: 85
To leave me but a little to myself.

Desdemona
Shall I deny you? No. Farewell, my lord.

Othello
Farewell, my Desdemona. I'll come to thee straight.

Desdemona
Emilia, come.—Be as your fancies teach you;
Whatever you be, I am obedient.   90

                                               Exit with Emilia.

Othello
Excellent wretch! Perdition catch my soul,
But I do love thee! And when I love thee not,
Chaos is come again.

Iago
My noble lord—

Othello
What dost thou say, Iago?   95

Iago
Did Michael Cassio, when you wooed my lady,
Know of your love?

Othello
He did, from first to last. Why dost thou ask?

Iago
But for a satisfaction of my thought;
No further harm.

Othello
Why of thy thought, Iago?   100

Iago
I did not think he had been acquainted with her.

104 aught: anything worthy of note. (OED obsolete)

107 for aught I know: Iago echoes Othello but in the negative sense of "as far as I know." (OED archaic)

114 he was of my counsel: someone in whom I confided and from whom I took advice.

116 purse thy brow: wrinkle your brow like a purse closed with drawstrings.

118 conceit: idea, notion.

120 My Lord, you know I love you: an echo of Simon Peter's answer to Jesus who asked him three times if he loved him: "Lord thou knowest that I love thee." (John 21.15-17) Three lines later in the New Testament, Peter asks Jesus, "Lord, who is he that shall betray thee?" Jesus indicates one of his disciples (Judas) but says let him stay with us, just as Othello keeps Iago by his side until the very end.

124 stops: pauses showing reluctance to answer.

126 tricks: traits or practices. (OED)

127 close delations: hidden denouncements or accusations. (OED)

Othello
  O, yes, and went between us very oft.
Iago
  Indeed?
Othello
  Indeed? Ay, indeed. Discern'st thou aught in that?
  Is he not honest?
Iago
  Honest, my lord?   105
Othello
  Honest. Ay, honest.
Iago
  My lord, for aught I know.
Othello
  What dost thou think?
Iago
  Think, my lord?
Othello
  "Think, my lord?" By heaven, he echo'st me,
  As if there were some monster in thy thought   110
  Too hideous to be shown. Thou dost mean something:
  I heard thee say even now, thou lik'st not that,
  When Cassio left my wife. What didst not like?
  And when I told thee he was of my counsel
  In my whole course of wooing, thou criedst "Indeed?"   115
  And didst contract and purse thy brow together
  As if thou then hadst shut up in thy brain
  Some horrible conceit. If thou dost love me,
  Show me thy thought.
Iago
  My lord, you know I love you.   120
Othello
  I think thou dost;
  And, for I know thou'rt full of love and honesty,
  And weigh'st thy words before thou giv'st them breath,
  Therefore these stops of thine fright me the more;
  For such things in a false disloyal knave   125
  Are tricks of custom, but in a man that's just
  They're close delations, working from the heart
  That passion cannot rule.

136 ruminate: mull over, meditate deeply upon.

143 apprehensions: probably the acquiring of knowledge, with a legal connotation. (OED obsolete).

144 leets: courts of record held once or twice a year by the lord of a manor. **law-days:** the actual sessions or days assigned to a court of law. Both terms point to the dramatist's easy familiarity with legal matters.

145 meditations lawful: pondering legal matters.

150 plague: affliction, shortcoming.

153 conceits: imagines, conceives of.

155 scattering: disorderly.

Iago
For Michael Cassio,
I dare be sworn I think that he is honest.
Othello
I think so too.
Iago
Men should be what they seem;   130
Or those that be not, would they might seem none!
Othello
Certain, men should be what they seem.
Iago
Why, then, I think Cassio's an honest man.
Othello
Nay, yet there's more in this?
I prithee, speak to me as to thy thinkings,   135
As thou dost ruminate, and give thy worst of thoughts
The worst of words.
Iago
Good my lord, pardon me.
Though I am bound to every act of duty,
I am not bound to that all slaves are free to.
Utter my thoughts? Why, say they are vile and false,   140
As where's that palace whereinto foul things
Sometimes intrude not? Who has a breast so pure
But some uncleanly apprehensions
Keep leets and law-days, and in session sit
With meditations lawful?   145
Othello
Thou dost conspire against thy friend, Iago,
If thou but think'st him wronged and make'st his ear
A stranger to thy thoughts.
Iago
I do beseech you,
Though I perchance am vicious in my guess
(As I confess it is my nature's plague   150
To spy into abuses, and oft my jealousy
Shapes faults that are not) that your wisdom
From one that so imperfectly conceits,
Would take no notice, nor build yourself a trouble
Out of his scattering and unsure observance.   155
It were not for your quiet nor your good,

149

161-164 Who steals my purse. . .poor indeed: Iago's speech is one of the most famous in Shakespeare. Ironically, however, Iago is mouthing this home truth while trying to violate it by destroying Othello's reputation and that of others. The prospect of ignominious cuckoldry, the concern for reputation, and the desire for revenge drive the play—much more so than simple jealousy—and tie it closely to Oxford's own life.

168 green-eyed: of bilious hue, indicative of fear or jealousy. (OED)

172 tells over: remembers, recounts.

176 fineless: probably, unlimited. A rare word, first used here. (OED)

178 my tribe: that is, my fellow citizens of a section of Venice, which was divided into six sections or neighborhoods ("tribes"), showing the dramatist's close knowledge of the city

181 still: always. **changes of the moon:** the waxing and waning of the moon was, for people in the Renaissance, a symbol of instability.

183 resolved: decided on a course of action. **goat:** a horned creature, thus an apt image for a man worried about being cuckolded.

Nor for my manhood, honesty, or wisdom,
To let you know my thoughts.

Othello

What dost thou mean?

Iago

Good name in man and woman, dear my lord,
Is the immediate jewel of their souls. 160
Who steals my purse steals trash; 'tis something, nothing;
'Twas mine, 'tis his, and has been slave to thousands.
But he that filches from me my good name
Robs me of that which not enriches him
And makes me poor indeed.

Othello

I'll know thy thoughts! 165

Iago

You cannot, if my heart were in your hand,
Nor shall not, whilst 'tis in my custody.

Othello

Ha?

Iago

O, beware, my lord, of jealousy.
It is the green-eyed monster which doth mock
The meat it feeds on. That cuckold lives in bliss 170
Who, certain of his fate, loves not his wronger;
But O, what damned minutes tells he over
Who dotes, yet doubts, suspects, yet fondly loves!

Othello

O misery!

Iago

Poor and content is rich, and rich enough, 175
But riches fineless is as poor as winter
To him that ever fears he shall be poor.
Good heaven, the souls of all my tribe defend
From jealousy.

Othello

Why, why is this?
Think'st thou I'd make a life of jealousy, 180
To follow still the changes of the moon
With fresh suspicions? No! To be once in doubt
Is once to be resolved. Exchange me for a goat,
When I shall turn the business of my soul

185 exsufflicate: Although the OED calls it a rare, obsolete word perhaps meaning puffed up or inflated, citing its use only here in *Othello*, more likely it's from the Italian *suffolare* meaning whispered or buzzed in the ear. (Variorum) This explication suggests a dramatist, like Oxford, who lived in Italy and knew Italian well. **blown:** rumored. (OED).

191 revolt: her turning from fidelity.

205 pranks: sexual escapades.

213 seel: from the aristocratic sport of falconry, to sew closed the eyes of a falcon as part of its training, here figuratively to hoodwink. (OED)
as close as   oak: probably, as tight as the close grain of the oak tree. (Variorum)

217 bound to thee: obligated to you as under a contract. (OED) In this personal crisis, Othello the military commander goes so far as to declare his fealty to a subordinate, reversing the normal relationship of authority and power.

To such exsufflicate and blown surmises 185
Matching thy inference. 'Tis not to make me jealous
To say my wife is fair, feeds well, loves company,
Is free of speech, sings, plays, and dances well;
Where virtue is, these are more virtuous.
Nor from mine own weak merits will I draw 190
The smallest fear or doubt of her revolt,
For she had eyes, and chose me. No, Iago,
I'll see before I doubt; when I doubt, prove;
And on the proof, there is no more but this—
Away at once with love or jealousy. 195

Iago
I am glad of this, for now I shall have reason
To show the love and duty that I bear you
With franker spirit. Therefore, as I am bound,
Receive it from me. I speak not yet of proof.
Look to your wife; observe her well with Cassio. 200
Wear your eye thus, not jealous nor secure.
I would not have your free and noble nature,
Out of self-bounty, be abused. Look to it.
I know our country disposition well;
In Venice they do let heaven see the pranks 205
They dare not show their husbands; their best conscience
Is not to leave it undone, but keep it unknown.

Othello
Dost thou say so?

Iago
She did deceive her father, marrying you;
And when she seemed to shake and fear your looks, 210
She loved them most.

Othello
And so she did.

Iago
Why, go to, then!
She that, so young, could give out such a seeming,
To seel her father's eyes up close as oak,
He thought 'twas witchcraft. But I am much to blame.
I humbly do beseech you of your pardon 215
For too much loving you.

Othello
I am bound to thee forever.

218 dashed your spirits: Iago's feigned and hypocritical concern for the trouble that he himself has caused.

225 success: outcome.

232 to affect: to prefer. (OED obsolete)

233 clime: climate (OED obsolete); here, figuratively, region or realm. In this single line, Iago cleverly sums up everything that would sow doubt about Desdemona in Othello's mind—disparity of country of origin, skin color, and social rank.

235 smell: suspect, sense.

239 recoiling to: returning to.

240 country forms: probably, the mores and practices of her country, Venice.

Iago
I see this hath a little dashed your spirits.
Othello
Not a jot, not a jot.
Iago
Trust me, I fear it has.
I hope you will consider what is spoke
Comes from my love. But I do see you're moved.   220
I am to pray you not to strain my speech
To grosser issues nor to larger reach
Than to suspicion.
Othello
I will not.
Iago
Should you do so, my lord,
My speech should fall into such vile success   225
Which my thoughts aimed not at. Cassio's my worthy friend.
My lord, I see you're moved.
Othello
No, not much moved.
I do not think but Desdemona's honest.
Iago
Long live she so! And long live you to think so!
Othello
And yet, how nature erring from itself—   230
Iago
Ay, there's the point! As (to be bold with you)
Not to affect many proposed matches
Of her own clime, complexion, and degree,
Whereto we see in all things nature tends—
Foh! One may smell in such a will most rank,   235
Foul disproportion, thoughts unnatural.
But pardon me. I do not in position
Distinctly speak of her, though I may fear
Her will, recoiling to her better judgment,
May fall to match you with her country forms   240
And happily repent.
Othello
Farewell, farewell:
If more thou dost perceive, let me know more.
Set on thy wife to observe. Leave me, Iago.

249 his place: perhaps a double meaning, that is, Cassio's place as Othello's lieutenant and his place in bed with Desdemona, a meaning that Othello does not catch.

253 strain his entertainment: probably, pleads for Cassio to be reinstated.

258 my government: my self-government, how I act.

262 If I do prove her haggard: the beginning of a much admired, extended metaphor from falconry, the sport of aristocrats. "Haggard" describes a young female hawk captured after getting its adult plumage, hence still wild, untamed. A pre-Shakespeare poem probably by Oxford, "If women could be fair. . ." laments the fickleness of woman with a hawking metaphor: "How oft from Phoebus do they flee to Pan, / Unsettled still like haggards wild they range, / These gentle birds that fly from man to man;/ Who would not scorn and shake them from the fist / And let them fly fair fools which way they list."

263 jesses: leather straps tied to the legs of a hawk and attached to a leash.

264 whistle her off: Send her off.   **down the wind:** The hawk is usually sent off upwind to take flight and pursue prey but downwind when turned loose because it's not performing well.

265 To prey at fortune: to hunt on her own in the wild.

267 chamberers: either men privileged to attend the bedchamber of a nobleman (OED obsolete), or gallants who frequent ladies' drawing rooms and/or bedrooms. (OED archaic and first such usage here) Thus, courtiers with privileged access to nobility.

269 gone: ruined, undone. (OED)   **abused:** wronged.

271 call these. . . ours: Aristocratic wives were, in effect, considered to be their husbands' property.

274 corner: even a small space, with a sexual connotation. (OED)

276 Prerogatived: privileged.

Iago
  My lord, I take my leave.
Othello
  Why did I marry? This honest creature doubtless   245
  Sees and knows more, much more, than he unfolds.
Iago [Returning] My lord, I would I might entreat your honor
  To scan this thing no further. Leave it to time.
  Although 'tis fit that Cassio have his place—
  For sure, he fills it up with great ability—   250
  Yet, if you please to hold him off awhile,
  You shall by that perceive him and his means.
  Note if your lady strain his entertainment
  With any strong or vehement importunity;
  Much will be seen in that. In the meantime,   255
  Let me be thought too busy in my fears
  (As worthy cause I have to fear I am)
  And hold her free, I do beseech your honor.
Othello
  Fear not my government.
Iago
  I once more take my leave.

                                                        Exit.
Othello
  This fellow's of exceeding honesty,   260
  And knows all qualities, with a learned spirit,
  Of humane dealings. If I do prove her haggard,
  Though that her jesses were my dear heartstrings,
  I'd whistle her off and let her down the wind
  To prey at fortune. Haply, for I am black   265
  And have not those soft parts of conversation
  That chamberers have, or for I am declined
  Into the vale of years (yet that's not much)
  She's gone. I am abused, and my relief
  Must be to loathe her. O curse of marriage,   270
  That we can call these delicate creatures ours
  And not their appetites? I had rather be a toad
  And live upon the vapor of a dungeon
  Than keep a corner in the thing I love
  For others' uses. Yet, 'tis the plague of great ones;   275
  Prerogatived are they less than the base.
  'Tis destiny unshunnable, like death.

278 forked plague: afflicted with the horns of the cuckolded.

279 quicken: show signs of life in the womb, hence from even before birth.

287 pain upon my forehead: no doubt caused by the great stress of the conflicting emotions of a general who is supposed to be decisive but is tormented by indecision about what to do about being cuckolded by Desdemona. This emotional turmoil may also lead to his epileptic fit in the next act. Figuratively, his headache suggests the growth of the cuckold's horns.

287 watching: going without sleep while on watch.

290 napkin: handkerchief. (OED) Honigmann says, "In Shakespeare's time handkerchiefs were luxury items, often (like this one) elaborately and expensively embroidered." Oxford would have been very familiar with such luxury items. On his return from Italy, he gave the queen a pair of embroidered and perfumed gloves that she liked so well she wore them when sitting for a portrait.

294 remembrance: keepsake.

297 conjured: beseeched earnestly. (OED).

299 work taken out: the embroidery pattern copied (not removed.) (OED)

Even then, this forked plague is fated to us
When we do quicken. Look where she comes.

Enter Desdemona and Emilia.

If she be false, O, then heaven mocks itself.   280
  I'll not believe it.
Desdemona
  How now, my dear Othello?
  Your dinner, and the generous islanders
  By you invited, do attend your presence.
Othello
  I am to blame.
Desdemona
  Why do you speak so faintly?   285
  Are you not well?
Othello
  I have a pain upon my forehead here.
Desdemona
  Why, that's with watching; It will away again.
  Let me but bind it hard, within this hour
  It will be well.
Othello
  Your napkin is too little.   290

[He puts the handkerchief from him, and it drops.]

Let it alone. Come, I'll go in with you.
Desdemona
  I am very sorry that you are not well.

Exeunt Othello and Desdemona.

Emilia
  I am glad I have found this napkin:
  This was her first remembrance from the Moor.
  My wayward husband hath a hundred times   295
  Wooed me to steal it, but she so loves the token
  --For he conjured her she should ever keep it--
  That she reserves it evermore about her
  To kiss and talk to. I'll have the work taken out,

159

302 his fantasy: whim or desire, with a connotation of deluding oneself by imaginary perceptions. (OED obsolete)

305 thing: Bawdy and insulting, Iago pretends that the "thing" is his wife's sexual organs. **common:** available for use by anyone.

315 to the advantage: took the opportunity.

And give it Iago. What he will do with it   300
Heaven knows, not I;
I nothing but to please his fantasy.

Enter Iago.

Iago
  How now? What do you here alone?
Emilia
  Do not you chide. I have a thing for you.
Iago
  You have a thing for me? It is a common thing—   305
Emilia
  Ha?
Iago
  To have a foolish wife.
Emilia
  O, is that all? What will you give me now
  For that same handkerchief?
Iago
  What handkerchief?
Emilia
  What handkerchief?   310
  Why, that the Moor first gave to Desdemona;
  That which so often you did bid me steal.
Iago
  Hast stolen it from her?
Emilia
  No, but she let it drop by negligence,
  And, to the advantage I, being here, took it up.   315
  Look, here it is.
Iago
  A good wench! Give it me.
Emilia
  What will you do with it, that you have been so earnest
  To have me filch it?
Iago
  [Snatching it] Why, what is that to you?
Emilia
  If it be not for some purpose of import,
  Give it me again. Poor lady, she'll run mad   320

322 acknown: acknowledge. (OED)

323 loose: let loose, drop.

328 conceits: thoughts, ideas.

330 act upon the blood: action on Othello's emotions.

331 Burn. . .sulphur: probably a reference in Pliny to sulphur mines burning continually on islands between Italy and Sicily. Oxford traveled in that region.

332 poppy: source of opium.   **mandragora:** the mandrake plant, from which a sleeping potion could be produced.

334 owedst: owned. (OED) that is, the "sweet sleep" that Othello enjoyed in the past.

337 Avaunt: Go away! (OED)

When she shall lack it.
Iago
Be not acknown on it.
I have use for it. Go, leave me.

Exit Emilia.

I will in Cassio's lodging loose this napkin
And let him find it. Trifles light as air
Are to the jealous confirmations strong   325
As proofs of Holy Writ. This may do something.
The Moor already changes with my poison:
Dangerous conceits are in their natures poisons,
Which at the first are scarce found to distaste,
But with a little act upon the blood   330
Burn like the mines of sulphur. I did say so.

Enter Othello.
Look where he comes!
Not poppy nor mandragora
Nor all the drowsy syrups of the world
Shall ever medicine thee to that sweet sleep
Which thou owedst yesterday.
Othello
Ha, ha, false to me?   335
Iago
Why, how now, General? No more of that.
Othello
Avaunt! Begone! Thou hast set me on the rack.
I swear 'tis better to be much abused
Than but to know it a little.
Iago
How now, my lord?
Othello
What sense had I of her stolen hours of lust?   340
I saw it not, thought it not, it harmed not me.
I slept the next night well, fed well, was free and merry;
I found not Cassio's kisses on her lips.
He that is robbed, not wanting what is stolen,
Let him not know it, and he's not robbed at all.   345
Iago
I am sorry to hear this.

348 pioners: diggers of trenches and tunnels for mines, the lowest rank of soldiers.   **tasted:** touched, had carnal knowledge of.

350-9 Farewell. . . .occupation's gone: an eloquent, detailed, colorful description of a professional military officer's love of the noise and excitement of "glorious war" –behavior that Oxford would have seen during his experience with the military.

357 mortal engines: deadly machines of war, cannons.

358 clamors: noise, thunder.

359 occupation: that is, his way of life; probably also his loss of Desdemona since "occupy" had a sexual connotation with a meaning to co-habit. (OED obsolete)

362 ocular: manifest to the eye. Perhaps from the Italian *occhi* in a passage in Cinthio.

367 the probation: the examination or testing of a person's conduct. (OED)

372 horror's head: probably, the peak or summit of horror.

377 God buy you: that is, may God save you. (OED, obsolete metaphor for "redeem" from theology).   **office:** position.   **fool:** Iago addressing himself.

Othello

I had been happy if the general camp,
Pioners and all, had tasted her sweet body,
So I had nothing known. O, now, forever
Farewell the tranquil mind! Farewell content!   350
Farewell the plumed troops and the big wars
That make ambition virtue! O, farewell!
Farewell the neighing steed and the shrill trump,
The spirit-stirring drum, the ear-piercing fife,
The royal banner, and all quality,   355
Pride, pomp, and circumstance of glorious war!
And O, you mortal engines, whose rude throats
The immortal Jove's dead clamors counterfeit,
Farewell! Othello's occupation's gone.

Iago

Is it possible, my lord?   360

Othello

Villain, be sure thou prove my love a whore.
Be sure of it. Give me the ocular proof,
Or by the worth of mine eternal soul,
Thou hadst been better have been born a dog
Than answer my waked wrath.

Iago

Is it come to this?   365

Othello

Make me to see it, or at the least so prove it
That the probation bear no hinge nor loop
To hang a doubt on, or woe upon thy life.

Iago

My noble lord—

Othello

If thou dost slander her and torture me,   370
Never pray more. Abandon all remorse;
On horror's head horrors accumulate;
Do deeds to make heaven weep, all earth amazed;
For nothing canst thou to damnation add
Greater than that.

Iago

O grace! O heaven forgive me!   375
Are you a man? Have you a soul or sense?
God buy you; take mine office. O wretched fool

381 profit: profitable lesson.

388 My name: In this outburst, Othello is solely concerned about his honor and reputation being "begrimed" and blackened. **fresh:** clean, sinless.

389 Dian's visage: the face of Diana, goddess of chastity.

397 supervisor: onlooker, spectator. (OED)

399 tedious: unpleasant, disagreeable.

400 prospect: position, spectacle.

401 bolster: probably, to lie on the same bolster or bed. (OED)

402 More than their own: that is, not their own beds.

405 prime: lusty, as in the prime and vigor of youth; here, ready for rutting. (OED) **goats and monkeys:** animals associated with lechery.

406 salt: in heat, said of dogs; (OED obsolete) hence lecherous. **gross:** monstrous, stupid.

That lov'st to make thine honesty a vice.
O monstrous world! Take note, take note, O world,
To be direct and honest is not safe.   380
I thank you for this profit, and from hence
I'll love no friend, since love breeds such offence.
Othello
Nay, stay. Thou shouldst be honest.
Iago
I should be wise, for honesty's a fool
And loses that it works for.
Othello
By the world,   385
I think my wife be honest and think she is not;
I think that thou art just and think thou art not.
I'll have some proof. My name, that was as fresh
As Dian's visage, is now begrimed and black
As mine own face. If there be cords, or knives,   390
Poison, or fire, or suffocating streams,
I'll not endure it. Would I were satisfied!
Iago
I see, sir, you are eaten up with passion:
I do repent me that I put it to you.
You would be satisfied?
Othello
Would? Nay, and I will.   395
Iago
And may; but how? How satisfied, my lord?
Would you, the supervisor, grossly gape on?
Behold her topped?
Othello
Death and damnation. O!
Iago
It were a tedious difficulty, I think,
To bring them to that prospect. Damn them then,   400
If ever mortal eyes do see them bolster
More than their own. What then? How then?
What shall I say? Where's satisfaction?
It is impossible you should see this,
Were they as prime as goats, as hot as monkeys,   405
As salt as wolves in pride, and fools as gross
As ignorance made drunk. But yet I say,

408 imputation: accusation. (OED)

412 office: job, assignment.

416 I lay with Cassio: It was not uncommon for military men to share a bed. Similar erotic dreams are found in classical literature. (See Ovid's *Heroides*). Iago undoubtedly concocts this story to suit his own purposes.

429 foregone conclusion: previous event; that is, a previous sexual coupling that Cassio is dreaming about, the climax ("conclusion") of the sexual act.

431 thicken: deepen, confirm.

432 I'll tear her all to pieces: Othello resolves to avenge his honor and reputation. Oxford knew the emotion. An early poem begins: "Fain would I sing, but fury makes me fret, / And rage hath sworn to seek revenge of wrong."

436 spotted with strawberries: embroidered with a pattern of strawberries. The red berries may be intended to evoke the blood spots on a virgin's wedding sheets. Neill argues for the contradictory, quadruple symbolism of the much-studied strawberry image: the love badge of Venus, sensuality exemplified in Bosch, the chastity and fertility of the Virgin Mary, and a Renaissance serpent of deceit. (155) This multiple symbolism would suggest an exceptionally well-read dramatist, like Oxford, hinting at Othello's conflicted emotions.

If imputation and strong circumstances
Which lead directly to the door of truth
Will give you satisfaction, you might have it.   410
Othello
Give me a living reason she's disloyal.
Iago
I do not like the office.
But since I am entered in this cause so far,
Pricked to it by foolish honesty and love,
I will go on. I lay with Cassio lately,   415
And being troubled with a raging tooth
I could not sleep. There are a kind of men
So loose of soul that in their sleeps will mutter
Their affairs. One of this kind is Cassio.
In sleep I heard him say, "Sweet Desdemona,   420
Let us be wary, let us hide our loves!"
And then, sir, would he grip and wring my hand,
Cry "O sweet creature!" then kiss me hard,
As if he plucked up kisses by the roots
That grew upon my lips; then laid his leg   425
Over my thigh, and sighed, and kissed, and then
Cried, "Cursed fate that gave thee to the Moor!"
Othello
O monstrous! Monstrous!
Iago
Nay, this was but his dream.
Othello
But this denoted a foregone conclusion.
'Tis a shrewd doubt, though it be but a dream.   430
Iago
And this may help to thicken other proofs
That do demonstrate thinly.
Othello
I'll tear her all to pieces.
Iago
Nay, but be wise. Yet we see nothing done,
She may be honest yet. Tell me but this:
Have you not sometimes seen a handkerchief   435
Spotted with strawberries in your wife's hand?
Othello
I gave her such a one. It was my first gift.

169

443 the slave: an Elizabethan term of contempt. (OED) Probably referring to Desdemona, but possibly to Cassio, too.

445 fond: foolish, doting.

446 black Vengeance: Here and in the lines that follow, Othello, now persuaded that he has been cuckolded and has lost his good name and reputation, resolves on murderous vengeance: He orders Iago to kill Cassio: he himself will kill Desdemona.

447 hearted throne: probably, enthroned in the heart.

448 fraught: cargo, hence burden. (OED).

449 aspics: asps, poisonous snakes.

453-6 Like to the Pontic Sea....Hellespont: This extended and apt metaphor indicates a writer well-versed with Pliny's work and the geography of the area known today as the Black Sea, the Sea of Marmora, and the Dardenelles.

462-79 Do not rise yet....your own for ever: This extended exchange between Othello and Iago, which closes the scene, suggests a mock marriage ceremony as they kneel together, pledging their love. Iago's final words are, "I am yours for ever." Some commentators have noted the strong homoerotic aspects of the play; Oxford was accused of homosexual acts, a crime in Elizabethan England, and was probably bi-sexual.

464 clip us: surround, encircle us, with a connotation of "hug." (OED archaic)

Iago

   I know not that; but such a handkerchief—
   I am sure it was your wife's—did I today
   See Cassio wipe his beard with.

Othello

   If it be that—   440

Iago

   If it be that, or any that was hers,
   It speaks against her with the other proofs.

Othello

   O, that the slave had forty thousand lives!
   One is too poor, too weak for my revenge.
   Now do I see 'tis true. Look here, Iago,   445
   All my fond love thus do I blow to heaven. 'Tis gone.
   Arise, black Vengeance, from the hollow hell.
   Yield up, O Love, thy crown and hearted throne
   To tyrannous Hate. Swell, bosom, with thy fraught,
   For 'tis of aspics' tongues.

Iago

   Yet be content.   450

Othello

   O, blood, blood, blood!

Iago

   Patience, I say. Your mind perhaps may change.

Othello

   Never, Iago. Like to the Pontic Sea,
   Whose icy current and compulsive course
   Ne'er feels retiring ebb, but keeps due on   455
   To the Propontic and the Hellespont,
   Even so my bloody thoughts with violent pace
   Shall ne'er look back, ne'er ebb to humble love,
   Till that a capable and wide revenge
   Swallow them up. Now, by yond marble heaven,   460
   [Kneeling] In the due reverence of a sacred vow
   I here engage my words.

Iago

   Do not rise yet.
   [He kneels] Witness, you ever-burning lights above,
   You elements that clip us round about,
   Witness that here Iago doth give up   465
   The execution of his wit, hands, heart,

468 in me remorse: perhaps a solemn obligation but such usage only here, per OED. Commentators have debated the meaning of the phrase.

479 I am your own for ever.: Ironically referring to the feudal service and obedience (at line 467) that a knight swears to his lord. Here, however, Iago pledges his service to Othello with the more modern, treacherous and cynical implication that the reverse is truly the case, i.e., that Othello has made a Faustian bargain to commit his soul to Iago, a commitment they seal, kneeling, in burlesque of a marriage ceremony.

3.4 enter. . .Clown: If they comment at all on this short exchange between the Clown and Desdemona about Cassio, critics say it is often omitted in performance. But in Shakespeare clowns and fools must be taken seriously. The Clown's bawdy punning on "lie" comically—but most ominously— foreshadows Othello's frenzied and nearly incoherent "lie with her?" outburst a few minutes later in his exchange with Iago about Cassio cuckolding him. (4.1.32-3)

1 sirrah: a term used to address servants or persons of low rank.

4 'tis stabbing: deserves stabbing.

8 devise: invent.

9 lie in mine own throat: to lie foully or infamously. (OED)

To wronged Othello's service. Let him command,
And to obey shall be in me remorse,
What bloody business ever.

Othello

I greet thy love,
Not with vain thanks, but with acceptance bounteous,   470
And will upon the instant put thee to it.
Within these three days let me hear thee say
That Cassio's not alive.

Iago

My friend is dead;
'Tis done at your request. But let her live.

Othello

Damn her, lewd minx! O, damn her, damn her!   475
Come, go with me apart. I will withdraw
To furnish me with some swift means of death
For the fair devil. Now art thou my lieutenant.

Iago

I am your own for ever.

Exeunt.

Scene 4. *Enter Desdemona, Emilia, and Clown.*

Desdemona

Do you know, sirrah, where Lieutenant Cassio lies?

Clown

I dare not say he lies anywhere.

Desdemona

Why, man?

Clown

He's a soldier, and for me to say a soldier lies, 'tis stabbing.

Desdemona

Go to. Where lodges he?   5

Clown

To tell you where he lodges, is to tell you where I lie.

Desdemona

Can anything be made of this?

Clown

I know not where he lodges, and for me to devise a lodging and
Say he lies here, or he lies there, were to lie in mine own throat.

10 edified: informed, instructed.

11 catechize: to question or interrogate systematically at length.

15 compass: appropriate limits.

20 crusadoes: Portuguese gold coins. **but:** except that.

24 the sun: probably a reference to the heat of the African sun.

25 humors: chief fluids of the body, said to determine one's temperament; alluding here to the mental qualities or disposition thought to arise from these humors. (OED).

Desdemona

Can you inquire him out, and be edified by report? 10

Clown

I will catechize the world for him; that is, make questions, and
by them answer.

Desdemona

Seek him, bid him come hither. Tell him I have moved my
Lord on his behalf and hope all will be well.

Clown

To do this is within the compass of man's wit, and therefore I 15
Will attempt the doing it.

Exit Clown.

Desdemona

Where should I lose that handkerchief, Emilia?

Emilia

I know not, madam.

Desdemona

Believe me, I had rather have lost my purse
Full of crusadoes. And but my noble Moor 20
Is true of mind and made of no such baseness
As jealous creatures are, it were enough
To put him to ill thinking.

Emilia

Is he not jealous?

Desdemona

Who, he? I think the sun where he was born
Drew all such humors from him. 25

Emilia

Look where he comes.

Enter Othello.

Desdemona

I will not leave him now till Cassio
Be called to him.—How is it with you, my lord?

Othello

Well, my good lady. *[Aside.]* O, hardness to dissemble!
How do you, Desdemona?

Desdemona

Well, my good lord.

175

32 fruitfulness and liberal heart: probably an intentional double meaning by Othello suggesting either a fertile, generous woman or a licentious libertine.

34 sequester: isolation or removal from society.

37 commonly: generally, but with a connotation here of sexually loose.

40-1 The hearts of old…not hearts.: that is, in feudal times women gave their hearts along with their hands, whereas women in these days of ("new heraldry") give their hands and heraldic rank in marriage but not their hearts.

43 chuck: a term of endearment.

45 rheum: head cold.

51 charmer: a sorceress, someone who worked spells.

Othello
  Give me your hand. This hand is moist, my lady.   30
Desdemona
  It yet hath felt no age nor known no sorrow.
Othello
  This argues fruitfulness and liberal heart.
  Hot, hot, and moist. This hand of yours requires
  A sequester from liberty, fasting and prayer,
  Much castigation, exercise devout;   35
  For here's a young and sweating devil here
  That commonly rebels. 'Tis a good hand, a frank one.
Desdemona
  You may indeed say so,
  For 'twas that hand that gave away my heart.
Othello
  A liberal hand. The hearts of old gave hands,   40
  But our new heraldry is hands, not hearts.
Desdemona
  I cannot speak of this. Come now, your promise.
Othello
  What promise, chuck?
Desdemona
  I have sent to bid Cassio come speak with you.
Othello
  I have a salt and sorry rheum offends me;   45
  Lend me thy handkerchief.
Desdemona
  Here, my lord.
Othello
  That which I gave you.
Desdemona
  I have it not about me.
Othello
  Not?
Desdemona
  No indeed, my lord.
Othello
  That's a fault. That handkerchief
  Did an Egyptian to my mother give: 50
  She was a charmer, and could almost read
  The thoughts of people. She told her, while she kept it,

57 new fancies: new women who caught his fancy.

61 perdition: sin, loss, ruin.

63 web: fabric.

64-5 A sybil. . .compasses: probably, a fortune-teller who was two hundred years old.

66 prophetic fury: frenzied inspiration. Honingmann suggests that the phrase is "perhaps Ariosto's *furor profetico* (*Orlando Furioso* c. 46, st. 80); if so, Shakespeare knew Ariosto in the original [Italian], for the English translation had no 'prophetic fury.'" Ariosto's *Orlando Furioso,* at 38,736 lines, is one of the longest poems in European literature; it was published in 1532. Oxford had easy access to this book in Lord Burghley's library or in Italy.

67-8 mummy: generally a medicine made from dead bodies, usually in Arabia. (OED) Here the unction or liquid was made from ("maidens' hearts") and used as a dye.

73 startingly: jumpily, with starts and stops. (OED)

74 Bless us!: an exclamation of surprise. (OED)

It would make her amiable and subdue my father
Entirely to her love; but if she lost it
Or made gift of it, my father's eye   55
Should hold her loathed and his spirits should hunt
After new fancies. She, dying, gave it me,
And bid me, when my fate would have me wived,
To give it her. I did so; and take heed on it;
Make it a darling like your precious eye.   60
To lose it or give it away were such perdition
As nothing else could match.

Desdemona
Is it possible?

Othello
'Tis true. There's magic in the web of it.
A sibyl, that had numbered in the world
The sun to course two hundred compasses,   65
In her prophetic fury sewed the work;
The worms were hallowed that did breed the silk,
And it was dyed in mummy which the skilful
Conserved of maidens' hearts.

Desdemona
Indeed? Is it true?

Othello
Most veritable; therefore look to it well.   70

Desdemona
Then would to God that I had never seen it!

Othello
Ha? Wherefore?

Desdemona
Why do you speak so startingly and rash?

Othello
Is it lost? Is it gone? Speak, is it out of the way?

Desdemona
Bless us!

Othello
Say you?

Desdemona
It is not lost; but what an if it were?   75

Othello
How?

81 misgives: I have misgivings, suspicions.

82 sufficient: capable.

87 Zounds!: short for God's wounds on the cross, from the quarto edition. The First Folio has, "Away!," probably the printer's substitute for the profanity.

91 year or two: that is, it takes more than a year or two.

Desdemona
  I say it is not lost.
Othello
  Fetch it, let me see it.
Desdemona
  Why, so I can, sir, but I will not now.
  This is a trick to put me from my suit.
  Pray you, let Cassio be received again.
Othello
  Fetch me the handkerchief!   80
  My mind misgives.
Desdemona
  Come, come: You'll never meet a more sufficient man.
Othello
  The handkerchief!
Desdemona
  I pray, talk me of Cassio.
Othello
  The handkerchief!
Desdemona
  A man that all his time
  Hath founded his good fortunes on your love,
  Shared dangers with you—   85
Othello
  The handkerchief!
Desdemona
  For sooth, you are to blame.
Othello
  Zounds!

                                                    Exit Othello.
Emilia
  Is not this man jealous?
Desdemona
  I never saw this before.
  Sure, there's some wonder in this handkerchief.
  I am most unhappy in the loss of it.   90
Emilia
  'Tis not a year or two shows us a man:
  They are all but stomachs, and we all but food;
  To eat us hungerly, and when they are full
  They belch us.

3.4

96 happiness: good fortune or luck in a particular affair. (OED's earliest meaning)

100 exist: that is, as Othello's lieutenant. Cassio speaks again in flowery, euphuistic language.

101 office: performance of a duty. (OED obsolete)

108-9 And shut myself...alms: simply, find something else to do.

111 advocation: efforts to advocate on Cassio's behalf.

116 the blank: the center, from the white spot at the center of a target, called the blank. (OED) Or perhaps point-blank range.

Enter Iago and Cassio.

Look you, Cassio and my husband.
Iago
   [To Cassio] There is no other way; 'tis she must do it.   95
   And, lo, the happiness! Go and importune her.
Desdemona
   How now, good Cassio! What's the news with you?
Cassio
   Madam, my former suit. I do beseech you
   That by your virtuous means I may again
   Exist and be a member of his love   100
   Whom I, with all the office of my heart,
   Entirely honor. I would not be delayed.
   If my offence be of such mortal kind
   That nor my service past, nor present sorrows,
   Nor purposed merit in futurity   105
   Can ransom me into his love again,
   But to know so must be my benefit;
   So shall I clothe me in a forced content,
   And shut myself up in some other course,
   To fortune's alms.
Desdemona
                        Alas, thrice-gentle Cassio,   110
   My advocation is not now in tune.
   My lord is not my lord; nor should I know him,
   Were he in favor as in humor altered.
   So help me every spirit sanctified
   As I have spoken for you all my best   115
   And stood within the blank of his displeasure
   For my free speech. You must awhile be patient.
   What I can do I will; and more I will
   Than for myself I dare. Let that suffice you.
Iago
   Is my lord angry?
Emilia
                     He went hence but now,   120
   And certainly in strange unquietness.
Iago
   Can he be angry? I have seen the cannon

125 Puffed: probably, blew away or blasted. (OED)

132 wrangle with inferior things: debate trivial matters; here ironically referring to her relations with Othello.

134 endues: causes to happen, affects. (OED)

138 Beshrew me: May evils befall me; a mild oath. (OED)

139 unhandsome: probably, unskillful.

140 Arraigning...suborned...witness...indicted: Oxford draws easily on his background in the law for this elaborate legal metaphor: Desdemona's charging of Othello with "unkindness" but finding that her testimony as a "witness" was corrupted ("suborned") and her indictment of him false.

142 conception: idea.

143 toy: fantastic notion. (OED obsolete.)

152 find him fit: calm, in a composed mood.

When it hath blown his ranks into the air,
And like the devil from his very arm
Puffed his own brother—and is he angry? 125
Something of moment then. I will go meet him.
There's matter in it indeed, if he be angry.
Desdemona
I prithee, do so.

Something, sure, of state,
Either from Venice, or some unhatched practice
Made demonstrable here in Cyprus to him, 130
Hath puddled his clear spirit; and in such cases
Men's natures wrangle with inferior things,
Though great ones are their object. 'Tis even so;
For let our finger ache, and it endues
Our other, healthful members even to a sense 135
Of pain. Nay, we must think men are not gods,
Nor of them look for such observancy
As fits the bridal. Beshrew me much, Emilia,
I was, unhandsome warrior as I am,
Arraigning his unkindness with my soul; 140
But now I find I had suborned the witness,
And he's indicted falsely.
Emilia
Pray heaven it be
State matters, as you think, and no conception
Nor no jealous toy concerning you.
Desdemona
Alas the day! I never gave him cause.
Emilia
But jealous souls will not be answered so; 145
They are not ever jealous for the cause,
But jealous for they're jealous. It is a monster
Begot upon itself, born on itself.
Desdemona
Heaven keep that monster from Othello's mind!
Emilia
Lady, amen. 150
Desdemona
I will go seek him. Cassio, walk hereabout.
If I do find him fit, I'll move your suit

185

162 continuate: with no interruptions.

163 strike off: cancel, explain.

164 Take me this work out: Copy the embroidery from this handkerchief.

166 friend: mistress.

168 Go to: Elizabethan for "Oh, come on."

171 remembrance: love token or keepsake

And seek to effect it to my uttermost.
Cassio
I humbly thank your ladyship.

Exit Desdemona with Emilia.

Enter Bianca.

Bianca
Save you, friend Cassio!
Cassio
What make you from home?   155
How is it with you, my most fair Bianca?
Indeed, sweet love, I was coming to your house.
Bianca
And I was going to your lodging, Cassio.
What, keep a week away? Seven days and nights?
Eightscore-eight hours? And lovers' absent hours   160
More tedious than the dial eight score times?
O weary reckoning!
Cassio
Pardon me, Bianca.
I have this while with leaden thoughts been pressed;
But I shall, in a more continuate time,
Strike off this score of absence. Sweet Bianca,
Take me this work out.
Bianca
O Cassio, whence came this?   165
This is some token from a newer friend.
To the felt absence now I feel a cause.
Is it come to this? Well, well.
Cassio
Go to, woman:
Throw your vile guesses in the devil's teeth,
From whence you have them. You are jealous now   170
That this is from some mistress, some remembrance.
No, in good troth, Bianca.
Bianca
Why, whose is it?
Cassio
I know not, neither. I found it in my chamber.

178 attend: wait for or stand-by for.

179 no addition: not to my benefit.

181 womaned: with a woman.

187 circumstanced: that is, under the circumstances.

I like the work well. Ere it be demanded
(As like enough it will) I would have it copied.   ˌ 175
Take it and do it, and leave me for this time.
Bianca
Leave you? Wherefore?
Cassio
I do attend here on the General,
And think it no addition, nor my wish,
To have him see me womaned.   180
Bianca
Why, I pray you?
Cassio
Not that I love you not.
Bianca
But that you do not love me.
I pray you, bring me on the way a little,
And say if I shall see you soon at night.
Cassio
'Tis but a little way that I can bring you,   185
For I attend here; but I'll see you soon.
Bianca
'Tis very good. I must be circumstanced.

Exeunt.

4.1.3 unauthorized: beyond the norms of society.

8 venial slip: a minor sin, easily forgiven.

16 They have. . .it not: an ambiguous remark that implies that women often seem to have honor when they do not.

20 the raven. . .infectious: referring to the folklore that ravens hovered over a house whose inhabitants were ill, especially with the plague.

21 boding: predicting, with the sense of threat.

Act 4

Scene 1. Enter Othello and Iago.

Iago
  Will you think so?
Othello
  Think so, Iago?
Iago
  What, to kiss in private?
Othello
  An unauthorized kiss?
Iago
  Or to be naked with her friend in bed
  An hour or more, not meaning any harm?
Othello
  Naked in bed, Iago, and not mean harm?   5
  It is hypocrisy against the devil.
  They that mean virtuously, and yet do so,
  The devil their virtue tempts, and they tempt heaven.
Iago
  If they do nothing, 'tis a venial slip.
  But if I give my wife a handkerchief—
Othello
  What then?   10
Iago
  Why then, 'tis hers, my lord, and being hers,
  She may, I think, bestow it on any man.
Othello
  She is protectress of her honor, too:
  May she give that?
Iago
  Her honor is an essence that's not seen;   15
  They have it very oft that have it not.
  But, for the handkerchief—
Othello
  By heaven, I would most gladly have forgot it.
  Thou said'st--O, it comes over my memory
  As doth the raven over the infected house,   20

24 abroad: out and about, rambling around.

25 importunate: troublesome, urgent.

26 voluntary dotage: foolish affection freely given.

27 convinced: conquered. (OED) **supplied:** freely given.

33-39 Lie with her. . . O devil!--: Acutely conflicted and under extreme emotional stress, Othello lapses into disorganized prose, rambles almost incoherently and falls into an epileptic fit. Medical experts note that severe stress frequently precedes an epileptic seizure. The sixteenth century dramatist shows unusually well-informed knowledge of epilepsy and its manifestations here and in the lines that follow.

s.d. Falls in a trance.: an epileptic seizure.

34 belie her: tell lies about her.   **fulsome**: disgusting, repulsive, with a connotation of obscene. (OED obsolete)

40 Work on, my medicine. . .Othello!: Iago, the scheming *Zanni* of *commedia dell'arte* and psychopathic, remorseless manipulator, relishes his talent for creating havoc for Othello and the worthy, chaste Desdemona. Cynically, his "medicine" is his evil power to deceive and manipulate.   **Othello!:** The only time in the entire play that Iago addresses Othello by name is when Othello is unconscious, and Iago does so with utter contempt, scorning him as a "credulous" fool.

Boding to all—he had my handkerchief.
Iago
Ay, what of that?
Othello
That's not so good now.
Iago
What if I had said I had seen him do you wrong?
Or heard him say—as knaves be such abroad,
Who having, by their own importunate suit,   25
Or voluntary dotage of some mistress,
Convinced or supplied them, cannot choose
But they must blab—
Othello
Hath he said anything?
Iago
He hath, my lord; but, be you well assured,
No more than he'll unswear.
Othello
What hath he said?   30
Iago
Why, that he did—I know not what he did.
Othello
What? What?
Iago
Lie—
Othello
With her?
Iago
With her, on her; what you will.
Othello
Lie with her? Lie on her? We say "lie on her" when they
Belie her. Lie with her: that's fulsome.—Handkerchief—
Confessions—handkerchief! To confess and be hanged for   35
His labor. First to be hanged and then to confess: I tremble
At it. Nature would not invest herself in such shadowing
Passion without some instruction. It is not words that
Shakes me thus. Pish! Noses, ears, and lips.—Is it possible?
Confess? Handkerchief? O devil—

Falls in a trance.

Iago
Work on, my medicine, work! Thus credulous fools are caught, 40

47 second fit. . .yesterday.: Because there is nothing in the play about an earlier seizure, Iago is no doubt lying, perhaps to show his control of the situation and get Cassio to leave so Iago can set up a weakened Othello for the eavesdropping trick.

49 lethargy: here, a coma-like state.

50 foams at mouth: During a seizure, the victim may droll or foam at the mouth.

51 savage madness: a lie to get the sensitive Cassio to leave.

54 on great occasion: on a matter of considerable importance.

55-6 hurt your head?. . . .mock me?: As is true for epileptics after a seizure, Othello is unaware that he has been unconscious. He picks up where he left off in his raving about Desdemona lying with Cassio and interprets Iago's question about his head as implying that he has the horns of the cuckold and that Iago is mocking him.

62 yoked: married or attached to a woman.

65 peculiar: unique, happening only to themselves.

And many worthy and chaste dames even thus,
All guiltless, meet reproach.—What, ho! My lord!
My lord, I say! Othello!

Enter Cassio.

How now, Cassio?
Cassio
What's the matter?   45
Iago
My lord is fallen into an epilepsy.
This is his second fit; he had one yesterday.
Cassio
Rub him about the temples.
Iago
The lethargy must have his quiet course.
If not, he foams at mouth, and by and by   50
Breaks out to savage madness. Look, he stirs.
Do you withdraw yourself a little while.
He will recover straight. When he is gone,
I would on great occasion speak with you.

Exit Cassio.
How is it, General? Have you not hurt your head?   55
Othello
Dost thou mock me?
Iago
I mock you not, by heaven.
Would you would bear your fortune like a man!
Othello
A horned man's a monster and a beast.
Iago
There's many a beast then in a populous city,
And many a civil monster.   60
Othello
Did he confess it?
Iago
Good sir, be a man.
Think every bearded fellow that's but yoked
May draw with you. There's millions now alive
That nightly lie in those unproper beds
Which they dare swear peculiar. Your case is better.   65

195

67 lip a wanton: kiss a loose woman.

71 list: listen (OED archaic)

75 ecstasy: a morbid unconsciousness, as in a trance or fit. (OED)

77 encave yourself: Conceal yourself, metaphorically as in a cave. With his clever manipulations, Iago has reduced Othello to a farcical figure in a comedy, eavesdropping to see whether he has been cuckolded. Although Cassio laughs and laughs, and although the eavesdropping scene could be right out of *commedia dell'arte*, Othello's predicament is not funny anymore.

78 fleers: mocking laughter, sneers. (OED)

82 cope: engage with, implying copulate with.

84 all-in-all in spleen: at the mercy of your impulses; for Elizabethans the spleen was thought to be the seat of sudden, violent impulses. (OED obsolete)

88 keep time: probably, control yourself.

90 housewife: a light, worthless woman, a hussy. (OED obsolete)

O, 'tis the spite of hell, the fiend's arch-mock,
To lip a wanton in a secure couch
And to suppose her chaste. No, let me know,
And knowing what I am, I know what she shall be.

Othello

O, thou art wise. 'Tis certain.

Iago

Stand you awhile apart;   70
Confine yourself but in a patient list.
Whilst you were here overwhelmed with your grief
(A passion most unsuiting such a man)
Cassio came hither. I shifted him away,
And laid good excuse upon your ecstasy,   75
Bade him anon return and here speak with me,
The which he promised. Do but encave yourself
And mark the fleers, the gibes, and notable scorns
That dwell in every region of his face;
For I will make him tell the tale anew,   80
Where, how, how oft, how long ago, and when
He hath, and is again to cope your wife.
I say, but mark his gesture: marry, patience,
Or I shall say you are all-in-all in spleen,
And nothing of a man.

Othello

Dost thou hear, Iago   85
I will be found most cunning in my patience;
But—dost thou hear?—most bloody.

Iago

That's not amiss;
But yet keep time in all. Will you withdraw?

[Othello stands apart.]

Now will I question Cassio of Bianca,
A housewife that by selling her desires   90
Buys herself bread and clothes. It is a creature
That dotes on Cassio—as 'tis the strumpet's plague
To beguile many and be beguiled by one.
He, when he hears of her, cannot restrain
From the excess of laughter. Here he comes.   95

97 unbookish: probably, naïve or credulous.

100 addition: something added to a man's name, hence a title or rank. Iago addressed Cassio as lieutenant, the rank Othello took away from him.

102 Ply Desdemona: Use her, bend her to your will.

105 caitiff: poor wretch.

114 customer: here, one who buys sexual favors from a prostitute. Cassio is talking about Bianca; Othello, however, thinks he refers to Desdemona.

Enter Cassio.

As he shall smile, Othello shall go mad;
And his unbookish jealousy must construe
Poor Cassio's smiles, gestures, and light behaviors
Quite in the wrong.—How do you now, Lieutenant?

Cassio

The worser that you give me the addition   100
Whose want even kills me.

Iago

Ply Desdemona well, and you are sure on it.
[Speaking lower] Now, if this suit lay in Bianca's power,
How quickly should you speed!

Cassio

Alas, poor caitiff!   105

Othello

[Aside] Look how he laughs already.

Iago

I never knew woman love man so.

Cassio

Alas, poor rogue! I think indeed she loves me.

Othello

[Aside] Now he denies it faintly, and laughs it out.

Iago

Do you hear, Cassio?

Othello

[Aside] Now he importunes him to tell it over.   110
Go to! Well said, well said.

Iago

She gives it out that you shall marry her. Do you intend it?

Cassio

Ha, ha, ha.

Othello

[Aside] Do you triumph, Roman? Do you triumph?

Cassio

I marry? What? A customer? Prithee, bear some charity to   115
My wit; do not think it so unwholesome. Ha, ha, ha!

Othello

[Aside] So, so, so, so! They laugh that win.

Iago

Why, the cry goes that you shall marry her.

119 scored me: marked or wounded me.

120 monkey: that is, Bianca. A term of playful contempt.

124 sea-bank: the sea coast, probably near the harbor below the fortifications.

129 nose: Cutting off a man's nose was a means of punishment or revenge; here also slang for penis.

132 another fitchew. . .a perfumed one: A fitchew is a polecat, which emits a bad smell when frightened or attacked, and also a name of contempt for a prostitute (OED). There is an ingenious pun on "fitchew" with the French *fichu*, a kerchief. Thus, Othello overhears Cassio describe Bianca as a prostitute and Desdemona as "another." And the word in English, "fitchew," that he uses for both women sounds like the French word for handkerchiefs, *fichus*, which were often "perfumed." The bi-lingual pun offers further support for Oxford's authorship of the play, for he was fluent in French and thus adept at this complex, perfumed fitchew-*fichu* word play.

139 hobbyhorse: a loose woman, a prostitute. (OED obsolete)

Cassio
Prithee, say true.
Iago
I am a very villain else.
Othello
[*Aside*] Have you scored me? Well.
Cassio
This is the monkey's own giving out. She is persuaded I will   120
Marry her out of her own love and flattery, not out of my
Promise.
Othello
[*Aside*] Iago beckons me. Now he begins the story.
Cassio
She was here even now; she haunts me in every place. I was
the other day talking on the sea-bank with certain Venetians,
and thither comes the bauble, and falls me thus about my   125
neck—
Othello
Crying, "O dear Cassio!" as it were; his gesture imports it.
Cassio
So hangs and lolls and weeps upon me, so shakes and pulls me. Ha,
ha, ha.
Othello
[*Aside*] Now he tells how she plucked him to my chamber.
O, I see that nose of yours, but not that dog I shall throw it to.
Cassio
Well, I must leave her company.   130
Iago
Before me, look, where she comes.

Enter Bianca with Othello's handkerchief.

Cassio
'Tis such another fitchew! Marry, a perfumed one.—What do
you mean by this haunting of me?
Bianca
Let the devil and his dam haunt you: What did you mean by
that same handkerchief you gave me even now? I was a fine   135
fool to take it. I must take out the work?—A likely piece of
work, that you should find it in your chamber, and not know

142 my handkerchief: that he had given to Desdemona.

144 After her: Improvising to advance his plotting, Iago takes advantage of Bianca's leaving to get rid of Cassio and release Othello from his eavesdropping.

157 nine years a-killing: that is, Cassio should die a slow death.

who left it there. This is some minx's token, and I must take
out the work? There; give it your hobbyhorse. Wheresoever you
had it, I'll take out no work on it.   140
Cassio
How now, my sweet Bianca? How now? How now?
Othello
[*Aside*] By heaven, that should be my handkerchief.
Bianca
If you'll come to supper tonight, you may; if you will not,
come when you are next prepared for.

                                                        Exit Bianca.
Iago
After her, after her.
Cassio
I must. She'll rail in the streets else.   145
Iago
Will you sup there?
Cassio
Yes, I intend so.
Iago
Well, I may chance to see you, for I would very fain speak
with you.
Cassio
Prithee, come. Will you?
Iago
Go to. Say no more.   150
                                                        Exit Cassio.
Othello
How shall I murder him, Iago?
Iago
Did you perceive how he laughed at his vice?
Othello
O, Iago!
Iago
And did you see the handkerchief?
Othello
Was that mine?
Iago
Yours, by this hand. And to see how he prizes the foolish   155
Woman your wife: she gave it him, and he hath given it his

168 invention: imagination.

169-70 so gentle. . .too gentle: a triple pun: "Gentle" meaning well-born and aristocratic, its earliest OED meaning; "gentle" referring to Desdemona's being yielding and compliant; and Iago's sarcastic "too gentle," referring to a horse that is tamed and is easily managed. (OED)

172 fond: foolish.   **patent to offend:** license or opportunity to sin or wrong you.

174 messes: probably, pieces of meat. (OED archaic); that is, make mincemeat of her.

178 expostulate: complain, remonstrate. (OED obsolete)

179 unprovide: probably, weaken, disarm, and take away my resolve.

Whore
Othello
I would have him nine years a-killing. A fine woman? A fair
Woman? A sweet woman?
Iago
Nay, you must forget that.
Othello
Ay, let her rot and perish, and be damned tonight, for she   160
Shall not live. No, my heart is turned to stone; I strike it, and
It hurts my hand. O, the world hath not a sweeter creature: she
Might lie by an emperor's side and command him tasks.
Iago
Nay, that's not your way.
Othello
Hang her! I do but say what she is: so delicate with her   165
Needle, an admirable musician. O, she will sing the
Savageness out of a bear. Of so high and plenteous wit and
Invention?
Iago
She's the worse for all this.
Othello
O, a thousand, a thousand times. And then, of so gentle a
condition.
Iago
Ay, too gentle.   170
Othello
Nay, that's certain. But yet the pity of it, Iago! O Iago, the
pity of it, Iago!
Iago
If you are so fond over her iniquity, give her patent to offend,
For if it touch not you it comes near nobody.
Othello
I will chop her into messes. Cuckold me?
Iago
O, 'tis foul in her.   175
Othello
With mine officer?
Iago
That's fouler.

183 undertaker: perhaps, one who acts as security for another. (OED obsolete) Sarcastically, Iago may be saying, "I'll take care of Cassio."

186 'Tis Lodovico: Several times in the play Iago tells Othello when someone approaches. Commentators have suggested that Othello may have been easily distracted or preoccupied, or that his eyesight was growing dim, which would allude metaphorically to his failure to perceive the trouble that the lying Iago is making for him.

191 instrument of their pleasures: document or letter with their wishes, that is, directives or military orders.

192 cousin: a relative.

Othello

Get me some poison, Iago, this night. I'll not expostulate with
Her, lest her body and beauty unprovide my mind again. This
Night, Iago.

Iago

Do it not with poison. Strangle her in her bed, 180
even the bed she hath contaminated.

Othello

Good, good: the justice of it pleases. Very good.

Iago

And for Cassio, let me be his undertaker. You
shall hear more by midnight.

Othello

Excellent, good. What trumpet is that same? 185

Iago

I warrant, something from Venice

Enter Lodovico, Desdemona, and attendants.

'Tis Lodovico, this, comes from the Duke.
See, your wife's with him.

Lodovico

Save you, worthy General!

Othello

With all my heart, sir.

Lodovico

The Duke and the senators of Venice greet you. 190

Othello

I kiss the instrument of their pleasures.

Desdemona

And what's the news, good cousin Lodovico?

Iago

I am very glad to see you, signor.
Welcome to Cyprus.

Lodovico

I thank you. How does Lieutenant Cassio? 195

Iago

Lives, sir.

Desdemona

Cousin, there's fallen between him and my lord
An unkind breach; but you shall make all well.

201 busy in the paper: absorbed in reading the letter.

203 atone: reconcile.

205 Are you wise?: that is, are you in your right mind, sane. (OED)

207 Deputing: appointing, with a connotation of substituting and replacing. (OED) The timing of the order is a stunning blow for Othello. The Duke and senate are recalling him simply because the military operations are over, and Cassio, his lieutenant, can be deputized to take over command of the forces. Ironically for Othello, however, the "deputing" order arrives just as he has become convinced, mistakenly, that Cassio has substituted for him as his deputy in Desdemona's bed and affections.

209 glad on it: glad about it.

211 mad: crazy, foolish, apparently mocking her, "I'm glad on it."

213 'Tis very much: You have gone too far.

216 earth could teem. . .crocodile: probably alluding to a notion that a crocodile would shed false tears to lure its victim (Othello), a notion included in John Sharpe's account of crocodiles seen during John Hawkins' second voyage (1564-5) to Africa and the New World. (Hakluyt, Variorum) Hence crocodile tears signified (Desdemona's) supposed hypocrisy. Also alluding to beliefs that snakes and flies, and here by extension crocodiles, were generated spontaneously from slime or mud ("the earth.")

Othello
  Are you sure of that?
Desdemona
  My lord?
Othello
  [reads] "This fail you not to do, as you will—"   200
Lodovico
  He did not call; he's busy in the paper.
  Is there division twixt my lord and Cassio?
Desdemona
  A most unhappy one. I would do much
  To atone them for the love I bear to Cassio.
Othello
  Fire and brimstone!
Desdemona
  My lord?
Othello
  Are you wise?   205
Desdemona
  What, is he angry?
Lodovico
  Maybe the letter moved him;
  For, as I think, they do command him home,
  Deputing Cassio in his government.
Desdemona
  Trust me, I am glad on it.
Othello
  Indeed?
Desdemona
  My lord?   210
Othello
  I am glad to see you mad.
Desdemona
  Why, sweet Othello—
Othello
  [Striking her] Devil!
Desdemona
  I have not deserved this.
Lodovico
  My lord, this would not be believed in Venice,
  Though I should swear I saw it. 'Tis very much.

221 Mistress!: a woman who has the upper hand and command over a man's heart. (OED) Here, no doubt said sarcastically.

229 well-painted passion: false attempt at innocence.

232 avaunt!: go away!

233 my place: an ambiguous and sardonic reference to Othello's place as commander on Cyprus and his place as Desdemona's husband.

235 Goats and monkeys: Othello echoes Iago's words in an earlier conversation.

237 all in all sufficient: very capable.

241 safe: firm, in good mental health.

Make her amends; she weeps.
Othello
  O devil, devil! 215
  If that the earth could teem with woman's tears,
  Each drop she falls would prove a crocodile.
  Out of my sight!
Desdemona
  I will not stay to offend you.
Lodovico
  Truly, an obedient lady.
  I do beseech your lordship, call her back. 220
Othello
  Mistress!
Desdemona
  My lord?
Othello
  What would you with her, sir?
Lodovico
  Who, I, my lord?
Othello
  Ay, you did wish that I would make her turn.
  Sir, she can turn, and turn, and yet go on 225
  And turn again. And she can weep, sir, weep.
  And she's obedient, as you say, obedient,
  Very obedient.—Proceed you in your tears.—
  Concerning this, sir—O, well-painted passion!—
  I am commanded home.—Get you away; 230
  I'll send for you anon.—Sir, I obey the mandate
  And will return to Venice.—Hence, avaunt!

Exit Desdemona.

  Cassio shall have my place. And, sir, tonight
  I do entreat that we may sup together.
  You are welcome, sir, to Cyprus.—Goats and monkeys! 235

Exit Othello.

Lodovico
  Is this the noble Moor whom our full senate
  Call all in all sufficient? Is this the nature
  Whom passion could not shake? Whose solid virtue
  The shot of accident nor dart of chance
  Could neither graze nor pierce?

242 He's that he is. . . .he were.: Once again, Iago delivers what seems to be a profound pronouncement but is cleverly obscure. Neill calls it "most teasingly opaque." The lines also recall Iago's "I am not what I am" and Oxford's "I am not as I seem to be" in one of his pre-Shakespeare poems. See note 1.1.64
breathe: mention, whisper.

246 stroke: blow, action.

247 blood: passions, emotions.

251 courses: courses of action.

253 mark: notice.

254 deceived: misled or mistaken.

4.2

4 no harm: nothing that would cause harm, i.e., nothing illicit.

Iago

He is much changed. 240

Lodovico

Are his wits safe? Is he not light of brain?

Iago

He's that he is. I may not breathe my censure
What he might be. If what he might he is not,
I would to heaven he were!

Lodovico

What, strike his wife?

Iago

Faith, that was not so well; yet would I knew 245
That stroke would prove the worst!

Lodovico

Is it his use?
Or did the letters work upon his blood
And new create his fault?

Iago

Alas, alas!
It is not honesty in me to speak
What I have seen and known. You shall observe him, 250
And his own courses will denote him so
That I may save my speech. Do but go after,
And mark how he continues.

Lodovico

I am sorry that I am deceived in him.

Exeunt.

Scene 2. Enter Othello and Emilia.

Othello

You have seen nothing then?

Emilia

Nor ever heard, nor ever did suspect.

Othello

Yes, you have seen Cassio and she together.

Emilia

But then I saw no harm, and then I heard
Each syllable that breath made up between them. 5

Othello

What, did they never whisper?

Emilia

Never, my lord.

10 her mask: fashionable, decorated half-masks with veil and headdress that were part of an aristocratic Venetian lady's wardrobe. Upper-class women wore them indoors and out, at balls and parties, and during various festivals, especially Carnival. This is one of many details of Venetian life and the customs of its aristocrats that would have been known and used in the play only by a dramatist who had been there.

12 durst: dare say. **honest:** in this context, chaste.

13 soul at stake: that is, stake my life on it.

16 serpent's curse: a reference to Genesis 3. 14, in which God condemns the serpent to crawl on its belly for deceiving Eve in the Garden of Eden.

20 bawd: a brothel's madam.

21 This is a subtle whore. . .her do it: Emilia because Othello addresses Emilia *in absentia* in the preceding line (although some commentators suggest Desdemona).

27 your function: that is, perform your duties, here as a prostitute at a whorehouse.

28 procreants: couples mating to procreate. (OED obsolete)

Othello
  Nor send you out of the way?
Emilia
  Never.
Othello
  To fetch her fan, her gloves, her mask, nor nothing?   10
Emilia
  Never, my lord.
Othello
  That's strange.
Emilia
  I durst, my lord, to wager she is honest,
  Lay down my soul at stake. If you think other,
  Remove your thought; it doth abuse your bosom.
  If any wretch have put this in your head,   15
  Let heaven requite it with the serpent's curse!
  For if she be not honest, chaste, and true,
  There's no man happy. The purest of their wives
  Is foul as slander.
Othello
  Bid her come hither. Go.

                               Exit Emilia.

  She says enough; yet she's a simple bawd   20
  That cannot say as much. This is a subtle whore,
  A closet lock and key of villainous secrets.
  And yet she'll kneel and pray; I have seen her do it.

                Enter Desdemona and Emilia.

Desdemona
  My lord, what is your will?
Othello
  Pray you, chuck, come hither.
Desdemona
  What is your pleasure?
Othello
  Let me see your eyes.   25
  Look in my face.
Desdemona
  What horrible fancy's this?

30 Your mystery: probably, your occupation. (OED obsolete) Othello treats Emilia like the madam of a brothel.

37 double damned: for your perjury and for your infidelity.

54-60 The fixed . . . discarded thence!: In this extended, multi-image metaphor, Othello bitterly laments that Desdemona by her supposed infidelity has "discarded" and shamed him. She has made him a "fixed figure. . .of scorn" before the world, which will seem to "point" steadily at him just as the imperceptibly moving and thus "fixed" hand of a clock points to the hour. These allusions again reflect Oxford's outrage that in London he had been made "a fable of the world" by rumors that while he was in Italy his wife had been unfaithful.

Othello

[To Emilia] Some of your function, mistress.
Leave procreants alone and shut the door;
Cough or cry "hem" if anybody come.
Your mystery, your mystery! Nay, dispatch.   30

Exit Emilia.

Desdemona

Upon my knees, what doth your speech import?
I understand a fury in your words,
  But not the words.

Othello

Why, what art thou?

Desdemona

Your wife, my lord; your true
And loyal wife.

Othello

Come, swear it, damn thyself, lest   35
being like one of heaven, the devils themselves
should fear to seize thee. Therefore be double damned:
swear thou art honest.

Desdemona

Heaven doth truly know it.

Othello

Heaven truly knows that thou art false as hell.

Desdemona

To whom, my lord? With whom? How am I false?   40

Othello

O, Desdemon! Away, away, away!

Desdemona

Alas the heavy day. Why do you weep?
Am I the motive of these tears, my lord?
If haply you my father do suspect
An instrument of this your calling back,   45
Lay not your blame on me. If you have lost him,
I have lost him too.

Othello

Had it pleased heaven
To try me with affliction, had they rained
All kinds of sores and shames on my bare head,
Steeped me in poverty to the very lips,   50

217

57 there: Desdemona.   **garnered up my heart:** stored or deposited it, as in a storehouse. Othello committed his "heart" (his reputation, his hopes and his "life") to Desdemona for safekeeping, and she has betrayed him.

62 knot and gender: copulate and produce offspring.   **complexion:** face.

66 shambles: slaughterhouse.

67 quicken: come to life.   **blowing:** swollen, rotten meat.

70 ignorant sin: sin of which I am unaware.

71 fair paper. . . book: Desdemona, in the sense of bound, blank pages.

73 public commoner: probably, common whore.

74 forges of my cheeks. . .deeds: A forge is an open hearth with bellows; metaphorically, Othello's cheeks are the bellows that would blow the fuel (her "deeds") into flames that would burn "modesty" to "cinders."

77 winks: closes its eyes. (OED earliest meaning), hence the moon goes dark, as during an eclipse.

83 vessel: from the Bible's description of a woman as a vessel of holiness and honor.

Given to captivity me and my utmost hopes,
I should have found in some place of my soul
A drop of patience. But, alas, to make me
A fixed figure for the time of scorn
To point his slow unmoving finger at.   55
Yet could I bear that too, well, very well.
But there where I have garnered up my heart,
Where either I must live or bear no life,
The fountain from the which my current runs
Or else dries up: to be discarded thence,   60
Or keep it as a cistern for foul toads
To knot and gender in. Turn thy complexion there,
Patience, thou young and rose-lipped cherubin—
I here look as grim as hell.

Desdemona

I hope my noble lord esteems me honest.   65

Othello

O, ay, as summer flies are in the shambles,
That quicken even with blowing. O thou weed,
Who art so lovely fair and smell'st so sweet
That the sense aches at thee, would thou hadst ne'er
been born!

Desdemona

Alas, what ignorant sin have I committed?   70

Othello

Was this fair paper, this most goodly book,
Made to write "whore" upon? What committed?
Committed? O thou public commoner,
I should make very forges of my cheeks,
That would to cinders burn up modesty,   75
Did I but speak thy deeds. What committed?
Heaven stops the nose at it and the moon winks;
The bawdy wind, that kisses all it meets,
Is hushed within the hollow mine of earth
And will not hear it. What committed?   80

Desdemona

By heaven, you do me wrong.

Othello

Are not you a strumpet?

Desdemona

No, as I am a Christian.

219

89 I cry you mercy: Sarcastically, "I beg your pardon."

92-3 office . . . gate of hell: that is, Emilia's duty is to guard the gates of hell, likely a bawdy, insulting reference to Desdemona's pudenda.

94 course: action together, with the suggestion of a sexual exchange. (OED)

95 keep our counsel: Don't talk about what you've overheard.

98 half asleep: numb, stunned. (OED)

103-4 answers. . . go by water: probably, cannot answer except with tears.

If to preserve this vessel for my lord
From any other foul unlawful touch
Be not to be a strumpet, I am none.   85
Othello
What, not a whore?
Desdemona
No, as I shall be saved.
Othello
Is it possible?
Desdemona
O, heaven forgive us!
Othello
I cry you mercy, then.
I took you for that cunning whore of Venice   90
That married with Othello. *[Calling out.]* You, mistress,
That have the office opposite to Saint Peter
And keep the gate of hell!

Enter Emilia.

You, you, ay, you!
We have done our course. There's money for your pains.
I pray you, turn the key and keep our counsel.   95

Exit Othello.

Emilia
Alas, what does this gentleman conceive?
How do you, madam? How do you, my good lady?
Desdemona
Faith, half asleep.
Emilia
Good madam, what's the matter with my lord?
Desdemona
With who?
Emilia
Why, with my lord, madam.   100
Desdemona
Who is thy lord?
Emilia
He that is yours, sweet lady.
Desdemona

105 wedding sheets: an ominous detail; wives were sometimes buried in their wedding sheets.

112 tasks: corrective measures, as in take to task. (OED)

113 chid: chided, scolded.

115 bewhored her: called her a whore.

121 callet: a lewd woman, a strumpet. (OED obsolete)

I have none. Do not talk to me, Emilia.
I cannot weep, nor answer have I none

But what should go by water. Prithee, tonight
Lay on my bed my wedding sheets, remember;   105
And call thy husband hither.
Emilia
Here's a change indeed.

                                            Exit.

Desdemona
'Tis meet I should be used so, very meet.
How have I been behaved, that he might stick
The smallest opinion on my least misuse?

Enter Iago and Emilia.

Iago
What is your pleasure, madam? How is it with you?   110
Desdemona
I cannot tell. Those that do teach young babes
Do it with gentle means and easy tasks.
He might have chid me so, for, in good faith,
I am a child to chiding.
Iago
What's the matter, lady?
Emilia
Alas, Iago, my lord hath so bewhored her,   115
Thrown such despite and heavy terms upon her,
As true hearts cannot bear it.
Desdemona
Am I that name, Iago?
Iago
What name, fair lady?
Desdemona
Such as she says my lord did say I was.
Emilia
He called her whore. A beggar in his drink   120
Could not have laid such terms upon his callet.
Iago
Why did he so?

125 forsook. . .matches: passed up opportunities to marry an aristocrat. In the next scene, Desdemona will recall one of them, Lodovico. (4.3.33)

128 Beshrew him: May evils befall him. (OED obsolete)

129 trick: a stupid, foolish act.

132 cogging, cozening slave: deceitful, defrauding rascal. (OED)

134 no such man: Ironically, Iago is the man.

136 halter: hangman's noose.

140 scurvy fellow: Ironically, Emilia describes the very man responsible, her husband, Iago, who is standing before her.

144 Speak within door: "Hush, don't speak so everyone can hear," but in this context an order to, "be quiet." Iago cannot tolerate the outspoken truth-telling of Emilia, the maid of commedia dell'arte, which will bring about his comeuppance and tragically her death.

145 squire: a personal servant, usually young; sometimes spoken with contempt. (OED)

149 Go to: In exasperation, "Stop your nonsense."

150-1 Good friend. . . I kneel: Of the many ironies in this play, this phrase may be the most poignant. Iago's scheming brought Othello the general to his knees before him and now Desdemona the aristocrat to her knees before him.

Desdemona

I do not know. I am sure I am none such.

Iago

Do not weep, do not weep. Alas the day!*Emilia*
Hath she forsook so many noble matches,   125
Her father and her country and her friends,
To be called whore? Would it not make one weep?

Desdemona

It is my wretched fortune.

Iago

Beshrew him for it!
How comes this trick upon him?

Desdemona

Nay, heaven doth know.

Emilia

I will be hanged if some eternal villain,   130
Some busy and insinuating rogue,
Some cogging, cozening slave, to get some office,
Have not devised this slander. I will be hanged else.

Iago

Fie, there is no such man. It is impossible.

Desdemona

If any such there be, heaven pardon him.   135

Emilia

A halter pardon him! And hell gnaw his bones!
Why should he call her whore? Who keeps her company?
What place? What time? What form? What likelihood?
The Moor's abused by some most villainous knave,
Some base notorious knave, some scurvy fellow.   140
O heaven, that such companions thou'dst unfold,
And put in every honest hand a whip
To lash the rascals naked through the world
Even from the east to the west.

Iago

Speak within door.

Emilia

O, fie upon them! Some such squire he was   145
That turned your wit the seamy side without
And made you to suspect me with the Moor.

Iago

You are a fool. Go to!

158 beggarly divorcement: that is, a divorced state in which I would be reduced to the status of a beggar.

159 Comfort forswear me: Even if I lose all hope of comfort.

162-4 It does. . . .make me: that is "I hate to say the word; there is nothing could make me do an act that would earn me the title ('addition') of whore."

171 stay the meat: that is, waiting to eat supper.

176 daff'st me: put me off; first usage here in this sense. From "doff," to put off clothing, esp. a hat. (OED obsolete)   **device:** ruse or trick.

177 conveniency: opportunity.

Desdemona
  Alas, Iago,
  What shall I do to win my lord again?
  Good friend, go to him; for, by this light of heaven, 150
  I know not how I lost him. Here I kneel.
  If ever my will did trespass against his love,
  Either in discourse of thought or actual deed,
  Or that mine eyes, mine ears, or any sense
  Delighted them in any other form; 155
  Or that I do not yet, and ever did,
  And ever will (though he do shake me off
  To beggarly divorcement) love him dearly,
  Comfort forswear me. Unkindness may do much,
  And his unkindness may defeat my life, 160
  But never taint my love. I cannot say "whore."
  It does abhor me now I speak the word;
  To do the act that might the addition earn
  Not the world's mass of vanity could make me.
Iago
  I pray you, be content. 'Tis but his humor. 165
  The business of the state does him offense,
  And he does chide with you.
Desdemona
  If it were no other—
Iago
  It is but so, I warrant.
[Trumpets within.]
  Hark, how these instruments summon you to supper: 170
  The messengers of Venice stay the meat.
  Go in, and weep not. All things shall be well.

                                  Exit Desdemona and Emilia.

                    Enter Roderigo.

  How now, Roderigo?
Roderigo
  I do not find that thou deal'st justly with me.
Iago
  What in the contrary? 175

186-9 The jewels. . . . find none.: Iago apparently has kept for himself the jewels that Roderigo entrusted to him to give to Desdemona and has lied to Roderigo about her promise to give Roderigo "sudden respect and acquaintance."

187 votarist: one who has taken religious vows, sometimes including a vow of chastity.

188 returned me: sent back to me.

193 fopped: made a fool of. (OED)

198 You have said now: that is, "Are you done?"

199 protest my intendment: state my intention.

202-3 most just exception: reasonable complaint.

Roderigo

Every day thou daff'st me with some device, Iago, and rather,
as it seems to me now, keep'st from me all conveniency than
suppliest me with the least advantage of hope: I will indeed
no longer endure it. Nor am I yet persuaded to put up in
peace what already I have foolishly suffered.   180

Iago

Will you hear me, Roderigo?

Roderigo

I have heard too much, for your words and performances are
no kin together.

Iago

You charge me most unjustly.

Roderigo

With naught but truth. I have wasted myself out of my   185
means. The jewels you have had from me to deliver to
Desdemona would half have corrupted a votarist. You have
told me she hath received them and returned me expectations
and comforts of sudden respect and acquaintance, but I find
none.

Iago

Well, go to, very well.   190

Roderigo

"Very well!" "Go to!" I cannot go to, man, nor 'tis not very
well. By this hand, I think it is scurvy, and begin to find
myself fopped in it.

Iago

Very well.

Roderigo

I tell you 'tis not very well. I will make myself known to   195
Desdemona. If she will return me my jewels, I will give over
my suit and repent my unlawful solicitation; if not, assure
yourself I will seek satisfaction of you.

Iago

You have said now?

Roderigo

Ay, and said nothing but what I protest intendment of doing.

Iago

Why, now I see there's mettle in thee, and even from this   200
instant to build on thee a better opinion than ever before.
Give me thy hand, Roderigo. Thou hast taken against me a

211 engines: instruments of torture, especially the rack. (OED obsolete)

216 Mauritania: in the 1500s, an Arab country at the far eastern end of North Africa, across the Strait of Gibraltar and the Mediterranean from Spain and the probable origin of the word "Moor." It would be the closest refuge for Islamic Moors expelled from Catholic Spain in the late 1400s. But there were no Venetian colonies in the area, so Othello would not have been assigned to Mauritania. Iago dupes Roderigo, playing on his gullibility, with a casual but seemingly plausible fabrication, which also hints that Othello is of Spanish-Moorish ancestry.

217 lingered: delayed, made to linger.

218 determinate: effective, decisive.

223 harlotry: a harlot, a slut.

224 his honorable fortune: probably his appointment as governor, which would entitle him to attendants and bodyguards.

231 grows to waste: a period of time approaches its end. (OED obsolete)

most just exception; but yet I protest I have dealt most
directly in thy affair.

Roderigo

It hath not appeared.   205

Iago

I grant indeed it hath not appeared, and your suspicion is not
without wit and judgment. But, Roderigo, if thou hast that in
thee indeed, which I have greater reason to believe now than
ever (I mean purpose, courage, and valor) this night show it.
If thou the next night following enjoy not Desdemona take me   210
from this world with treachery and devise engines for my life.

Roderigo

Well, what is it? Is it within reason and compass?

Iago

Sir, there is especial commission come from Venice to depute
Cassio in Othello's place.

Roderigo

Is that true? Why, then Othello and Desdemona return again
to Venice.   215

Iago

O, no; he goes into Mauritania and takes away with him the
fair Desdemona, unless his abode be lingered here by some
accident; wherein none can be so determinate as the removing
of Cassio.

Roderigo

How do you mean, removing of him?

Iago

Why, by making him uncapable of Othello's place—knocking
out his brains.   220

Roderigo

And that you would have me to do?

Iago

Ay, if you dare do yourself a profit and a right. He sups
tonight with harlotry, and thither will I go to him. He
knows not yet of his honorable fortune. If you will watch his
going thence, which I will fashion to fall out between twelve   225
and one, you may take him at your pleasure. I will be near to
second your attempt, and he shall fall between us. Come,
stand not amazed at it, but go along with me: I will show you
such a necessity in his death that you shall think yourself
bound to put it on him. It is now high suppertime, and the   230

235 satisfied: convinced.

10 incontinent: immediately, with a connotation of its earliest meaning, lacking self-restraint in sexual matters. (OED)

16 Good Father: God in heaven.

night grows to waste. About it.
Roderigo
I will hear further reason for this.
Iago
And you shall be satisfied.   235

                                                    Exeunt.

Scene 3. *Enter Othello, Lodovico, Desdemona, Emilia, and attendants.*

Lodovico
I do beseech you, sir, trouble yourself no further.
Othello
O, pardon me; it will do me good to walk.
Lodovico
Madam, good night. I humbly thank your ladyship.
Desdemona
Your honor is most welcome.
Othello
Will you walk, sir? O, Desdemona!
Desdemona
My lord?
Othello
Get you to bed on the instant. I will be returned forthwith.
Dismiss your attendant there. Look it be done.   5
Desdemona
I will, my lord.
                    Exit Othello, with Lodovico and attendants.
Emilia
How goes it now? He looks gentler than he did.
Desdemona
He says he will return incontinent,   10
He hath commanded me to go to bed,
And bade me to dismiss you.
Emilia
Dismiss me?
Desdemona
It was his bidding. Therefore, good Emilia,
Give me my nightly wearing, and adieu.
We must not now displease him.   15

24 Barbarie: perhaps an old form of Barbara or an obsolete form of Barbary. (OED) If the latter, then a North African woman, presumably black like Othello, was a maid in Desdemona's household, was abandoned by her lover and died from grief and shame.

25 mad: insane.

26 song of "Willow": a traditional ballad with many verses and variations. The willow tree symbolized grief for the loss of a loved one. (See Appendices.)

27 fortune: fate.

31 dispatch: hurry.

33 proper man: worthy, respectable, genteel, handsome, with a connotation of suitable. (OED) Lodovico and Desdemona are both Venetian aristocrats. He was probably one of the rejected suitors mentioned by Emilia in the previous scene. (4.2.125) Desdemona is suddenly recalling that she might have married him, one of her own standing in the aristocracy, rather than a black Moorish mercenary who has caused her so much grief. "Proper man" also appears in act one where Iago describes Cassio as a "proper man" and realizes he could use the respectable, genteel Cassio to sow suspicion in the mind of Othello that his aristocratic wife might prefer someone from her own station in life. (1.3.368)

45 hie thee: hasten.

47 Let nobody blame him. . .scorn I approve: foreshadowing that she will not blame Othello for killing her and will accept his "scorn." The Willow song has led her, seemingly unwittingly, into singing about her fate. (See Appendices for an interpretation of this song.)

48 Nay, that's not next: The line Desdemona has omitted is, "He was born to be fair; I, to die for his love." And her fate is to die for Othello's love.

Desdemona

All's one. Good Father how foolish are our minds!
If I do die before thee, prithee shroud me
In one of those same sheets.

Emilia

Come, come, you talk.

Desdemona

My mother had a maid called Barbarie.
She was in love, and he she loved proved mad   25
And did forsake her. She had a song of "Willow,"
An old thing 'twas, but it expressed her fortune,
And she died singing it. That song tonight
Will not go from my mind; I have much to do
But to go hang my head all at one side   30
And sing it like poor Barbarie. Prithee, dispatch.

Emilia

Shall I go fetch your nightgown?

Desdemona

No, unpin me here.
This Lodovico is a proper man.

Emilia

A very handsome man.

Desdemona

He speaks well.

Emilia

I know a lady in Venice would have walked
barefoot to Palestine for a touch of his nether lip.   35

Desdemona

[Singing]
The poor soul sat sighing by a sycamore tree,
Sing all a green willow;
Her hand on her bosom, her head on her knee,
Sing willow, willow, willow.   40
The fresh streams ran by her and murmured her moans;
Sing willow, willow, willow;
Her salt tears fell from her, and softened the stones;
Lay by these.
[Singing]
Sing willow, willow, willow—
Prithee, hie thee. He'll come anon.   45
[Singing]

52 couch with more men: probably, have sexual relations with more men, from the French *coucher*.

57 abuse: cheat on.

67 joint ring: one of two finger rings made in separable halves that fit the halves of the other, thus proving the true love of the man and woman who wear them. (Variorum)

68 lawn: a kind of fine linen from Laon, France; the OED's earliest definition of the word.

68-9 petty exhibition: modest gift.

Sing all a green willow must be my garland.
Let nobody blame him; his scorn I approve—
Nay, that's not next.—Hark! Who is it that knocks?

Emilia

It's the wind.

Desdemona

[Singing]

  I called my love false love; but what said he then?   50
Sing willow, willow, willow;
"If I court more women, you'll couch with more men."
So, get thee gone. Good night. Mine eyes do itch;
Doth that bode weeping?

Emilia

'Tis neither here nor there.

Desdemona

I have heard it said so. O, these men, these men!   55
Dost thou in conscience think—tell me, Emilia—
That there be women do abuse their husbands
In such gross kind?

Emilia

There be some such, no question.

Desdemona

Wouldst thou do such a deed for all the world?

Emilia

Why, would not you?

Desdemona

No, by this heavenly light.   60

Emilia

Nor I neither by this heavenly light; I might do it as well in the
dark.

Desdemona

Wouldst thou do such a deed for all the world?

Emilia

The world's a huge thing. It is a great price for a small vice.

Desdemona

In troth, I think thou wouldst not.   65

Emilia

In troth, I think I should, and undo it when I had done. Marry,
I would not do such a thing for a joint ring, nor for measures
Of lawn, nor for gowns, petticoats, nor caps, nor any petty
Exhibition. But for all the whole world: why, who would not

77 as many to the vantage: probably, as many more. (OED obsolete)

78 store: furnish. (OED first meaning). Emilia may be saying that there are women who would cheat on their husbands to furnish the life ("world") they "played for" by their adultery. Venetian courtesans who were married could take rich lovers for a lavish life style.

81 pour our treasures into foreign laps: that is, pour the semen that is rightfully ours into other women. Honigmann suggests, "perhaps alluding to the myth of Danae, who was impregnated by Zeus disguised as a shower of gold."

83 throwing restraint: restricting the freedom of the wives.

84 scant our former having: take away our possessions.

85 galls: bitterness of spirit, rancor. (OED) Here, probably the spirit to hold a grudge, express displeasure.

87 sense: sensations, feelings.

91 affection: passion, lust. (OED obsolete)

98 Not to pick. . .bad mend: probably, not to merely sort the worse evil from the lesser but to use the evil to improve ("mend").

Make her husband a cuckold to make him a monarch? I   70
Should venture purgatory for it.
Desdemona
Beshrew me if I would do such a wrong for the whole world.
Emilia
Why, the wrong is but a wrong in the world, and having the
World for your labor, 'tis a wrong in your own world, and
You might quickly make it right.   75
Desdemona
I do not think there is any such woman.
Emilia
Yes, a dozen, and as many to the vantage
As would store the world they played for.
But I do think it is their husbands' faults
If wives do fall. Say that they slack their duties   80
And pour our treasures into foreign laps,
Or else break out in peevish jealousies,
Throwing restraint upon us? Or say they strike us,
Or scant our former having in despite?
Why, we have galls, and though we have some grace,   85
Yet have we some revenge. Let husbands know
Their wives have sense like them. They see, and smell,
And have their palates both for sweet and sour,
As husbands have. What is it that they do
When they change us for others? Is it sport?   90
I think it is. And doth affection breed it?
I think it doth. Is it frailty that thus errs?
It is so, too. And have not we affections,
Desires for sport, and frailty, as men have?
Then let them use us well; else let them know,   95
The ills we do, their ills instruct us so.
Desdemona
Good night, good night. Heaven me such uses send
Not to pick bad from bad, but by bad mend!

                                                  Exeunt.

1 bulk: a framework projecting from the front of a shop; a stall. (OED)

2 bare: unsheathed.   **Put it home:** to its target.

11 quat: pimple, small boil; a contemptuous term for a young man (OED). **to the sense:** to the quick (OED obsolete), alluding to Roderigo's weakness or susceptibility to be irritated and provoked into action.

14 Live Roderigo: that is, if Roderigo lives.

16 bobbed: probably, taken by deception. (OED, citing it here as its only usage.)

21 unfold: expose.

23 'tis he. . .thou diest; The foolish Roderigo botches the ambush, which starts out as a slapstick brawl typical of *commedia dell'arte* but quickly turns vicious. Iago instantly improvises to further his scheme. In the dark, he tries to kill Cassio, making it appear the work of Roderigo, but only wounds him, and then fatally wounds Roderigo. Iago sows confusion, brilliantly manipulating everyone in this scene, including Othello and Lodovico; and even making himself the hero.

25 coat: either armor or a thick, padded coat.

26 make proof: test.

Act 5

Scene 1. Enter Iago and Roderigo.

Iago
  Here, stand behind this bulk. Straight will he come.
  Wear thy good rapier bare, and put it home.
  Quick! Quick! Fear nothing. I'll be at thy elbow.
  It makes us or it mars us. Think on that,
  And fix most firm thy resolution.   5
Roderigo
  Be near at hand. I may miscarry in it.
Iago
  Here, at thy hand. Be bold, and take thy stand.

                                              [Iago stands aside.]

Roderigo
  I have no great devotion to the deed;
  And yet he hath given me satisfying reasons.
  'Tis but a man gone. Forth, my sword. He dies.   10
Iago
  I have rubbed this young quat almost to the sense,
  And he grows angry. Now, whether he kill Cassio
  Or Cassio him, or each do kill the other,
  Every way makes my gain. Live Roderigo,
  He calls me to restitution large   15
  Of gold and jewels that I bobbed from him
  As gifts to Desdemona.
  It must not be. If Cassio do remain,
  He hath a daily beauty in his life
  That makes me ugly; and besides, the Moor   20
  May unfold me to him; there stand I in much peril.
  No, he must die. But so. I hear him coming.

                          Enter Cassio.
Roderigo
  I know his gait, 'tis he.—Villain, thou diest!
Cassio
  That thrust had been mine enemy indeed,
  But that my coat is better than thou know'st.   25

31-6 'Tis he . . . be spotted: Iago has apparently made sure Othello would be nearby and would witness the melee. **'Tis he**: that is, Cassio. Othello thinks Cassio is dying. In Othello's brief appearance here in the dark, he is not seen or heard by Cassio and Roderigo; neither of the wounded men responds to him. His words are an aside, and once again Othello finds himself in the ignoble position of an eavesdropper, this time complicit in murderous street fighting. He has not acted as a professional military officer and stopped the fighting, as he did in Venice in act 1. He wants revenge.

33 Minion: strumpet, mistress, referring to the absent Desdemona.

34 your unblest fate hies: that is, your death, unblessed, comes quickly nearer ("hies").

37 No passage?: No passersby? (OED rare)

42 heavy: overcast and dark.

43 counterfeits: faked, not true cries of distress.

I will make proof of thine.

[He wounds Roderigo.]

Roderigo
O, I am slain!

[He falls. Iago, from behind, wounds Cassio in the leg, and exits.]
Cassio
I am maimed forever. Help, ho! Murder! Murder!

Enter Othello.
Othello
The voice of Cassio! Iago keeps his word.
Roderigo
O, villain that I am!
Othello
[Aside] It is even so.
Cassio
O, help, ho! Light! A surgeon!   30
Othello [Aside]
'Tis he. O brave Iago, honest and just,
That hast such noble sense of thy friend's wrong!
Thou teachest me. Minion, your dear lies dead,
And your unblest fate hies. Strumpet, I come.
For of my heart those charms, thine eyes, are blotted.   35
Thy bed, lust-stained, shall with lust's blood be spotted.

Exit Othello.

Enter Lodovico and Gratiano
Cassio
What ho! No watch? No passage? Murder! Murder!
Gratiano
'Tis some mischance. The voice is very direful.
Cassio
O, help!
Lodovico
Hark!   40
Roderigo
O, wretched villain!
Lodovico
Two or three groan. 'Tis a heavy night;
These may be counterfeits. Let's think it unsafe

46 in his shirt: night clothes. (OED) Quickly improvising after he wounds Roderigo and Cassio, Iago leaves and then returns in his night clothes to make it appear that he had no part in the fighting.

54 spoiled: injured.

58 O treacherous villains: Ironically, it is Iago who is the treacherous villain, and he knows it. Roderigo will realize it a moment later when he calls for help and Iago stabs him, fatally.

59 What are you. . .some help.: calling on Lodovico and Gratiano.

62 slave: An Elizabethan term of contempt.

To come into the cry without more help.
Roderigo
   Nobody come? Then shall I bleed to death.   45

                    Enter Iago, with a light.
Lodovico
   Hark!
Gratiano
   Here's one comes in his shirt, with light and weapons.
Iago
   Who's there? Whose noise is this that cries on murder?
Lodovico
   We do not know.
Iago
   Did not you hear a cry?
Cassio
   Here, here! For heaven's sake, help me!
Iago
   What's the matter?   50
Gratiano
   This is Othello's ancient, as I take it.
Lodovico
   The same indeed, a very valiant fellow.
Iago
   What are you here that cry so grievously?
Cassio
   Iago? O, I am spoiled, undone by villains!
   Give me some help.   55
Iago
   O me, Lieutenant! What villains have done this?
Cassio
   I think that one of them is hereabout,
   And cannot make away.
Iago
   O treacherous villains!
   What are you there? Come in, and give some help.
Roderigo
   O, help me there!   60
Cassio
   That's one of them.

63 damned Iago: Too late, Roderigo realizes he has been duped by Iago. The comedy is over for him. **Bloody thieves**: Iago makes it appear he suspects several attackers, serving to deflect any suspicions that he engineered the melee.

66 prove us, praise us: probably, "when you test us you will know our value and sing out praises."

71 brother: apparently to falsely persuade the others, if they had any doubts, that he was on Cassio's side in the melee.

Iago
  O murderous slave! O villain!

Roderigo
  O damned Iago! O inhuman dog!
Iago
  Kill men in the dark?—Where be these bloody thieves?—
  How silent is this town!—Ho! Murder, murder!—
  What may you be? Are you of good or evil?   65
Lodovico
  As you shall prove us, praise us.
Iago
  Signor Lodovico?
Lodovico
  He, sir.
Iago
  I cry you mercy. Here's Cassio hurt by villains.
Gratiano
  Cassio?   70
Iago
  How is it, brother?
Cassio
  My leg is cut in two.
Iago
  Marry, heaven forbid!
  Light, gentlemen! I'll bind it with my shirt.

                    Enter Bianca
Bianca
  What is the matter, ho? Who is it that cried?
Iago
  Who is it that cried?
Bianca
  O, my dear Cassio!   75
  My sweet Cassio! O, Cassio, Cassio, Cassio!
Iago
  O, notable strumpet! Cassio, may you suspect
  Who they should be that have thus mangled you?
Cassio
  No.

81 garter: here, a belt or a sash. (OED obsolete) **chair:** an enclosed chair carried on two poles, a sedan. (OED obsolete) The origin of the sedan chair, which later came to describe a litter or stretcher, may be traceable to Italy of the early seventeenth (or perhaps sixteenth) century, where it had "long been in use." (OED) If so, Oxford was probably the first to introduce into English the use of "chair" to describe a sedan chair, which by extension could be used as a stretcher.

84 trash: Roderigo, as earlier, in acts 2 and 3.

93 accidents: unexpected, unfortunate incidents. (OED obsolete)

97 well said: well done, perhaps with some sarcasm.

100 Save you your labor: that is, don't try to help Cassio. **He. . .slain here:** Roderigo.

103 bear. . .air: Outdoors air was thought to be bad for a wound.

Gratiano

I am sorry to find you thus. I have been to seek you.   80

Iago

Lend me a garter. So.—O, for a chair
To bear him easily hence!

Bianca

Alas, he faints! O, Cassio! Cassio! Cassio!

Iago

Gentlemen all, I do suspect this trash
To be a party in this injury—   85
Patience awhile, good Cassio.—Come, come;
Lend me a light.
Know we this face or no?
Alas, my friend and my dear countryman
Roderigo? No.—yes, sure.—Yes, 'tis Roderigo. Roderigo?

Gratiano

What, of Venice?   90

Iago

Even he, sir. Did you know him?

Gratiano

Know him? Ay.

Iago

Signor Gratiano? I cry you gentle pardon.
These bloody accidents must excuse my manners
That so neglected you.

Gratiano

I am glad to see you.

Iago

How do you, Cassio? O, a chair, a chair!   95

Gratiano

Roderigo!

Iago

He, he, 'tis he.
O, that's well said; the chair.
Some good man bear him carefully from hence;
I'll fetch the general's surgeon.
[To Bianca] For you, mistress,
Save you your labor.—He that lies slain here, Cassio,   100
Was my dear friend. What malice was between you?

Cassio

None in the world, nor do I know the man.

105 gastness of her eye: terrified look. (OED obsolete)

106-8 Nay, if you stare. . .guiltiness will speak: Improvising quickly, Iago tells the others that Bianca's appalled "stare" (she is beginning to suspect the truth) is a guilty look.

116 know: find out, discover.

124 dressed: bandaged.

127 happed: happened, with a connotation of unlucky misfortune. (OED)

128 go on afore: Most likely, Iago is courteously bidding Lodovico and Gratiano go ahead of himself.

129 foredoes me: ruins me. (OED obsolete)

Iago
[To Bianca.] What, look you pale?—O, bear him out of the air--
Stay you, good gentlemen.—Look you pale, mistress?—
Do you perceive the gastness of her eye?— 105
Nay, if you stare, we shall hear more anon.—
Behold her well; I pray you, look upon her.
Do you see, gentlemen? Nay, guiltiness
Will speak, though tongues were out of use.

Enter Emilia.

Emilia
Alas, what's the matter?
What's the matter, husband? 110
Iago
Cassio hath here been set on in the dark
By Roderigo and fellows that are escaped.
He's almost slain, and Roderigo dead.
Emilia
Alas, good gentleman! Alas, good Cassio!
Iago
This is the fruit of whoring. Prithee, Emilia, 115
Go know of Cassio where he supped tonight.
[To Bianca.] What, do you shake at that?
Bianca
He supped at my house, but I therefore shake not.
Iago
O, did he so? I charge you go with me.
Emilia
O, fie upon thee, strumpet! 120
Bianca
I am no strumpet, but of life as honest
As you that thus abuse me.
Emilia
As I? Fie upon thee!
Iago
Kind gentlemen, let's go see poor Cassio dressed.—
Come, mistress, you must tell us another tale. 125
Emilia, run you to the citadel
And tell my lord and lady what hath happed.—
Will you go on afore? *[Aside.]* This is the night
That either makes me or foredoes me quite.

251

5.2.1 the cause: the situation moving a person to action, e.g. in law the grounds for action. (OED)

2 chaste stars: In classical mythology, the Moon is Diana, the goddess of chastity, and the stars are the train of virgins attending her. (Variorum)

8 If I quench. . . minister: "If I extinguish my torch. . ."

5 monumental alabaster: the white stone often used for funeral monuments.

10 thy light: Desdemona's life.

13 relume: illuminate again. (OED first usage)

17 Justice: The traditional figure of Justice, a woman, held scales to weigh the evidence and a sword to punish. Othello believes that Justice requires him to punish Desdemona, despite his love for her, because he thinks, mistakenly, that she cuckolded him and destroyed his reputation.

26 bethink yourself: recollect, call to mind. (OED).

28 Solicit for it straight: plead for it now.

Scene 2.Enter Othello with a light, and Desdemona in her bed.

Othello
It is the cause, it is the cause, my soul.
Let me not name it to you, you chaste stars!
It is the cause. Yet I'll not shed her blood,
Nor scar that whiter skin of hers than snow,
And smooth as monumental alabaster. 5
Yet she must die, else she'll betray more men.
Put out the light, and then put out the light.
If I quench thee, thou flaming minister,
I can again thy former light restore,
Should I repent me. But once put out thy light, 10
Thou cunning'st pattern of excelling nature,
I know not where is that Promethean heat
That can thy light relume. When I have plucked thy rose,
I cannot give it vital growth again;
It needs must wither. I'll smell thee on the tree. 15
O balmy breath, that dost almost persuade
Justice to break her sword! One more, one more.
Be thus when thou art dead, and I will kill thee,
And love thee after. One more, and that's the last.
So sweet was never so fatal. I must weep, 20
But they are cruel tears. This sorrow's heavenly;
It strikes where it doth love. She wakes.
Desdemona
Who's there? Othello?
Othello
Ay, Desdemona.
Desdemona
Will you come to bed, my lord?
Othello
Have you prayed tonight, Desdemon?
Desdemona
Ay, my lord. 25
Othello
If you bethink yourself of any crime
Unreconciled as yet to heaven and grace,
Solicit for it straight.

32 heaven forfend: heaven forbid.

36 Humh! A low sound of disagreement or dissatisfaction. (OED)

38 eyes roll so: Perhaps Othello, under stress in his conflicted agony, borders on another fit.

Desdemona

Alack, my lord, what do you mean by that?

Othello

Well, do it, and be brief. I will walk by. 30

I would not kill thy unprepared spirit.

No, heaven forfend! I would not kill thy soul.

Desdemona

Talk you of killing?

Othello

Ay, I do.

Desdemona

Then heaven have mercy on me!

Othello

Amen, with all my heart.

Desdemona

If you say so, I hope you will not kill me. 35

Othello

Humh.

Desdemona

And yet I fear you; for you are fatal then

When your eyes roll so. Why I should fear I know not,

Since guiltiness I know not; but yet I feel I fear.

Othello

Think on thy sins.

Desdemona

They are loves I bear to you. 40

Othello

Ay, and for that thou die'st.

Desdemona

That death's unnatural that kills for loving.

Alas, why gnaw you so your nether lip?

Some bloody passion shakes your very frame.

These are portents; but yet I hope, I hope, 45

They do not point on me.

Othello

Peace, and be still!

Desdemona

I will so. What's the matter?

Othello

That handkerchief which I so loved and gave thee

Thou gav'st to Cassio.

53 presently: immediately, without delay. (OED obsolete or archaic)

55 choke the strong conception: silence the idea.

60 warranty: authorization. (OED rare)

63 stone my heart: turn my heart to stone, harden my heart. (OED, first use here)

68 confess: here, to declare, testify to.

Desdemona
No, by my life and soul!
Send for the man and ask him.
Othello
Sweet soul, take heed, take heed of perjury.   50
Thou art on thy deathbed.
Desdemona
Ay, but not yet to die.
Othello
Yes, presently.
Therefore confess thee freely of thy sin;
For to deny each article with oath
Cannot remove nor choke the strong conception   55
That I do groan withal. Thou art to die.
Desdemona
Then Heaven have mercy on me!
Othello
I say, amen.
Desdemona
And have you mercy, too! I never did
Offend you in my life; never loved Cassio
But with such general warranty of heaven   60
As I might love. I never gave him token.
Othello
By heaven, I saw my handkerchief in his hand.
O perjured woman! Thou dost stone my heart,
And makes me call what I intend to do
A murder, which I thought a sacrifice.   65
I saw the handkerchief.
Desdemona
He found it, then.
I never gave it him. Send for him hither;
Let him confess a truth.
Othello
He hath confessed.
Desdemona
What, my lord?
Othello
That he hath used thee.
Desdemona
How? Unlawfully?

71 stopped: silenced.

72 taken order: taken measures, made arrangements. (OED)

73 interprets: explains to herself, figures out. (OED)

80 strive: struggle, resist.

82 Being done. . .no pause: perhaps, the verdict rendered, the punishment must be immediate.

83 *Smothers her.*: Earlier, Iago had suggested that Othello "strangle her in her bed." (4.1.180) The stage direction "*Smothers her*" in the First Folio (1623), and the quarto's "*He stifles her*" the year before, may not have been written by the dramatist and may have been added by scribes. Stanley Wells and Gary Taylor say in their *William Shakespeare, a Textual Companion* (1997) that "stage directions may have been tampered with by the scribe," although they do not cite smothering/stifling. (478) The play-text dialogue does not indicate the manner of the slaying, so the Elizabethan actors playing Othello and Desdemona may have been left to improvise—strangling, smothering, stifling, stabbing, or more than one method.

88 So, so.: He renews his attack.

Othello
  Ay.
Desdemona
  He will not say so.   70
Othello
  No, his mouth is stopped;
  Honest Iago hath taken order for it.
Desdemona
  O, my fear interprets. What? Is he dead?
Othello
  Had all his hairs been lives, my great revenge
  Had stomach for them all.
Desdemona
  Alas, he is betrayed and I undone.   75
Othello
  Out, strumpet! Weep'st thou for him to my face?
Desdemona
  O, banish me, my lord, but kill me not!
Othello
  Down, strumpet!
Desdemona
  Kill me tomorrow; let me live tonight!
Othello
  Nay, if you strive—   80
Desdemona
  But half an hour!
Othello
  Being done, there is no pause.
Desdemona
  But while I say one prayer!
Othello
  It is too late.

                                                          Smothers her. Emilia
  [Within] My lord! My lord! What, ho! My lord! My lord!
Othello
  What noise is this? Not dead? Not yet quite dead?   85
  I that am cruel am yet merciful;
  I would not have thee linger in thy pain.
  So, so.
Emilia
  [Within] What, ho! My lord! My lord!

                                            259

90 By and by.: directly, right away. (OED obsolete)

91 like: likely that. **she:** Emilia. In the lines that follow, Othello's "she" refers sometimes to Emilia, sometimes to Desdemona.

92 high: high-pitched, loud. The sounds most likely come from the fighting outside (off-stage).

97-9 huge eclipse. . . .yawn: seemingly, an apocalyptic eclipse of the sun and moon at the same time, hence "huge," accompanied by an terrifying earthquake that opens a chasm ("yawn") in the earth's crust. Pliny and *Revelations* in the Bible described earthquakes accompanying eclipses.

107 very error of the moon: that is, the errant moon has gone off course.

Othello
  Who's there?
Emilia
  [Within] O, good my lord, I would speak a word with you!
Othello
  Yes, 'tis Emilia.—By and by.—She's dead.   90
  'Tis like she comes to speak of Cassio's death.—
  The noise was high. Ha! No more moving?
  Still as the grave. Shall she come in? Were it good?—
  I think she stirs again. No. What's best to do?
  If she come in, she'll sure speak to my wife.   95
  My wife! My wife! What wife! I have no wife.
  O, insupportable! O, heavy hour!
  Methinks it should be now a huge eclipse
  Of sun and moon, and that the affrighted globe
  Should yawn at alteration.
Emilia
  [Within] I do beseech you   100
  That I may speak with you, O, good my lord.
Othello
  I had forgot thee. O, come in, Emilia.—
  Soft, by and by. Let me the curtains draw.—
  [To Emilia, outside] Where art thou? What's the matter with thee now?

                            Enter Emilia.
Emilia
  O, my good lord, yonder's foul murders done!   105
Othello
  What? Now?
Emilia
  But now, my lord.
Othello
  It is the very error of the moon;
  She comes more nearer earth than she was wont,
  And makes men mad.
Emilia
  Cassio, my lord, hath killed a young Venetian   110
  Called Roderigo.
Othello
  Roderigo killed?
  And Cassio killed?

114-15 Then murder's. . .grows harsh: a metaphor from music; that is, when the expected murder of Cassio went sour or off-key the sweet music of revenge turned harsh. This kind of subtle metaphor would occur to a writer like Oxford, who was an accomplished amateur musician, as were many aristocrats.

118 Out: a cry of lamentation or reproach, sometimes combined with "alas," as here. (OED)

121-3 A guiltless death. . .O, farewell.: Many of the details of Desdemona reviving and then dying and Emilia's cries for help were probably drawn from a story by Matteo Bandello about a wife-murder; they are not in Cinthio, nor in the French or English translations. (Shaheen 164) Bandello's *Novelle*, or tales, were published in Italian, in 1554 and in 1573, two years before Oxford was in Italy. (See Influences and Sources.) Commentators have debated how Desdemona could have revived for a minute or so after having been strangled, smothered, or stifled (or stabbed), and then died. Five physicians in the late nineteenth century offered a variety of medical explanations. The most renowned surgeon at the time, D. Hayes Agnew, argued that "surgical writers refer to instances in which, after violence applied to the neck and the person apparently suffocated, partial recovery has followed with ability to speak, and yet death suddenly followed from shock." (Variorum 302-7) Many commentators, however, have explained her reviving as simply for dramatic effect.

122 kind lord: probably, lawful, rightful lord (OED obsolete), not today's usual meaning of "kind."

130 folly: wickedness, unchastity. (OED).

131 belie her: lie about her, falsely representing her. (OED)

132 false as water: from Genesis 49.4, unstable as water, hence untrustworthy.

Othello
Not Cassio killed? Then murder's out of tune,
And sweet revenge grows harsh.
Desdemona
O, falsely, falsely murdered!   115
Emilia
Alas, what cry is that?
Othello
That? What?
Emilia
Out and alas! That was my lady's voice.
Help, help, ho, help! O, lady, speak again!
Sweet Desdemona., O, sweet mistress, speak.   120
Desdemona
A guiltless death I die.
Emilia
O, who hath done this deed?
Desdemona
Nobody; I myself. Farewell.
Commend me to my kind lord. O, farewell!
Othello
Why, how should she be murdered?
Emilia
Alas, who knows?
Othello
You heard her say herself it was not I.   125
Emilia
She said so. I must needs report the truth.
Othello
She's like a liar gone to burning hell!
'Twas I that killed her.
Emilia
O, the more angel she,
And you the blacker devil.
Othello
She turned to folly, and she was a whore.   130
Emilia
Thou dost belie her, and thou art a devil.
Othello
She was false as water.

134 top her: lie on top of, copulate with.　　**else**: if you don't believe me.

141 chrysolite: from the Greek words for gold and stone; probably from Pliny, who wrote that "the topaz or chrysolite hath a singular green color by itself for which it is esteemed very rich, and when it was first found it surpassed all others in price." He goes on to say that a king of Egypt had a statue of his wife made of chrysolite and put it in a chapel named "the Golden Temple." (Variorum.)

142 sold: deliver up someone, e.g. a hostage, the earliest OED meaning, chiefly from Old English and now obsolete, with a connotation of giving up a person treacherously.

145 iterance: repetition over and over.

146 made mocks with: made a mockery of. (OED obsolete)

153 most filthy bargain: probably a racist insult.

Emilia
Thou art rash as fire to say
That she was false. O, she was heavenly true!
Othello
Cassio did top her. Ask thy husband else.
O, I were damned beneath all depth in hell   135
But that I did proceed upon just grounds
To this extremity. Thy husband knew it all.
Emilia
My husband?
Othello
Thy husband.
Emilia
That she was false to wedlock?
Othello
Ay, with Cassio. Nay, had she been true,
If heaven would make me such another world   140
Of one entire and perfect chrysolite,
I'd not have sold her for it.
Emilia
My husband?
Othello
Ay, 'twas he that told me first.
An honest man he is, and hates the slime
That sticks on filthy deeds.
Emilia
My husband?
Othello
What needs this iterance, woman? I say thy husband. 145
Emilia
O, mistress, villainy hath made mocks with love.
My husband say that she was false?
Othello
He, woman;
I say thy husband. Dost understand the word?
My friend, thy husband; honest, honest Iago.   150
Emilia
If he say so, may his pernicious soul
Rot half a grain a day. He lies to the heart.
She was too fond of her most filthy bargain.

157 Peace, you were best: that is, you best be quiet.

159 gull: someone duped by deception.

160 dirt: filth or excrement. (OED earliest meaning)

163 The Moor has killed my mistress!: Emilia, the outspoken maid of *commedia dell'arte,* doesn't hesitate to expose Othello's crime and then the deception and the "odious damn lie" of her husband, Iago. (176)

166 on your neck: as your responsibility, alluding to hanging or beheading. (OED obsolete)

Othello
  Ha?
Emilia
  Do thy worst!   155
  This deed of thine is no more worthy heaven
  Than thou wast worthy her.
Othello
  Peace, you were best.
Emilia
  Thou hast not half that power to do me harm
  As I have to be hurt. O, gull! O, dolt!
  As ignorant as dirt! Thou hast done a deed—   160
  I care not for thy sword; I'll make thee known,
  Though I lost twenty lives.—Help! Help, ho, help!
  The Moor hath killed my mistress! Murder, murder!

                  Enter Montano, Gratiano, and Iago.
Montano
  What is the matter? How now, General?
Emilia
  O, are you come, Iago? You have done well,   165
  That men must lay their murders on your neck.
Gratiano
  What is the matter?
Emilia
  [To Iago] Disprove this villain, if thou be'st a man.
  He says thou toldst him that his wife was false.
  I know thou didst not; thou'rt not such a villain.   170
  Speak, for my heart is full.
Iago
  I told him what I thought, and told no more
  Than what he found himself was apt and true.
Emilia
  But did you ever tell him she was false?
Iago
  I did.   175
Emilia
  You told a lie, an odious, damned lie!
  Upon my soul, a lie, a wicked lie.
  She false with Cassio?
  Did you say with Cassio?

179 charm your tongue: be quiet. (OED obsolete)

182 O heavens forfend!: God forbid!

188 I think upon it: I remember now.

198 lift up eye: Women were meant to keep their eyes downcast unless they looked upward to heaven.

202 Desdemon: Gratiano, as Othello had done previously, uses the diminutive form of Desdemona's name. Because Othello addresses Gratiano as uncle, the latter is likely a member of Brabantio's family.

Iago
  With Cassio, mistress. Go to, charm your tongue.
Emilia
  I will not charm my tongue; I am bound to speak.   180
  My mistress here lies murdered in her bed—
All
  O, heavens forfend!
Emilia
  And your reports have set the murder on.
Othello
  Nay, stare not, masters. It is true indeed.
Gratiano
  'Tis a strange truth.   185
Montano
  O, monstrous act!
Emilia
  Villainy, villainy, villainy!
  I think upon it—I think I smell it! O, villainy!
  I thought so then—I'll kill myself for grief—
  O, villainy, villainy!   190
Iago
  What, are you mad? I charge you, get you home.
Emilia
  Good gentlemen, let me have leave to speak.
  'Tis proper I obey him, but not now.
  Perchance, Iago, I will ne'er go home.
Othello
  O! O! O!   195

                                                    Othello falls on the bed.
Emilia
  Nay, lay thee down and roar,
  For thou hast killed the sweetest innocent
  That ever did lift up eye.
Othello
  O, she was foul!
  I scarce did know you, uncle. There lies your niece,
  Whose breath indeed these hands have newly stopped.   200
  I know this act shows horrible and grim.
Gratiano
  Poor Desdemon. I am glad thy father's dead.

203 mortal: fatal.

203-4 pure grief. . .in twain: Grief killed him by shearing ("Shore") or cutting his "old thread" of life. In early Greek mythology, Atropos, one of the three Fates, ended the life of a mortal by cutting their thread of life with her "abhorred shears."

207 reprobance: the state of being a reprobate, probably in the theological sense of rejected by God, hence damned. (OED) Gratiano suggests that were Brabantio still alive to see his daughter murdered by Othello he might have been so grieved that he would have committed suicide, which would have damned him, and which is the very act that Othello will commit and be damned for it.

217 'Twill out: The truth will come out.

218 as liberal as the north: probably, as freely and strongly as the north wind blows. (Variorum)

222 dull: obtuse, stupid.

Thy match was mortal to him, and pure grief
Shore his old thread in twain. Did he live now,
This sight would make him do a desperate turn,   205
Yea, curse his better angel from his side,
And fall to reprobance.
Othello
'Tis pitiful. But yet Iago knows
That she with Cassio hath the act of shame
A thousand times committed. Cassio confessed it;   210
And she did gratify his amorous works
With that recognizance and pledge of love
Which I first gave her. I saw it in his hand;
It was a handkerchief, an antique token
My father gave my mother.   215
Emilia
O, heaven! O heavenly powers!
Iago
Come, hold your peace.
Emilia
'Twill out! 'Twill out! I? peace?
No. I will speak as liberal as the north.
Let heaven and men and devils, let them all,
All, all, cry shame against me, yet I'll speak.   220
Iago
Be wise, and get you home.
Emilia
I will not.
Gratiano
Fie, your sword upon a woman?
Emilia
O thou dull Moor!
That handkerchief thou speak'st of
I found by fortune and did give my husband;
For often, with a solemn earnestness,   225
More than indeed belonged to such a trifle,
He begged of me to steal it.
Iago
Villainous whore!
Emilia
She give it Cassio? No, alas! I found it,
And I did give it my husband.

231 coxcomb: a fool who thinks he can deceive people. (OED). A coxcomb was a cap worn by a court fool or jester.

232 stones: thunderbolts, lightning. (OED obsolete); Othello would like to have lightning bolts to hurl at Iago and destroy him.

233 precious: egregious, arrant, with a connotation of worthless. (OED)

237 notorious: obvious. (OED).

239 without: from the outside.   **him**: Othello.

242 whipster: a vague term of contempt for an insignificant person. (OED); today, a whipper-snapper.

243 But why should Honor outlive Honesty?: Several glosses have been offered for this line, including, "Why should my reputation ('honor') be more important than my integrity ('honesty')?" Or, "Why should I, representing military honor and bravery, outlive Desdemona, representing honesty and chastity?" The dramatist may have intended the ambiguity.

245 play the swan and die in music: an allusion to the fable that the swan, mute through its life, sings immediately before dying.

Iago
Filth, thou liest!
Emilia
By heaven, I do not, I do not, gentlemen.   230
O, murderous coxcomb, what should such a fool
Do with so good a woman?
Othello
Are there no stones in heaven
But what serve for the thunder?—Precious villain!

                    [He runs at Iago. Iago stabs Emilia.]
Gratiano
The woman falls! Sure, he hath killed his wife.
Emilia
Ay, ay. O, lay me by my mistress' side.   235
                                                         Exit Iago.

Gratiano
He's gone, but his wife's killed.
Montano
'Tis a notorious villain. Take you this weapon,
Which I have here recovered from the Moor.
Come, guard the door without. Let him not pass,
But kill him rather. I'll after that same villain,   240
For 'tis a damned slave.

                    Exeunt Montano and Gratiano.
Othello
I am not valiant neither,
But every puny whipster gets my sword.
But why should Honor outlive Honesty?
Let it go all.
Emilia
What did thy song bode, lady?
Hark, canst thou hear me? I will play the swan,   245
And die in music. "Willow, willow, willow."
Moor, she was chaste. She loved thee, cruel Moor.
So come my soul to bliss as I speak true.
So speaking as I think, alas, I die.
                              She dies.
Othello
I have another weapon in this chamber;   250

251 sword of Spain, the Isebrookes temper: In aristocratic and military circles, well-tempered swords from Spain were considered the best. "Isebrookes" was a variant spelling of Innsbruck, which produced fine, well-tempered steel. As a professional military officer, Othello describes with precision his sword made by Spanish swordsmiths from the best, well-tempered steel from Innsbrook. In the First Folio, the word is "ice-brookes," which seems inapt but has been adopted by some editors as alluding to tempering steel by plunging it in ice-cold streams. 'Isebrookes" in the quarto is more likely to have been the word written by the dramatist, who knew about such matters.

256 naked: without a weapon or suit of armor. (OED)

262 your stop: your efforts to check or restrain me. (OED)

265 butt: ending point or destination. (OED obsolete)

266 seamark: either the high-tide line or a navigation mark such as a lighthouse, marking the endpoint of a voyage. (OED) In either case, another example of the dramatist's ready knowledge of nautical and navigational matters.

268-9 Man. . . .retires: that is, if you were to arm ("man") yourself with nothing by a reed (a "rush"), I would collapse. In mock tournaments conducted by aristocrats, the combatants were armed with rushes in place of spears. (Variorum)

271 at compt: at a day of reckoning or final account, the Last Judgment.

274 slave!: Othello addressing himself, as contemptible.

It was a sword of Spain, the Isebrookes temper—
O, here it is. Uncle, I must come forth.
Gratiano
If thou attempt it, it will cost thee dear.
Thou hast no weapon, and perforce must suffer.
Othello
Look in upon me then and speak with me,   255
Or, naked as I am, I will assault thee.
Gratiano
What is the matter?
Othello
Behold, I have a weapon;
A better never did itself sustain
Upon a soldier's thigh. I have seen the day
That, with this little arm and this good sword,   260
I have made my way through more impediments
Than twenty times your stop. But, O, vain boast!
Who can control his fate? 'Tis not so now.
Be not afraid, though you do see me weaponed;
Here is my journey's end, here is my butt   265
And very seamark of my utmost sail.
Do you go back dismayed? 'Tis a lost fear;
Man but a rush against Othello's breast
And he retires. Where should Othello go?
[To Desdemona.] Now, how dost thou look now? O, ill-starred wench! 270
Pale as thy smock! When we shall meet at compt,
This look of thine will hurl my soul from heaven,
And fiends will snatch at it. Cold, cold, my girl?
Even like thy chastity. O, cursed, cursed slave!
Whip me, ye devils,   275
From the possession of this heavenly sight;
Blow me about in winds, roast me in sulfur,
Wash me in steep-down gulfs of liquid fire.
O, Desdemon! Dead! Desdemon dead!. O! O!

Enter Lodovico, Cassio [carried in a litter],
Montano, and Iago [prisoner], with officers.
Lodovico
Where is this rash and most unfortunate man?   280
Othello
That's he that was Othello. Here I am.

275

283 feet, but that's a fable: Othello refers to the folk legends that the devil had hoofed feet.

288 in the practice: through the treachery or evil machinations (of Iago). (OED, earliest recorded sense)

291 an honorable murderer. . .all in honor: Challenged to explain himself, Othello instinctively defends his reputation for honor, showing no regret for having foolishly believed that Desdemona cuckolded him, no remordse for having killed her.

294 consent: agree, plan together.

300-1 What you know. . .never will speak word.: As in *commedia dell'arte*, Iago, the witty, clever, scheming *Zanni*, comes to an ignominious end. His manipulations of all the main characters got out of hand, and he can say nothing without admitting that all his improvising and scheming gained him nothing and resulted in appalling murders and a suicide. With his last words in the play, he also shows a total lack of empathy and remorse—the mark of a true psychopath.

302 Torments: tortures.

Lodovico
  Where is that viper?
  Bring the villain forth.
Othello
  I look down towards his feet, but that's a fable.
  If that thou be'st a devil, I cannot kill thee.
Lodovico
  Wrench his sword from him.
Iago
  I bleed, sir, but not killed.   285
Othello
  I am not sorry neither. I'd have thee live,
  For, in my sense 'tis happiness to die.
Lodovico
  O, thou Othello, thou was once so good,
  Fallen in the practice of a cursed slave,
  What shall be said to thee?
Othello
  Why, anything.   290
  An honorable murderer, if you will,
  For nought I did in hate, but all in honor.
Lodovico
  This wretch hath part confessed his villainy.
  Did you and he consent in Cassio's death?
Othello
  Ay.   295
Cassio
  Dear General, I never gave you cause.
Othello
  I do believe it, and I ask your pardon.
  Will you, I pray, demand that demi-devil
  Why he hath thus ensnared my soul and body?
Iago
  Demand me nothing. What you know, you know.   300
  From this time forth I never will speak word.
Lodovico
  What, not to pray?
Gratiano
  Torments will ope your lips.
Othello
  Well, thou dost best.

311 discontented paper: a letter expressing Roderigo's dissatisfaction with the turn of events.

314-15 Iago. . .satisfied him: Iago probably ("belike") was able to intervene before Roderigo sent the letter and thus was able to satisfy Roderigo with some kind of explanation.

316 caitiff: miserable wretch.

321 wrought to his desire: worked to fit his scheme.

322 O, fool, fool, fool!: Othello castigating himself.

324-5 Brave me. . .I was cast: that is, challenge and threaten me (the night of melee) so that I would be dismissed ("cast") as unqualified. (OED)

330 this slave: Iago.

Lodovico

Sir, you shall understand what hath befallen,
Which, as I think, you know not. Here is a letter   305
Found in the pocket of the slain Roderigo,
And here another. The one of them imports
The death of Cassio to be undertook
By Roderigo.

Othello

O, villain!

Cassio

Most heathenish and most gross.   310

Lodovico

Now here's another discontented paper,
Found in his pocket too. And this, it seems,
Roderigo meant to have sent this damned villain;
But that belike Iago in the interim
Came in and satisfied him.   315

Othello

O, the pernicious caitiff!
How came you, Cassio, by that handkerchief
That was my wife's?

Cassio

I found it in my chamber;
And he himself confessed but even now
That there he dropped it for a special purpose   320
Which wrought to his desire.

Othello

O, fool, fool, fool!

Cassio

There is besides in Roderigo's letter
How he upbraids Iago, that he made him
Brave me upon the watch, whereon it came
That I was cast; and even but now he spake,   325
After long seeming dead, Iago hurt him,
Iago set him on.

Lodovico

[*To Othello*] You must forsake this room, and go with us.
Your power and your command is taken off,
And Cassio rules in Cyprus. For this slave,   330
If there be any cunning cruelty
That can torment him much and hold him long,

337 I have done the state some service: In his final speech before killing himself, Othello's expresses no compassion for Desdemona or regret that he falsely suspected her of infidelity. He stills thinks of himself in grandiose terms, showing only a self-centered concern for his reputation and excusing himself for loving "not wisely but too well." The speech hints disturbingly at the *Capitano* of *commedia dell'arte,* who brags about his military exploits, especially against the Turks.

345 base Judean: The quarto has "Indian." Commentators debate whether the word should be "Indian" or "Judean." "Judean" was a rare word in Elizabethan times. (Variorum) Shaheen argues persuasively for "Judean" and cites a source in Italian. Oxford was in a position to see the Italian source and use the rare word.

346 tribe: "Tribe" in *The Merchant of Venice* refers to groups or clans of Jewish people in Venice, thus supporting the "Judean" reading above. In the Shakespeare plays, "tribe" never refers to Indians.

348-9 Drops tears...Arabian trees...medicinal gum: probably myrrh, a gum resin from certain trees and used in perfumes. (OED) In Ovid's *Metamorphoses* (possibly translated by Oxford and published as by his uncle, Arthur Golding), the sisters of Phaeton weep tears that turn into amber, a fossil resin from the pine tree.

350 Aleppo: a trading center in Syria about two hundred miles from Famagusta on Cyprus. Aleppo was the Middle East headquarters for the Levant, or Turkey, company chartered in 1581.

351 Where a malignant. . .smote him, thus: After reminding them of his service to Venice as military commander, Othello recalls how he had oncedefended a Venetian and stabbed a Turk; but now, by killing his Venetian wife he has disgraced himself and become, like the Turk, the Moorish enemy of the Venetians. So he stabs himself as he stabbed the Turk, "thus."

359 Spartan dog: from Ovid's *Metamorphoses*, wherein the hunter Actaeon is turned into his quarry and is devoured by his own hounds led by a Spartan dog, which, like Iago, changes from servant to destroyer.

360 fell: fierce, savage.

361 loading of this bed.: Fatally wounded, Othello kissed Desdemona and lies dead with her on their bed.

It shall be his. You shall close prisoner rest
Till that the nature of your fault be known
To the Venetian state.—Come, bring him away. 335
Othello
Soft you; a word or two before you go.
I have done the state some service, and they know it.
No more of that. I pray you, in your letters,
When you shall these unlucky deeds relate,
Speak of me as I am; nothing extenuate, 340
Nor set down aught in malice. Then must you speak
Of one that loved not wisely but too well;
Of one not easily jealous but, being wrought,
Perplexed in the extreme; of one whose hand,
Like the base Iudean, threw a pearl away 345
Richer than all his tribe; of one whose subdued eyes,
Albeit unused to the melting mood,
Drop tears as fast as the Arabian trees
Their medicinal gum. Set you down this,
And say besides, that in Aleppo once, 350
Where a malignant and a turbaned Turk
Beat a Venetian and traduced the state,
I took by the throat the circumcised dog
And smote him, thus.

[He stabs himself.]

Lodovico
O bloody period!
Gratiano
All that is spoke is marred. 355
Othello
I kissed thee ere I killed thee. No way but this,
Killing myself, to die upon a kiss. *He dies.*
Cassio
This did I fear, but thought he had no weapon;
For he was great of heart.
Lodovico
[To Iago] O, Spartan dog,
More fell than anguish, hunger, or the sea: 360
Look on the tragic loading of this bed.
This is thy work. The object poisons sight;
Let it be hid. Gratiano, keep the house,
And seize upon the fortunes of the Moor,

For they succeed on you.
[To Cassio.]
To you, Lord Governor,   365
Remains the censure of this hellish villain,
The time, the place, the torture. O, enforce it!
Myself will straight aboard, and to the state
This heavy act with heavy heart relate.

Exeunt

Dating the Play

Oxford probably began writing *Othello* in the years after he returned to London from Italy in 1576, revising it several times in the 1580s when he was in his thirties. (William of Stratford was in his teens and early twenties.) Although there is no direct, historical evidence to date any Shakespeare play–no diaries, dated manuscripts, letters and such–there is substantial, indirect evidence to date the composition of *Othello* in the late 1570s and into the 1580s.

On March 3, 1579, three years after Oxford returned from Italy, *A Moor's Masque* with Oxford in one of the roles was performed at court. Masques were entertainments that combined music, speeches and dialogue and that were performed and danced by court figures costumed and masked. *A Moor's Masque* is a lost, anonymous work that may well have been based on an early, first-draft scene that Oxford would rewrite for *Othello*. Since Oxford and three other lords performed in *A Moor's Masque* and he was the only dramatist among the four, he probably wrote and directed it.

Throughout the decade that followed, Oxford was active in the theater world. He was the patron of two acting companies, which performed regularly at court. Scores of plays and masques were performed at court, although the records of payments to the acting companies give the titles only about half the time and do not identify the dramatists. In 1583, Oxford leased space in a former Dominican monastery, the Blackfriars, and founded the first indoor commercial theater in London. Oxford would become known as an accomplished playwright, and it would seem reasonable to infer that his plays, including *Othello*, were among the untitled, anonymous plays performed at court and in the Blackfriars theater in the late 1570s and throughout the 1580s.

That *Othello* was essentially completed by 1593 is suggested by accounting records in Henslowe's Diary for four performances of a play called "The Mawe," in late 1593 and early 1594. "Mawe" may well have been a drawled pronunciation of "Moor." Henslowe's spelling was wildly idiosyncratic, often based on the sound of a word, as was spelling in general in Elizabethan England.

Several historical and literary events described in the Influences and Sources section also suggest initial composition of the play, or parts of it, in the late 1570s with revisions continuing into the 1580s. These events include the maneuvering in 1570 of the Turkish fleet towards Rhodes and then Cyprus; the Turks' invasion of west and central Cyprus but not Famagusta until 1571; Catholic Spain's threat to Protestant England and England's rapprochement with the Islamic Ottoman empire in the mid-1570s; the publication of the two novels in euphuistic style in 1579-80; and perhaps Anjou's courting of Queen Elizabeth during these years, his ceremonious installation as Duke of Brabant

285

in 1582, and his disastrous defeat in its capital the following year. These topical allusions in the play would have been outdated and quite stale for aristocratic audiences ten or twenty years later, when Stratfordians date its composition and performance.

It is likely that uppermost in Oxford's mind would have been his sojourn in Venice in 1575-6, his experience there of *commedia dell-arte*, his probable visit to Famagusta in 1575, and his suspicion after his return from Italy of his wife's infidelity and then their reconciliation in 1581.

While no single piece of evidence is definitive, the cumulative effect of all the evidence strongly indicates that the dramatist wrote *Othello* in the late 1570s and during 1580s.

For lack of specific evidence, Stratfordian scholars most often date the composition of a Shakespeare play a year or two before its first appearance in the records, and this is how they date *Othello*. They estimate that the play was written in 1603-04, immediately before the first record of its performance, November 1, 1604. That dating is not only quite arbitrary, but the performance record in the Revels Accounts is suspect as a probable nineteenth-century forgery, which is nevertheless accepted as valid. To support that dating, Stratfordian commentators note that three books they consider minor sources had recently been translated into English: Contarini in 1599, Leo Africanus in 1600, and Pliny in 1601. As stated in the Influences and Sources section, however, these books had been published in Venice (in Italian and Latin) before Oxford arrived and were certainly available to him there and/or in Burghley's library in London.

Some Stratfordians also cite as a source Richard Knolles' *General History of the Turks*, published in the fall of 1603, which has details about the Turkish fleet's movements. Honigmann, however, points out in his 1993 article that Knolles acknowledges that he compiled historical facts from earlier sources. Honigmann found one, suggested that there were undoubtedly others, and ruled out Knolles as an influence. In his Arden edition, Honigmann never mentions Knolles as a possible source. He suggested a composition date of 1601-02 based largely on echoes of *Othello* that he finds in the first quarto of *Hamlet*.

Dating the composition of any Shakespeare play is difficult and can only be approximate. Both Oxfordian and Stratfordian scholars continue to search for evidence to support their datings. On balance, however, the late 1570s and the 1580s seem to make the most sense for the dates of composition and revision of *Othello*.

The publication history of *Othello* is unusual. The single-play quarto edition was not published until 1622, the year before it was published again as one of the thirty-six Shakespeare plays in the First Folio. Almost all of the other quarto editions of Shakespeare plays had been published two decades earlier, during

Oxford's lifetime. The text of this Oxfordian edition is based on the Globe text of 1864, which conflates to some extent the quarto and First Folio play texts. The First Folio text contains about 150 lines that are not in the quarto. Only the most significant differences between the quarto and First Folio texts are noted in this Oxfordian edition.

Appendices

The Dramatist's Knowledge
of the Military in Othello

Commentators on *Othello* have recognized the exceptional knowledge of the military demonstrated by the dramatist. In *Othello*, he creates an authentic military commander who makes all the right moves when performing his duties as a general. Indeed, it is a natural and ready knowledge of command and military ranks that only someone who had served in the military, as Oxford did, would be able to acquire and use with such facility. The following discussion and excerpt support this view of the dramatist as having served as a military officer and having inside knowledge of the operations and politics of the military, as well as of the rigors and subtleties of military command.

To cite just a few examples:

In *Shakespeare: the Invention of the Human*, Harold Bloom recognizes that Othello is "the skilled professional who maintains the purity of arms by sharply dividing the camp of war from that of peace. . . . Sound as Othello's military judgment clearly was, he did not know Iago, a very free artist of himself" (434).

In her book *Othello, a contextual history,* Virginia Mason Vaughn says that "everything we see of Othello in the first half of the play. . .makes him a truly professional military leader, a man who harmoniously combines heroic standards of virtue and valor with professional knowledge and experience. According to Jorgensen, Othello is 'one of the most respected and capable military executives in Shakespeare'" (48). The Jorgensen quotation is from *Shakespeare's Military World,* still considered the most authoritative of the half-dozen books and many articles on the knowledge of the military demonstrated in the Shakespeare plays.

Oxford had that "professional knowledge and experience" of the military that Vaughn extols. He had many friends in the military, including his two favorite cousins, Francis and Horatio Vere, professional military officers known as "the Fighting Veres." Oxford served twice in the military. When he was nineteen turning twenty he joined the forces of the Earl of Sussex, who was putting down the Catholic "Northern Rebellion." He served up to seven months on England's border with Scotland. Back in England he was one of two commanders in a mock battle staged for the entertainment of the queen at Warwick. There were two make-shift forts, battering rams, explosions, and fireworks including "a dragon flying, casting out huge flames" that set fire to one of the flimsy forts. When he was thirty-five, he was briefly a commander of

English troops in a campaign in the Netherlands against the Spanish. In 1579, the anonymous "Defense of the Military Profession" was dedicated to Oxford. The booklet argued the need for a standing army of trained professionals.

In his article on "Othello's Occupation" in *Shakespeare Quarterly* (spring 1975), C. F. Burgess of Virginia Military Academy describes how the dramatist understood the distinctive mind-set of a military officer. He argues that commentators on the play have not given sufficient attention to Othello's background as an experienced military commander and general to explain his motives and actions. He concludes: "When Othello is seen in proper perspective—that is, as a military man—the matter of his apparent gullibility in trusting Iago, of which so many critics have made so much, takes on an entirely new dimension. Othello has been conditioned to expect absolute loyalty and honesty from his subordinates. It is not only logical that Othello should put his faith in Iago; given what he thinks he knows of his ancient, it is inevitable" (212-13).

On the dramatist's knowledge of military ranks, Michael Neill observes in his edition of *Othello* that the rank of lieutenant was "something of a novelty (OED's earliest example is dated 1578)" (461). That dating is two years after Oxford returned from Italy. Neill goes on to note that "tension between holders of this new rank [lieutenant] and their ensigns seems to have been common," and he cites two later authorities, Thomas Digges' *Stratioticos* (1590) and Edward Davies' *The Art of War and England's Traynings* (1620). Clearly, Oxford had the military experience to be familiar with all these aspects of the military.

In her article, "Lieutenancy, Standing In, and *Othello*" in ELH 57, Julia Genster notes the contrasting use of "lieutenant" in the play. The word comes from the French *lieu*, meaning "place," and *tennant* "holding" or "taking." An official role for Cassio as Othello's lieutenant is to stand in for Othello in his absence, to take his place. At the same time, Othello erroneously suspects Cassio of standing in for him, taking his place in Desdemona's affections and in her bed. This excerpt opens Genster's article:

> In its treatment of military offices, with their ordinal structures and their real and emblematic functions, *Othello* is consistently alive to the ways in which these offices give rise to certain orderings of perception, for the characters within the drama and for the audience without. Arrangements and rearrangements of power—political, social, sexual – are, amid what Frank Whigham has called the "surge of social mobility that occurred at the boundaries between ruling and subject classes in late sixteenth-century England," a habitual Shakespearean concern.(1) The exact configurations of military power are not. M. R. Ridley reminds us that "Shakespeare's use

of military rank is both limited and loose." (2) And yet in *Othello* arrangements of social and sexual power are played out particularly close to the terms of office, of place. Who occupies what offices, military and sexual, how long and how well they hold them, how they gain or lose them: These questions arise so frequently in the drama that they become a kind of ideational tic – a tic which all the characters touch upon, but which Iago palpates with cunning, expert, obsessive urgency. What interests Iago, what interests Shakespeare, are the ways in which the ranks that place soldiers in legible relation to one another may be mapped on to the structures of personal identity, of social and sexual governance.

The metaphoric dovetailing of sexual and military orders is a Renaissance commonplace, as writers probe the Petrarchan vocabulary of erotic attitudes. But *Othello* suggests what we do not find suggested to the same degree elsewhere in Shakespeare's works: the ways that particular military offices with their attendant duties may be made to constitute emblematic and rhetorical places, which are then inscribed upon other structures, domestic or social. All of the play's characters are interested in the possibilities that the different networks may be brought into correspondence, but Iago is the most adept reader in and reader out of place inscriptions. Recasting the clown's riddling in Iago's terms, to tell where a person lodges in one structure is to tell where he may be belied in, dislodged from, another.

In Iago's and in the play's preoccupation with military places as loci for rhetorical invention and particularly in the office whose assignment is the most frequently interrogated – that of the lieutenancy – Shakespeare presents a figure, an image, which provides a vantage point on the play. (The word appears twenty-six times in *Othello*, which makes it half as frequent as "honest." (3) In this drama where "all relations are embedded in power and sexuality," lieutenancy, in its definition, its practice, its very etymology, extends its force over the play as whole. (4)

As that etymology reminds us, the lieutenant is the place holder for his commanding officer. (5) The lieutenant is at once a sign of his commander's power and a powerful reminder of his potential absence, since the lieutenant either receives the commands of his superior officer or substitutes for him. In choosing a subordinate a captain is, in effect, choosing a second self; he is empowering someone to play him, to be him in his absence. In *Othello* the image is most ferocious when it provides the putative cuckold with the emblem of his own cuckolding: Someone unauthorized is standing in for him, holding his place, doing his office. Yet the cuckold is present, imaginatively, watching as the adulterous love displaces him. He is both present and usurped, as Iago's sharpened pun makes clear: "Would you, the supervisor, grossly gape on,/ Behold her topped?" (3.3.401-402). In the ocular proof that Iago offers to his mind's eye, Othello is both supervisor, Cassio's commander, and yet as supervisor, overseer, doubly impotent. The cuckold's mind is haunted by the figure of his own absence from the pictures so powerfully present to his imagination.

Lieutenancy appears here at its most obvious and most corrosive, as it collapses military and domestic structures. It describes more generally, however, a suggestive angle on Iago's mind and the power that he is able to exercise over the play's other characters, and on the competition between Iago and Desdemona for Othello and for us. Lieutenancy thus thematizes that potential collapse of different structures of signification into one another; for the characters within the drama it figures both their hopes and their terrors; for the audience it patterns their engagement and their defense.

NOTES

1. Frank Whigham, *Ambition and Privilege: The Social Tropes of Elizabethan Courtesy Theory* (Berkeley: Univ. of California Press 1984), xi.
2. M. R. Ridley, ed. *Othello* (London: The Arden Edition of the Works of Shakespeare, 1958), 6n.
3. The word appears fourteen times elsewhere in Shakespeare, the preponderance (eight) in the tavern scene in 2 *Henry IV*. It was pronounced then, as now in England, as lef-tenant: see Fausto Cercignani, *Shakespeare's Words and Elizabethan Pronunciation* (Oxford: The Claredon Press, 1981), 206. The word "ancient" appears more frequently here than elsewhere: nine times here, ten times in other works.
4. The quotation is from Stephen Greenblatt, *Renaissance Self-Fashioning from More to Shakespeare* (Chicago: University. of Chicago Press, 1980), 236.
5. The play on the etymology has been noticed by two other critics, whose works appeared after I had finished the draft of this essay. Joel Fineman notes the play on place holder: "The Sound of O in *Othello*: The Real of the Tragedy of Desire," *October* 45 (1988): 86n. Tom McBride analyzes the "social spaces" of *Othello* to redress a critical imbalance which has, in his view, unduly privileged psychic

over social loci: "Othello's Orotund Occupation," *Texas Studies in Literature and Language* 30 (1988): 412-30.

The Dramatist's Knowledge of Music
As Shown in *Othello*

By Ren Draya

Every Shakespeare play demonstrates the author's extensive use of aural imagery and sounds: trumpet fanfares, battle alarms, a crow cawing, a knocking at the door. And there is music. Often, the dramatis personae include "musicians," as in Two Gentlemen of Verona, Much Ado About Nothing, Twelfth Night, and Othello. The plays are replete with references to music and to musical instruments, with snatches of lyrics, and with full songs. Each musical reference or song advances the plot, illuminates character, or enhances a mood.

In the history plays and many of the tragedies, the fanfares, drum rolls, trumpet calls and flourishes show that this writer was familiar with the rituals and pageantry of court life. Battle scenes contain alarums, tuckets, sennets—details that remind us that this author also had military training. We have no proof, no documentation, that the Stratford man had experience in court or in the military, nor that he received any musical education. Oxford, on the other hand, had military experience, served in court, and was well versed in music

For the well-born Elizabethan aristocrat, good manners called for training in musical skills and an enjoyment of songs. In his book on vocal songs in Shakespeare, Peter Seng points out that "the attitudes of the upper classes are reflected in the handbooks of nurture and education for their offspring; nearly all of these books prescribe some training in musical skills" (xii). As an aristocrat educated by tutors, the seventeenth earl of Oxford would have received extensive training in music. Thus, the more than four hundred references and allusions to music in the Shakespeare plays, including more than a hundred songs, point to someone with an exceptional education in music, someone like Oxford.

Oxford's contemporaries noted his proficiency in music. One said he was so musical that "using the science [of music] as a recreation, your Lordship has overgone most of them that make it a profession" (quoted in Lord 4). John Farmer, organist and master of the children of the choir at Christ Church Cathedral in Dublin, dedicated his two books of madrigals to Oxford—one in 1590, the other in 1599. Farmer wrote that he was "emboldened for your Lordship's great affection to the noble science" of music (quoted in Ogburn 720).

Music is incorporated in Shakespeare plays several times in one way or another—instrumental music, a complete song, phrases from lyrics, allusions to song titles, and especially metaphors and other figures of speech from the world of music. A typical example of a musical metaphor is in *Othello*, when Iago cynically watches the loving reunion between Othello and Desdemona:

[*Aside*] O, you are well tuned now!
But I'll set down the pegs that make this music.
(2.1.198-9)

A stringed instrument, such as a lute, is tuned by turning wooden pegs to which the strings are attached. Iago thus announces himself as being in control. He plans to loosen the strings of the well-tuned affection between Othello and Desdemona and ruin their love "music." At the start of the next act, "rough music" will signal that their love is doomed. Powerful musical metaphors come readily to a dramatist well-trained in music.

The first instance of instrumental music in *Othello* is a trumpet call or "tucket" that announces the arrival of Othello on Cyprus, an effective way of representing action occurring off stage. "The Moor! I know his trumpet," says Iago (2.1.176). A tucket with a particular melody and rhythm served as a personal calling card, almost an aural heraldic device, for a general or traveling aristocrat. Later, a flourish by trumpets announces the arrival of Lodovico from Venice. Lodovico comes as an emissary of the Doge and would thus be entitled to a fairly elaborate flourish (Long 145). And this tucket is integral to the drama. In *Songs from Shakespeare's Tragedies,* Frederick Sternfeld notes that the ceremonial flourishes for Lodovico accomplishes a change in mood; the music reestablishes a formal, diplomatic atmosphere after the disruption caused when Othello publicly strikes Desdemona.

In act 4, trumpet flourishes serve both a dramatic and a ceremonial purpose when they interrupt Iago as he offers to Desdemona a dissembling excuse for Othello's striking her. He falsely tells her that Othello's preoccupation with state business is the reason he impatiently struck her. At this moment, trumpets sound from the Citadel, announcing supper (4.2.165-170). In *Shakespeare's Use of Music*, John H. Long analyzes the moment:

Iago, of course, is not invited. He uses the interim to plot with Roderigo. Othello and Desdemona dine with Lodovico and the other emissaries. How hollow must this pomp sound to Othello, whose occupation is gone, whose commission has been revoked, and who is resolved to do away with his wife as soon as the banquet concludes! To Desdemona, perhaps, the trumpet music gives hope, suggesting to her those affairs of state which Iago has just said might be the cause of her husband's distemper (146).

Whether or not Long's interpretation is a hundred percent correct, it makes us realize that the dramatist clearly was familiar with formal state suppers. The sounding of trumpets during these dinners and for diplomatic events was customary in Queen Elizabeth's reign, events Oxford would have attended.

There is one more piece of instrumental music in *Othello*, an *aubade* at the start of act 3. An *aubade* is an early-morning serenade traditionally played by street musicians to awaken newlyweds. Musicians hired by Cassio start to perform under the window of Othello and Desdemona's bedroom. But the musicians are either inept or are deliberately making noisy discords. A Clown, evidently Othello's servant, enters and interrupts them. He scolds them with bawdy insults and tells them "to make no more noise" (3.1.13). Michael Neill says in his line note, "The function of this episode, with its obscene badinage, is to taint Cassio's serenade with some of the quality of the 'rough music' [the French *charivari* music made with pots and pans] with which early modern communities expressed disapprobation of inappropriate weddings" (279).

The audience will immediately realize the ironic foreshadowing here. No matter how well Cassio thinks he knows Othello, he does not know that the Moor dislikes music. Thus he has chosen the wrong way to regain Othello's approval. This failure means that Cassio is bound to fail in trying to regain his lieutenancy, and Desdemona will not be a successful petitioner for him. Her failure is emblematic of the dire breach growing between this bride and her powerful husband.

Two vocal songs are integral to the plot. The first, in act 2 scene 3, is a drinking song—more accurately, parts of two drinking songs—which Iago uses to entice Cassio to relax. It establishes a convivial atmosphere and also creates the illusion of the passage of time. Seng notes that Iago does not rely on someone else singing but actually is himself the singer, which again highlights the fact that Iago is in control. Iago sings, Iago causes Cassio to drink too much, Iago thus ensures Cassio's disgrace. Cassio, who has admitted he does not have a good head for drink, mistakenly sees Iago as his friend.

Just before the song, Cassio says, "they have given me a rouse already" (2.3.58). A rouse is a large glass or mug for drinking toasts (OED). Montano, the governor of Cyprus, is present as the soldiers drink. Thus, Iago's drinking song calls our attention to two unusual features: A high ranking official has let his hair down and is drinking along with the various guards and lower-ranked soldiers; and Lieutenant Cassio joins in the seemingly good-natured fun, perhaps encouraged by the fact that Montano is part of the company and certainly urged on by the jovial but scheming Iago.

"And let me the cannikin clink, clink," sings Iago (2.3.61-4). His diminutive "cannikin" adds to the sense of innocent fun, but it also rhymes with "manikin," originally "a little figure of a man, contemptuously" (OED). Iago has nothing but contempt for Cassio and may be hinting that Cassio is a man who lacks stature and can be manipulated.

> And let me the cannikin clink, clink
> And let me the cannikin clink
> A soldier's a man,
> O man's life's but a span,
> Why then, let a soldier drink.
> (2.3.60-4)

For the line "O, man's life's but a span," Seng notes the similarity to Psalm 36, "thou has made my days as it were a span long." This suggests that a kind of throw-away fatalism is being tossed in the face of Cassio. It's as if the fuzzy-headed Cassio is being told, "No big deal, lieutenant: Your life is just a set of years. If you're a man and a soldier, what's wrong with a few friendly drinks?" Audiences realize that Cassio hasn't a chance. The second part of the drinking song is brilliantly appropriate:

> King Stephen was and-a worthy peer,
> His breeches cost him but a crown;
> He held them sixpence all too dear,
> With that he called the tailor lown.
> He was a wight of high renown,
> And thou art but of low degree;
> 'Tis pride that pulls the country down,
> Then take thy auld cloak about thee.
> (2.3.76-83)

Scholars disagree on the origin of this song, and variations can be found from different time periods with different kings being named. Some believe it's a traditional ballad, some claim it was originally from Scotland or the North of England. "Lown" is a Scottish word for rogue. Oxford was in Scotland when he was nineteen turning twenty. Some can find no proof that the song was handed down at all, which would mean that Oxford wrote it specifically for *Othello*.

Whatever its origin, the song is no casual adjunct to the action. The line "Tis pride that pulls the country down" reminds us of one of the major themes in *Othello*—that of reputation, pride and position, the concerns of aristocrats. This jolly drinking song voices Iago's own impatience with privilege. He resents the attitude of someone in a high position, someone like Cassio who has the position Iago wanted. Cassio is not clear-headed and thus does not notice the implicit warning. Relaxed and perhaps trying to be "one of the guys," Cassio becomes too drunk to make clear decisions. He picks a fight—or is goaded into picking a fight—and the ensuing ruckus awakens Othello and results in Cassio's dismissal as lieutenant.

Perhaps the most famous music in the play—and the most affective for audiences—is Desdemona's plaintive "Willow Song." This is indeed a traditional folk ballad, from England. Desdemona calls it "an old thing." Several melodies are associated with the "Willow Song," all of them haunting; one of them is contained in a 1540 collection now housed in the British Museum. With its many verses, the song gives a conventional treatment of unrequited love and is eminently suitable to the sadness and confusion Desdemona is feeling at this point in the play.

Inclusion of the song points to the author's knowledge of music as well as his ability to seize a dramatic moment and highlight its ironies and complexities. Suddenly, after many scenes of males wielding power, we are given an accumulation of women: this quiet scene between Desdemona and Emilia, the mention of Desdemona's mother and of a disappointed maid. The song reflects the intimate setting, for a well-born woman would not sing in public but can do so in her own chamber. Desdemona explains:

> My mother had a maid called Barbarie,
> She was in love and he she loved proved mad
> And did forsake her. She had a song of Willow,
> An old thing it was, but it expressed her fortune,
> And she died singing it. That song tonight
> Will not go from my mind.
>
> (4.3.24-31)

It is the perfect song for Desdemona. She _is_ in love and Othello's actions do indeed seem those of a madman. The name Barbarie suggests the Barbary coast—home of the Moors and thus a link to Othello himself. As Desdemona is readied for bed, she continues to sing,

> Sing all a green willow must be my garland.
> Let nobody blame him, his scorn I approve.
>
> (4.3.51)

There is utter irony here. It was an old custom for those forsaken in love to wear a willow garland, the weeping willow tree a traditional symbol of tears and sadness. Desdemona's use of "must be" accentuates the sense that she is fated to be a victim. "Let nobody blame him" foretells Desdemona's refusal as she lies dying in act 5 to identify her husband as her murderer. And, adding almost unbearable poignancy at the end of the tragedy—accentuated by Othello's knowledge, finally, of her innocence and his own errors in believing Iago—Emilia will ask the rhetorical question, "What did thy song forebode, lady?" and sing "willow, willow, willow" as she dies. Two needless deaths, two innocent women each killed by her husband.

In the act 4 context of the "Willow Song," Desdemona breaks off her singing with "Nay, that's not next" (4.3.39-54). One way of interpreting this moment is that she has simply forgotten the sequence of stanzas or has mixed up the lines to a verse. Her realization signals the moment of deepest pathos in the play, for (depending on which version of the ballad one consults) the line Desdemona has omitted is "She was born to be fair, I to die for his love," Or, "He was born to be fair, I to die for his love." All the permutations of this line produce irony. Desdemona was born to be fair, i.e., true and loyal to her husband; and she is fair, if "fair" refers to her white complexion. If we insert the masculine pronoun, "He was born to be fair," the irony still holds, for in neither way is Othello fair. Desdemona is destined to die because of his love, albeit at this point a love twisted by jealousy and deceit.

Another way of interpreting this moment is to accept that the singer in the old ballad was a man and that the dramatist changed it to the voice of a woman to fit Desdemona's unhappy predicament. After she sings, "Let nobody blame him, his scorn I approve," which is what she believes and what she will say even as she lies dying, she abruptly breaks off with "Nay, that's not next." She suddenly realizes that the next line, if it's in the voice of a woman, foreshadows her death: "He was born to be fair; I, to die for his love." She was just about to sing what she fears to admit to herself: I, Desdemona, was born to die for his, Othello's, love. She does not sing that ominous line. Either interpretation is a masterful, dramatic stroke, conveying her shock of recognition, a shock that aristocratic audiences educated in songs and music and knowing the fatal line, which Desdemona skips over, would also recognize.

Oxford's knowledge of songs and instrumental music adds emphasis and power to the play's sad tale of a doomed elopement, unfounded suspicion and misguided revenge. The author easily drew an apt metaphor from a stringed instrument. He knew how trumpet calls and flourishes signified various events at court and served as personal calling cards for aristocrats and generals. He had a stock of songs upon which he could draw to heighten dramatic moments in his plays. *Othello* is just one of the Shakespeare plays that show an exceptional knowledge of music—knowledge that Oxford would have acquired in his upbringing as a nobleman.

Bibliography

Brooke, Tucker. *The Shakespeare Songs*. New York: Morrow, 1929.

Hosley, Richard. "Was There a Music Room in Shakespeare's Globe?" *Shakespeare Survey 13*. Cambridge UP, 1960.

Honigmann, E.A.J., ed. *Othello*, by William Shakespeare. London: Arden (reprint), 2002.

Long, John H. *Shakespeare's Use of Music: A Study of the Music And Its Performance in the Original Production of Seven Comedies*. Gainesville: Univ. of Florida Press, 1955.
Shakespeare's Use of Music: the Histories and Tragedies. Gainesville: Univ. of Florida Press, 1971.

Lord, Suzanne. *Music from the Age of Shakespeare: A Cultural History*. Westport CT: Greenwood, 2003.

Neill, Michael, ed. *Othello, the Moor of Venice*. Oxford UP, 2006. And see appendix D, "The Music in the Play," by Linda Phyllis Austern

Noble, Richmond. *Shakespeare's Use of Song*. Oxford UP, 1923.

Ogburn, Charlton. *The Mysterious William Shakespeare, the Myth and the Reality*. McLean VA: EPM, 1984.

Pechter, Edward, ed. *Othello, authoritative text, sources and contexts, criticism*. New York: Norton, 2004.

Seng, Peter. *The Vocal Songs in the Plays of Shakespeare: A Critical History*. Harvard UP, 1967.

Sternfeld, Frederick. *Songs from Shakespeare's Tragedies*. Oxford UP, 1964.

(This expanded article is adapted from the author's presentation at the thirteenth annual Shakespeare Authorship Studies Conference at Concordia University, Portland, Oregon, in April 2009.)

The Dramatist's Knowledge of Famagusta Harbor and Fortifications on Cyprus

By Richard F. Whalen

Most of *Othello* takes place on the island of Cyprus in the Mediterranean, and a dozen short and quite incidental passages at the start of act 2 suggest that the author of the play may have voyaged to Cyprus, landing at the fortified harbor of Famagusta, the island's principal port. These passages accurately reflect the topography of the harbor and battlements at Famagusta, which is not named in the play text. Until now, the off-hand description of the port in the dialogue has not received the attention it deserves, especially since it would seem that only someone who had been to Famagusta could describe so accurately its topography. Although there are no historical records that the author of *Othello* visited Cyprus, the seventeenth Earl of Oxford had the opportunity, the time and the financial means to voyage to Cyprus when he was traveling in Italy in 1575-6.

The dozen passages are in scene 1 act 2, when Othello, Iago, Desdemona and Cassio arrive from Venice in Othello's fleet of warships in the aftermath of a violent storm at sea. As the scene opens, Montano and three gentlemen on the battlements above the harbor are waiting anxiously for them to arrive. Their comments and those of others in the scene reflect the topography of the Famagusta harbor and wharf with the battlements and citadel directly above the wharf, according to two bird's-eye view drawings labeled "Venice. Depicting Famagusta." One is dated "1572 F Valegio," and the other "1600 G. Rossacio." (GoogleEarth shows essentially the same topography today.)

As act 2 opens, Montano, the Venetian governor of Cyprus, enters and asks two gentlemen, "What from the cape can you discern at sea?" A cape, according to the OED, can be a projection from a headland. One gentleman says, "Nothing at all," that is, no ships in sight yet. Four lines later, Montano refers to the storm that "shook our battlements." So they are standing on battlements that project out, like a cape.

The walls of the Famagusta battlements are, and were, thirty feet thick, and the men are standing on the gun platform behind the top of the battlements. They would not be on the front edge. Standing behind the thick battlements, the men would be able to see the harbor entrance and rock ledges some distance away but not the wharf directly below them.

Twenty lines later, a third gentleman arrives and reports that a Venetian ship "is here put in." He says that Cassio "is come on shore," that the storm destroyed the Turkish fleet and that Cassio hopes that Othello's ship has survived the storm. So, Cassio is still down at the wharf, "on shore." He has not yet joined Montano on the battlements above.

Twelve lines later, Montano says, "Let's to the seaside," confirming that he is above the wharf, not at it. Seventeen lines later the townsfolk are "on the brow of the sea," crying "a sail!" So they are on the same heights above the harbor and can see in the distance that a ship is arriving.

Five lines later, Cassio, who has arrived from the wharf, says to one of Montano's gentleman-companions: "I pray you, sir, go forth and give us truth who 'tis that is arrived." A second Venetian ship has arrived in the harbor, but someone must go down to the wharf to see who is on board.

Nine lines later, the gentleman-companion returns, and Cassio asks him: "How now? Who has put in?" Again, the dialogue shows that Montano, his gentlemen-companions and Cassio are high above the harbor and cannot see the part of the harbor that is close to shore and the wharf directly below them. They must rely on reports brought up to them from the wharf.

Iago's ship with Desdemona has arrived, and in a flight of overwrought rhetoric Cassio says that her ship safely passed "the guttered rocks and congregated sands." These are the rock and sand ledges that in fact do surround and protect Famagusta harbor with its narrow entrance, which her ship safely navigated. It's a topographical detail that typically would be noticed and used in the play by someone who had sailed into the harbor.

Desdemona, Iago and others arrive on the battlements and are welcomed by Cassio. Someone shouts, "a sail, a sail!' and an arriving ship fires a cannon shot. A gentleman says, "They give this greeting to the citadel; this likewise is a friend." So the setting includes a citadel, a fortified castle with battlements overlooking the harbor, but not overlooking the wharf where ships might tie up. Cassio says, "See for the news," and a gentleman leaves to go down to the wharf.

When Iago hears the trumpets that signal Othello's arrival, Desdemona says, "Let's meet him and receive him," but Cassio says "Lo, where he comes." Desdemona and the others were prepared to go down to meet Othello, but he arrives before they begin their descent.

After Othello tells Desdemona how happy he is to see her, he says, "Come, let's to the castle." Before leaving the battlements, however, he tells Iago, "I prithee, good Iago, go to the bay and disembark my coffers." And Iago says to an attendant, "Do thou meet me presently at the harbor. Bring thou the master [of the ship] to the citadel; he is a good one." So, yet again, it's clear that they are not at the harbor but above it. Iago must "go the bay" to get Othello's luggage.

The dialog by several speakers in 210 lines at the start of act 2 exactly reflects the actual topography of the port of Famagusta, then and now. The entrance to the large harbor is narrow, with ledges on both sides. The wharf is directly below the battlements out of sight for anyone standing on the battlements high above. And the fortifications include a castle.

It is hard to imagine that a playwright who had not been to Famagusta would set the scene for the arrival of Othello's fleet with so many passing mentions that put the speakers on the battlements directly above the harbor wharf, such that they must rely on messenger reports to know who has arrived on land.

Shakespeare scholars have entirely overlooked or chosen to ignore the evidence that the dramatist knew the unique topography of Famagusta. Edmund Malone, in his 1790 edition of Shakespeare, was the first to recognize that the port was Famagusta. (357) Before Malone, editors assumed the Venetians were at Nicosia, the capital of Cyprus but thirty miles from the sea. A few editors in the centuries after Malone recognized that the play's unnamed port was Famagusta, but modern-day editors, do not even name it, much less note the striking evidence in a dozen passages that the dramatist seems to have been there.

It might be argued that Oxford did not have to go to Cyprus for the unique details of Famagusta's harbor and fortifications. In Venice, he was well-placed to see the 1572 Valegio bird's-eye drawing or other maps and paintings of Famagusta and its harbor. He could have heard about the details from the many Venetian sea captains who had been to Cyprus. These possibilities, however, seem too conjectural and especially unlikely given the ease with which the dramatist incidentally but vividly and repeatedly works the Famagusta harbor topography into the dialogue a dozen times, particularly Cassio's reference to the harbor entrance. It's hard to conceive why Oxford (or any dramatist) would have taken the trouble to do so if he hadn't been there. The details read as first-hand observations. (In any case, it's extremely unlikely that William of Stratford, who was never in Italy, somehow could have picked up those details in England and decided for some reason to use them.)

When the seventeenth Earl of Oxford was traveling on the Continent, he wrote home from Paris that he hoped to take "two or three months to see Constantinople and some part of Greece." (Letter to Burghley 17 March 1575 in Cecil papers 8.24) But there is no historical evidence that he visited those countries.

Although various letters from him and others attest to his whereabouts in Italy most of the time, nothing tells where he was for about four months, from mid-May to mid-September of 1575. Four months out of touch is a long time, suggesting that during those months he was on a galley visiting cities on the Adriatic and Mediterranean.

Other Shakespeare plays show that the dramatist may well have voyaged to Ragusa on the Adriatic and to Sicily in the Mediterranean. *Twelfth Night* is set in Ragusa (today's Dubrovnik) on the Croatian coast across the Adriatic from Italy (Anderson 85-6 end notes). *Much Ado About Nothing* is set in Messina on Sicily off the toe of Italy. And most of *Othello* is set in Famagusta on Cyprus in the Mediterranean.

Oxford and his entourage lived for nearly half a year in Venice, which had a ship-building industry and was home port for scores of commercial galleys. If he had wished, he could have chartered for his exclusive use a swift galley with new sails and strong oarsmen to take him to Ragusa and Sicily, and also to Famagusta on Cyprus, a regular port of call for Venetian galleys.

(This article is based on a paper delivered at the Shakespeare Authorship Studies Conference at Concordia University, Portland, Oregon, in April 2009.)

Annotated Bibliography for *Othello*

This bibliography is limited to the articles and books that have been most valuable for this Oxfordian edition of *Othello*. It does not attempt to list the very extensive literature on the play and on sixteenth-century history and politics that were consulted for background.

Adams, Maurianne S. " 'Ocular Proof' in *Othello* and Its Source." *PMLA* 79 no. 3 (1964). For the dramatist's knowledge of Italian.

Adler, Doris. "The Rhetoric of Black and White." *Shakespeare Quarterly* 25, no. 2 (spring 1974).

Anderson, Mark. *Shakespeare by Another Name: The Life of Edward de Vere, Earl of Oxford, the Man Who Was Shakespeare.* New York: Gotham, 2005. Esp. valuable for Oxford's trip to Italy and *A Moor's Masque*. See chapters 4 and 5 and the extensive end notes for them.

Andrews, Kenneth R. *Trade, Plunder and Settlement.* Cambridge UP, 1984. For England's breakthrough into trade with the Turkey in 1575-6, see chapter 4, esp. pp. 88-9.

Auden, W. H. *The Dyer's Hand and Other Essays.* New York: Random House, 1960. His essay, "The Joker in the Pack," on Iago and Roderigo recognizes the comedy that is integral to the tragedy.

Bevington, David. *Shakespeare: The Seven Ages of Human Experience.* 2nd edition. Malden MA: Blackwell, 2005. See pp. 49, 171.

Bloom, Harold. *Shakespeare: The Invention of the Human.* New York: Riverhead-Penguin Putnam, 1998. See chapter 24 "*Othello*," esp. pp. 445-55 on cuckoldry, reputation and improvisation.

___. *Bloom's Shakespeare Through the Ages: Othello.* Ed. Harold Bloom. New York: Checkmark, 2008. A selection of commentaries, including Bloom on Cassio as a courtier (9), W. H. Auden on Iago as the "Joker in the Pack" (267), and Cassio as a ladies' man (272-3).

Bristol, Michael. "Charivari and the Comedy of Abjection in *Othello*." *Othello: Authoritative Text, Sources and Contexts Criticisms.* Ed. Edward Pechter. New York: Norton, 2004. Reprinted from *Renaissance Drama*, new series, 21 (1990). For his view of the play as a "seriocomic or carnivalesque masquerade."

Bull, George. *Michelangelo, a Biography.* New York: St. Martin's Griffin, 1998. For Ludovico Beccadelli's eminence in Venice.

Bullough, Geoffrey. *Narrative and Dramatic Sources of Shakespeare.* Vol. 7. New York: Columbia UP, 1962.

Chambers, D.S. *The Imperial Age of Venice, 1380-1580.* New York: Harcourt, 1970.

Clubb, Louise George. *Italian Drama in Shakespeare's Time.* Yale UP, 1989.

Doran, Madeleine. "Good Name in *Othello.*" *Studies in English Literature* 7, no. 2 (spring 1967). For Iago's manipulation of Othello's concern for his reputation.

Duchartre, Pierre Louis. *The Italian Comedy.* Trans. by Randolph T. Weaver. Dover, 1966.

Emery, John P. "Othello's Epilepsy." *The Psychoanalytic Review* 46 (1959). For the agitation that precedes an epileptic seizure and for comment on Othello's "trance" in act 4.

Everett, Barbara. "'Spanish' Othello: The Making of Shakespeare's Moor." *Shakespeare Survey 35* (1982) For Othello as the braggart soldier of fortune of *commedia dell'arte.*

Fernie, Ewan. *Shame in Shakespeare.* London and New York: Routledge, 2002. See chapter 6 *Othello*, esp. 136-8, 147.

Furness, Horace Howard, ed. *A New Variorum Edition of Othello.* Philadelphia: Lippincott, 1886. See pp. 303-7 for several nineteenth-century medical opinions on Desdemona's death, and p. 357 for his note that Famagusta on Cyprus is the setting for acts 2-5.

Gilvary, Kevin. "Shakespeare and Italian Comedy." *Great Oxford: Essays on the Life and Work of Edward de Vere, 17th Earl of Oxford, 1550-1604.* Ed. Richard Malim. Kent UK: Parapress, 2004. A survey of the influence of *commedia dell'arte.*

Gross, Kenneth. *Slander and Skepticism in* Othello. *ELH* 56, no. 4 (winter 1989). Esp. pp 821, 826.

Guilfoyle, Cherrell. "Othello, Otuel and the English Charlemagne Romances." *Review of English Studies* 38 (1987). For a possible influence on the play and source for Othello's name.

Hall, Kim, ed. *Othello, the Moor of Venice: Texts and Contexts.* New York: Bedford/St. Martin's, 2007. Includes a generous selection of excerpts from scores of writings pertaining to the play.

Hess, W. Ron. *The Dark Side of Shakespeare.* Vol. 3 App. H, forthcoming. Private communication to the editors with a "transcription, translation and interpretation of the *Tirata Della Giostra* from *Dell 'Arte Rappresentativa Premeditata ed all' Improvisa, Parti Due*, compiled by Andrea Perrucci in 1699," and with copious commentary by Hess on Oxford named nine times in a *commedia erudite* script of a fictional jousting tournament.

Honigmann, E. A. J. "The First Quarto of *Hamlet* and the Date of *Othello,*" *Review of English Studies* 44, new series, no. 174 (1993). For his view of Knolles as a supposed source.

___. Ed. *Othello.* London: Nelson, 1999. Reprinted in the Arden Shakespeare series, 2002. An excellent, comprehensive edition for Oxfordian researchers.

Hughes, Stephanie H. "New Light on the Dark Lady." *The Shakespeare Oxford Newsletter.* (Fall 2000.) For the name of Iago's wife, from Emilia Bassano Lanier.

Jardine, Lisa. "Gloriana Rules the Waves: or, the Advantage of Being Excommunicated (and a Woman)." *Transactions of the Royal Historical Society* 14. Cambridge UP online (2005) An account of England's "strategic rapprochement with the Ottoman Empire," drawing extensively on S. A. Skilliter's *William Harborne and the Trade with Turkey 1578-1582, a Documentary Study of the First Anglo-Ottoman Relations.* Oxford UP, 1997.

Jeffrey, V. M. "Shakespeare's Venice." *Modern Language Review (*January 1932). For the specific location in Venice of the "Sagittary," the lodging for Othello and Desdemona, quoted by Ridley and confirmed by Richard Roe on site (private communication).

Jolly, Eddi. " 'Shakespeare' and Burghley's Library." *The Oxfordian 3* (2000).

Kinney, Arthur. "Shakespeare's *Comedy of Errors* and the Nature of Kinds." *Studies in Philology* 85.1 (1988). See p. 156 for *commedia* "posterior to Shakespeare."

Kahn, Coppelia. *Man's Estate: Masculine Identity in Shakespeare.* Berkeley CA: University of California Press, 1981.

Lea, K. M. *Italian Popular Comedy, a Study in the* commedia dell'arte, *1560-1620 with Special Reference to the English Stage.* 2 vols. New York: Russell, 1962.

May, Steven W. *The Elizabethan Courtier Poets: The Poems and Their Contexts.* University of Missouri Press, c. 1991. Reprint by the University of North Carolina, 1999. For Oxford's poems and May's assessment of him as the courtier poet who was the "chief innovator" in subject matter and execution and one of the two "most creative" courtiers who wrote amorous lyrics. (54, 68) See also de Vere, ed. by Chiljian.

Magri, Noemi. *Othello* in "The Dating Project." *The De Vere Society Newsletter.* 16.1 (February 2009). For "Mawe" in Henslowe's Diary.

de Mendonça, Barbara Heliodora C. "*Othello*: a Tragedy Built on a Comic Sructure." *Shakespeare Survey 2.* Cambridge UP, 1968. For the influence of *commedia del'arte* on *Othello*.

Miller, Ruth Loyd. "'The Family of Love' and Iago's Sermon in *Othello*." In *Hidden Allusions in Shakespeare's Plays: a Study of the Early Court Revels and Personalities of the Times* by Eva Turner Clark. Port Washington NY: Kennikat for Minos Publishing, 3d revised edition,

1974. For Miller's dating of the play 1578-81.

Moore, John R. "Othello, Cassio, and Iago as Soldiers." *Philological Quarterly* 21 (1952).

Nelson, Alan. *Monstrous Adversary, the Life of Edward de Vere, 17th earl of Oxford.* Liverpool UP, 2003. For letters by and about Oxford in Italy, see chap. 26.

Nicoll, Allardyce. *The World of Harlequin, a Critical Study of the Commedia del'Arte.* Cambridge UP, 1963. See pp 119 and 223 for his ambiguous conclusions regarding its influence on Shakespeare.

Noble, Richmond. *Shakespeare's Biblical Knowledge.* London: 1935.

Neill, Michael, ed. *Othello, the Moor of Venice.* Oxford UP, 2006. In this most recent and most fully annotated edition, Neill says that "Contemporary criticism has been more sympathetic to what it sees as Shakespeare's deliberate manipulation of comic conventions," citing four scholarly works. (5) He also argues that from an Early Modern perspective that "'place,' that is, rank might well have seemed a more important dimension of Othello's tragedy than 'race.'" (112, 147 ff) See also Neill on "Military Designations" (461-3) and Linda Phyllis Austern on "The Music in the Play." (445-54)

Ogburn, Dorothy and Charlton. *This Star of England, "William Shakespeare," Man of the Renaissance.* New York: Coward-McCann, 1952. See chapters 39 and 40 for the evidence they compile to date *Othello* in the 1580s.

Poisson, Rodney. "Othello's 'Base Judean'": a Better Source for the Allusion." *Shakespeare Quarterly* 26, no. 4 (autumn 1975).

Richards, Kenneth and Laura. *The* Commedia dell'Arte, *a Documentary History.* Oxford: Blackwell for the Shakespeare Head Press, 1990. Translations of "the most important documents" plus introductory essays to each chapter. They note that the "visiting Italian players [in England] of the 1570s may well have been the last between then and the closing of the theaters in 1642, for no concrete evidence of their presence later [in England] has come down" (263).

Ridley, M. R., ed. *Othello*, in the Arden edition. London: Methuen, 1958. For his analysis of the play's leading characters, esp. for Iago's improvisation and delight in getting revenge.

Ross, Lawrence J. "Three Readings in the Text of *Othello.*" *Shakespeare Quarterly* 14 (spring 1963). For Othello's Spanish sword of Innsbruck steel.

Shaheen, Naseeb. "Shakespeare's Knowledge of Italian." *Shakespeare Survey* 47 (2002). For Bandello as a source and for the dramatist's knowledge of Italian.

Sipahigil, T. "'Sagitary/Sagittar' in *Othello*." *Shakespeare Quarterly* 27, no. 2 (spring 1976)

Smith, Winifred. The *Commedia dell'Arte: a Study in Italian Popular Comedy*. New York: Columbia UP, 1912.

Steele, Eugene. "Verbal Lazzi in Shakespeare's Plays." *Italica* 53, no. 2 (summer 1976). For the influence of *commedia dell'arte* on the Shakespeare plays in general.

de Vere, Edward, 17th earl of Oxford. *Letters and Poems*. Ed. Katherine Chiljian. San Francisco: Horatio Society, 1998. See esp. his letters at pp. 17-18, 21-2, 25, 36; and early poems at pp. 162, 163, 164, 167, 186. See also May.

Wallace, Charles William. *The Evolution of the English Drama up to Shakespeare*. Berlin: Reimer, 1912. Pp. 72-5, 199. For a performance of "a mores maske" in 1579, listed in his Table of Plays and Masks before Queen Elizabeth, see pp 72-5, 199.

Webb, Henry J. "The Military Background in *Othello*." *Philological Quarterly* 30 (1950).

___. *Elizabethan Military Science: the Books and the Practice*. Madison WI: University of Wisconsin Press, 1965.

Whalen, Richard F. "Commedia dell'Arte in Othello: Italian Theater Unknown in England but Known to Oxford." Forthcoming in Brief Chronicles.

Acknowledgments

We owe an immense debt of gratitude to the many Oxfordian scholars who have researched Oxford's life and *Othello*. We fully recognize that without their work this Oxfordian edition of the play would not be possible. *Othello*, of course, has inspired many volumes of commentary by traditional Shakespeare scholars over the past two centuries, and we are indebted to them for their many discoveries and insights that have been helpful as we crafted this Oxfordian edition. Especially valuable were the Variorum edition of 1886, the Arden editions by M.R. Ridley (1958) and E.A.J. Honigmann (1999), and Michael Neill's edition from the Oxford University Press (2006).

There is no way we could acknowledge here everyone whose work has proved especially valuable or who went out of their way to provide assistance and encouragement, but we would like to mention the following: our fellow Oxfordian edition editors Michael Delahoyde and Roger Stritmatter; Fran Gidley, Ron Hess, Noemi Magri, Kevin Gilvary and especially Dick Roe for their work on Oxford-Shakespeare in Italy; Cape Cod Shakespeareans David Connor, Newton Froelich, Jon Greenberg and Steven Kagle; and Paul Altrocchi, Robert Brazil, Frank Davis, Gary Goldstein, John Hamill, Ramon Jimenez, Earl Showerman, Richard Smiley and Peter Usher.

Ren Draya is grateful for the editorial and computer assistance generously provided by colleagues at Blackburn College, including Carol Schaefer, head librarian; Chuck Sutphen, director of computer service; and English majors Emily Jo Johnston, Jillian Stambaugh and Marie Sutterfield.

Finally, both editors of this edition want to recognize and thank their spouses, Dan McCandless and Carol Pearson Whalen, for their patience and loving support.